U.S. Army Headgear

U.S. Army Headgear

1812-1872

John P. Langellier & C. Paul Loane

Foreword by Don Troiani

Schiffer Military History
Atglen, PA

Dedicated To:

The supportive and understanding ladies
who make it possible to follow our obsessions.

Judy, Katie, Deanna, and Erica.

Book Design by Ian Robertson.

Library of Congress Catalog Number: 2002110742

Printed in China.
ISBN: 0-7643-1672-9

We are interested in hearing from authors with book ideas on related topics.

Published by Schiffer Publishing Ltd.
4880 Lower Valley Road
Atglen, PA 19310
Phone: (610) 593-1777
FAX: (610) 593-2002
E-mail: Schifferbk@aol.com.
Visit our web site at: www.schifferbooks.com
Please write for a free catalog.
This book may be purchased from the publisher.
Please include $3.95 postage.
Try your bookstore first.

In Europe, Schiffer books are distributed by:
Bushwood Books
6 Marksbury Avenue
Kew Gardens
Surrey TW9 4JF
England
Phone: 44 (0) 20 8392-8585
FAX: 44 (0) 20 8392-9876
E-mail: Bushwd@aol.com.
Free postage in the UK. Europe: air mail at cost.
Try your bookstore first.

CONTENTS

FOREWORD

In 1960, Connecticut native Waverly Lewis published a modest illustrated catalog of his personal headgear collection to serve as a general guide for collectors and antiquarians.[1] This work, along with occasional articles in the journal of the Company of Military Historians, served for many years as the only references for those interested in U.S. military headdress. Nearly a decade later a more systematic study by Edgar Howell and Donald Kloster followed.[2] This influential monograph remained the standard for more than a quarter century.

Now John Langellier and C. Paul Loane have collaborated to produce another resource that not only builds upon the information provided by their predecessors, but also contributes fresh material to the body of existing knowledge. These two highly respected and long-time students of American military history have spent decades locating and analyzing specimens in both public and private collections in the United States and Europe. They have woven their individual research into a concise narrative, accompanied by an extensive selection of illustrations and informative captions. Their overview takes the reader on a journey through more than a half century of change, illustrating the variety of factors that contributed to the evolution of U.S. military headgear during this dynamic period.

This important survey is especially strong for the pivotal Civil War period. In short, *U.S. Army Headgear 1812-1872* is the undoubted bible of American Civil War headgear. As the North and South fought to decide the fate of a nation, the antebellum patterns of the Regular Army, fads and fashions of the militia, influences of foreign countries, and contrivances of inventive civilians all found their way into the Union Army. The result was a colorful, sometimes chaotic assemblage of styles which, as the authors clearly depict, was reflective of the robust individualism of the American soldier throughout history.

Langellier and Loane have now given us a long awaited and noteworthy addition to the field. As such, their exceptional and intriguing book deserves a special place in the literature concerning our country's military heritage.

Don Troiani

Notes:

1 Waverly P. Lewis, *U.S. Military Headgear 1770-1880* (Devon, CT: Printed by the Author, 1960).

2 Edgar M. Howell and Donald E. Kloster, *United States Army Headgear to 1854: Catalog of United States Army Uniforms in the Collections of the Smithsonian Institution* (Washington, DC: Smithsonian Institution Press, 1969).

ACKNOWLEDGMENTS & ABBREVIATIONS

A work of this scope can only be completed with the help of many colleagues and friends, each of whom added to the body of knowledge. The authors are indebted to these individuals and to a number of generous institutions. This includes Don Troiani, who provided the foreword and shared his excellent collection and library. Likewise, John Henry Kurtz allowed us great access to his noteworthy collection and reviewed a portion of the manuscript. Similarly, Robert Borrell, Sr., Dr. Edward Burka, Alex de Quesada, Jr., James Frasca, Jan Gordon, Dr. Elizabeth Atwood Lawrence, Craig Nannos, and Joe Parr opened their collections to us. Also, Len Benson, Joseph Fulginitti, John Gunderson, Joshua Landish, Gary Leister, William McKenna, Howard Madaus, Richard Mendoza, Dean Nelson, John Ockerbloom, Herb Peck, Pat Regis, Richard Roash, Victor Romano, Wayne Sherman, and R. Bryce Workman provided key pieces or information for this endeavor. Dr. William Schultz and Dr. Michael McAfee gave permission for use of numerous photographs from their extensive collections. At the Minnesota Historical Society's Ft. Snelling, Stephen Osman was unstinting as always. Many members of the Company of Military Historians, including Walter Bradford, J. Duncan Campbell, Gordon Chappell, René Chartrand, Ray Darida, Fredrick Gaede, David Sullivan, Marco Zlatich, and the late Detmar Finke proved of great assistance as well.

Michael Strong, the curator of the Cumberland County Historical Society, in Carlisle, Pennsylvania, likewise provided assistance. Harold Yoder, Vickie Heffner, and Dave Terefenko of the Berks County, PA, Historical Society made it possible to photograph a rare French fatigue cap in the society's collection. The Wisconsin Veterans Museum, Illinois State Historical Library, Delaware Historical Society, and New Jersey's Camden County Historical Society, Gloucester County Historical Society, and Salem County Historical Society all willingly allowed items from their fine collections to be examined and photographed, as did the Alexander Library of Rutgers-The State University of New Jersey, and the Civil War Library and Museum of the Military Order of the Loyal Legion in Philadelphia. Michael Winey and Randy Hackenberg of the U.S. Army Military History Institute also provided valuable assistance, as did Bruce Bazelon and the staff at Harrisburg's Pennsylvania Historical and Museum Commission. At Gettysburg National Military Battlefield Park, Curator Michael Vice, along with Assistant Curator Craig Blindenbacher and Paul Shevchuk, an NPS volunteer, rendered many kindnesses. Ronn Palm generously allowed the reproduction of many images from his suberb collection, and Bill Synnamon was another helpful resource in Gettysburg. Brian White called our attention to new information on the seamless felt hat, and Greg Schuler generously forwarded important information about that and other items of Illinois uniforms. Anna von Lunz and William "Bill" Brown of the National Park Service assisted with photographs of an 1813-pattern infantry cap in the collections of Fort McHenry National Monument and Historic Shrine. Peter Harrington of the Anne S. K. Brown Collection at Brown University, A. Wilson Greene formerly of Chalmette Battlefield National Military Park, and Gilbert Gonzales of the Rutherford B. Hayes Presidential Center and Library were most helpful. Don Kloster facilitated requests from the Smithsonian Institution's Museum of American History. Luther Hansen of the U.S. Army Quartermaster Museum furnished a number of fine images from Ft. Lee, Virginia. Moreover, Denison J. Beach and Virginia L. Smyers of Harvard University's Houghton Library, expedited copies of watercolors from the Henry Elkins Winder Collection.

Kurt Cox and Glen Swanson undertook photography on several occasions. Additional help with photography was provided by Largemoor Studios in Camden, N.J. Moreover, Dr. Vincent Transano made useful comments on portions of the manuscript. Other organizations cooperated in various ways as well, all of which are listed below.

Pictorial Sources

ADEQ Alex de Quesada Historical Resources, Inc. Collection
AL Alexander Library, Rutgers University, New Brunswick, NJ
BCHS Berks County Historical Society, Reading, Pa.
BL Bancroft Library, University of California, Berkeley
BUL Brown University Library, Providence, RI
CBNMP Chalmette Battlefield National Military Park (National Park Service) Arabi, La.
CHS Camden County Historical Society, Camden, NJ
CCHS Cumberland County Historical Society, Carlisle, PA
CF Chuck Fowler
CMH The Company of Military Historians, Rutland, MA
CPL C. Paul Loane
CSPRD California State Parks and Recreation Department, Sacramento, CA
CWLM Civil War Library and Museum, Philadelphia, PA
DHS Delaware Historical Society, Wilmington, Del.

DT	Don Troiani
EB	Edward Burka, MD
EG	Eugene Groves
FAM	Frontier Army Museum, Ft. Leavenworth, KS
FMNMAHS	Ft. McHenry National Monument and Historic Shrine, (National Park Service) Baltimore, MD
FWSQ	Ft. Winnebago Surgeon's Quarters, Portage, WI
FWS&HM	Ft. Worth Science and History Museum, Ft. Worth, TX
GC	Gordon Chappell
GGNRA	Golden Gate National Recreation Area, (National Park Service) San Francisco, CA
GHS	Gloucester Co. Historical Society, Woodbury, N.J.
GL	Gary Leister
GMHQM	General Meade Headquarters Museum, Gettysburg, PA
GNMB	Gettysburg National Military Battlefield, (National Park Service) Gettysburg, PA
HL	Houghton Library, Harvard University, Cambridge, MA by permission of the Henry Elkins Widener Collection
HM	Howard Madeus
HP	Herb Peck
HSD	Historical Society of Delaware, Wilmington, DE
ISHL	Illinois State Historical Library
JB	Jack Blades
JCN	J. Craig Nannos
JDC	Colonel James D. Campbell, Jr.
JCG	Jan C. Gordon
JG	John Gunderson
JF	Joseph Fulginitti
JCF	James C. Frasca
JG	Jerome Greene
JHK	John Henry Kurtz
JML	Joshua M. Landish
JO	John Ockerbloom
KHC	Kurt Hamilton Cox
KSHS	Kansas State Historical Society, Topeka, KS
LB	Leonard Benson
LC	Library of Congress, Washington, DC
MJM	Michael J. McAfee, Ph.D.
MNHS	Minnesota Historical Society, Minneapolis, MN
NA	National Archives
PEI	Peabody Essex Institute, Salem, MA
PHMC	Pennsylvania Historical and Museum Commission, Harrisburg, Pa.
PR	Pat Regis
NA	National Archives, College Park, MD
NYSHS	New York State Historical Society, New York, NY
RB	Robert Borrell, Sr.
RP	Ronn Palm
RBHPC&L	Rutherford B. Hayes Presidential Center and Library, Fremont, OH
RM	Richard Mendoza
RR	Richard Roash
SCHS	Salem County Historical Society, Salem, NJ
SHSW	State Historical Society of Wisconsin, Madison, WI
SFTC	Santa Fe Trail Center, Larned, KS
SI	Smithsonian Institution, Museum of American History, Armed Forces Collection, Washington, DC
TC	Tøhusmuseet (Royal Arsenal Museum), Copenhagen, Denmark
USA	U.S. Army (former Presidio Army Museum Collection, Presidio of San Francisco, CA)
USACMH	Army Museum Central Collection, U.S. Army Center of Military History, Washington, DC
USAMHI	U.S. Army Military History Institute, Carlisle Barracks, PA
USAQM	U.S. Army Quartermaster Museum, Ft. Lee, VA
USHS	Utah State Historical Society, Salt Lake City, UT
USMCM	U.S. Marine Corps Museum, Washington, DC
VR	Victor Romano
VJM	V.J. Moran
WC	Wes Clark
WCC	Western Costume Company, North Hollywood, CA
WJS	William J. Schultz, M.D.
WM	William McKenna
WPM	West Point Museum, U.S. Military Academy, West Point, NY
WS	Wayne Sherman
WSA	Wyoming State Archives, Cheyenne, WY
WVM	Wisconsin Veterans Museum

End Notes

AGO	Adjutant General's Office
A&NJ	*Army and Navy Journal*
ARSW	*Annual Report of the Secretary of War*
CCF	Consolidated Correspondence Reports
GO	General Orders
HQA	Headquarters of the Army
LR	Letters Received
LS	Letters Sent
OQMG	Office of the Quartermaster General
RG	Record Group
SO	Special Orders
WD	War Department

1

Forging a Nation 1783-1832

After the successful conclusion of the American Revolution, the victorious Continental Army began to dwindle. Indeed, by November 25, 1783, George Washington personally led only one regiment of infantry and a pair of artillery battalions. Early the next year the secretary of war indicated that only 700 men remained on the rolls. Soon thereafter the civil authorities acted, finding even this small force too large for the emerging republic to maintain. On June 3, 1784, only twenty-five enlisted men were to be retained as a garrison for Fort Pitt, while another fifty-five were to be stationed at West Point. A handful of officers were to command this token complement. As an auxiliary, Connecticut, New Jersey, New York, and Pennsylvania were asked to provide 700 men for a year to occupy abandoned British forts on the frontier.

Except for Pennsylvania, the states were slow in responding to fill their quotas. With potential threats from European powers and internal conflicts with Native Americans dictating another course of action, this situation could not long endure. As a result, late in 1786 Congress again addressed the country's needs for a standing army. This time the lawmakers raised the strength to 1,340 privates and non-commissioned officers, as well as retained the state levy of 700 men. The combined units eventually would be forged into a *legion*, a concept that took its inspiration from the army of the early Roman republic. Additionally, the concept was one that had a practical basis, in that the sublegions consisted of a force with its own integral infantry, artillery, and mounted elements, someone akin to regimental combat teams of a later era.

"The Legion of the United States," as it ultimately was authorized, was to consist of 5,120 personnel who would be divided evenly into four sub-legions. Nothing approaching that figure came into being, however. In 1796 the legion concept was abandoned.

With that the more traditional regimental system returned. Four regiments of infantry, two companies of light dragoons, and a corps of artillerists and engineers constituted what by then had become the United States Army under the federal government, with the president serving as the commander-in-chief. In 1797, a limited staff came into being to provide support and administrative functions, while during the following year, a potential war with France spurred Congress to confer authority on the president to enlist as many as 30,000 troops as an "Eventual Army," if hostilities erupted. Fortunately, a peaceful solution averted conflict.

Confident that all was well, President John Adams saw to it that reductions of the standing army took place, so that near the end of December 1801, only 4,052 men remained in uniform. The following year, when Thomas Jefferson replaced Adams in office, his newly installed administration initiated further cutbacks, leaving only a total of 3,212 officers and soldiers on the rolls soon after his assumption of duties.

Slightly later in Jefferson's term, on March 16, 1802, the United States Congress further scaled down the army by authorizing only twenty

Left: Lieutenant Colonel Charles Hamilton Smith, a British officer who clandestinely observed the American military, painted this image of "Cavalry of the United States of America in 1812," depicting enlisted dragoons wearing a black leather helmet ornamented with a white metal crest, plate, and visor. A white turban and long, white horsehair mane completed this dramatic piece of headgear. By permission of the Harry Eakins Widener Collection. HL

Above: A surviving example of a dragoon helmet, probably produced sometime between 1808 and 1811, bears an 1812 pattern plate with charging dragoon, but one struck of silver plated copper, rather than the more typical white metal. The turban is cloth painted to represent leopard skin. Inside, a leather sweatband is attached to a linen bag with a drawstring. Regulations called for a blue plume with white tip, most of which is missing on this specimen, which may have been a privately purchased helmet for an officer. Photographs by Gilbert Gonzales. RBHPL

Right: This light dragoon helmet also bears the 1812 pattern plate, but the body is the type procured by contracts c. 1815. The detail of the chain strap of scales and the white metal front plate are typical features of U.S. Army examples of the era for this type of headgear. DT

Another Charles Hamilton Smith watercolor portrayed an "Officer of Dragoons, United States Service, 1814" with the black leather helmet body decorated with crest, visor, turban, plate, chin strap and side bars, white mane, and "houppe." By permission of the Harry Eakins Widener Collection. HL

C.H. Smith's rendition of infantry officers and enlisted men in 1816 depicted the former group wearing black bicorn hats with white plumes, while the common soldiers donned 1813 pattern infantry caps with white metal plates, feathers, cords, and tape, or painted trim on the edge of the front piece. HL

Cockades similar to this leather one were described by Callender Irvine, the commissary general of purchases. This specimen may have been produced for the chapeau de bras of artillery officer during the 1808-1812 period. JCN

companies of artillery, a like number of infantry companies, and a meager engineer contingent, along with a cadet corps at the newly established military academy located at West Point, New York. The paper strength was 172 officers and 3,040 soldiers, although a lesser number actually were mustered than the ceilings allowed by law.[1]

During this formative period in the U.S. Army's history, shifts in military fashion had begun to occur, in large part influenced by styles worn in Europe during the Napoleonic wars. One transplanted practice was the replacement of the old tri-corner hat with bicorns, or chapeaus as they came to be known.* These were worn "athwartships" (sideways) a la the Little Corporal himself, at a slight angle, or in a front to back arrangement called "fore and aft" by the British.[2] As interpreted in the United States, by the uniform regulations adopted on January 30, 1787, the American cocked hats were to have white trim for infantrymen and yellow trim for artillerymen, with round 4-inch black leather cockades.[3] Feathers that rose six inches above the brim further designated the wearer's branch. Originally black feathers topped in red were assigned to artillerymen, and red, black, and white ones set off the First, Second, and Third U.S. Infantry regiments respectively.[4] An 1800 directive further instructed infantry officers to have:

*For the purpose of this volume, a hat is considered to be a head covering that has a brim all around the horizontal, conical, or cylindrical part, which covers the head, while a cap is understood to not have a brim, although it regularly has a visor or bill.

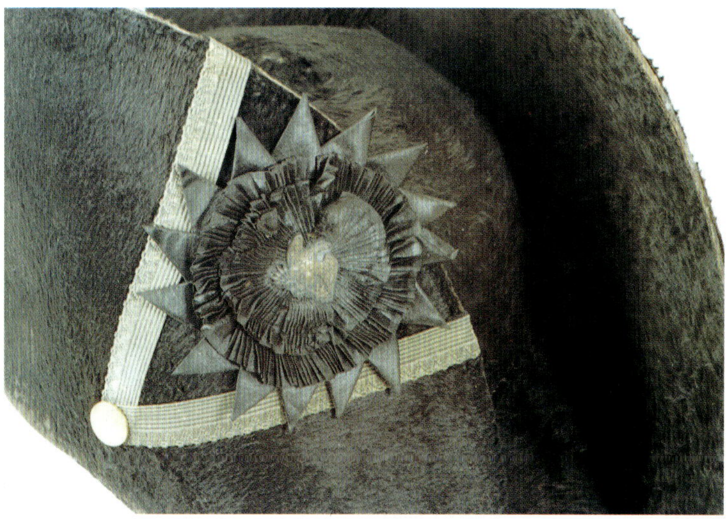

Officer's bicorn typical of the type worn by infantry officers during the 1805-1815 era, with a detail of the cockade with eagle device. DT

Left, right, and interior lining views of the British-inspired cap, which was authorized for U.S. infantrymen in 1813. Unlike its English counterpart, which had a body of fur felt, the American model was of leather, and the front piece was applied separately on the first models. DT

Later contract versions of the 1813 pattern cap were distinguished by the front piece being made integral to the body. The caps remained regulation through the early 1820s, and in some instances were modified for fatigue wear. This example bears a small paper label inside that reads "Redfern"—a Philadelphia based maker that produced this cap around 1818 or 1819. Note the "US" on the cap plate has been removed carefully by scraping and pounding, thereby inferring the piece was sold as surplus for the use of militia in the 1820s. JDC

> Hats, full cocked, with narrow black binding, fan on hind part eight inches broad—sides and corners six inches broad; Black cockade of four inches diameter having a white eagle in center, the cockade to rise an inch above the brim—loop and button black.[5]

The chapeau remained in vogue through the turn of the nineteenth century for general officers and staff officers—even continuing as a regulation item for the former group into the 1930s, although the shape and size shifted from one era to the next.[6] Gradually, however, this type of head dress began to be phased out for infantrymen, at least for company grade or platoon officers (second lieutenants through captains), as the cocked hat gave way to a cap. On the other hand, cocked hats with black leather cockades bearing a gold eagle in the center, a gold loop fastened with a gold button, and a white plume that rose six inches above the hat for enlisted men and eight for officers remained regulation for artillery troops at least until 1812.[7] Further, it is possible that the leather cockades for the enlisted artillery chapeau may have been substituted for the applied gold eagle.[8] An existing example, perhaps dating from as early as 1808, features a tooled leather eagle surmounting a canon with an arc of fifteen stars that was an integral part of the leather cockade.[9]

According to a March 30, 1800, general order (that may have served as interim uniform regulations), general officers were to have the chapeau, too. In this instance, the color of the plume was dictated by rank and branch. The eagle and trim were gold, the former element being attached to the traditional cockade.[10]

While the chapeau continued as a mainstay for generations, in various forms other types of headgear came onto the scene. In due course, these overshadowed the cocked hat. As one example, mounted units that remained active for a brief period into the early 1800s traditionally had been distinguished by leather helmets. These were to be "crowned with black horse hair," and have "a brass front, with a mounted Dragoon in the Act of Charging."[11] Officers of this "Corps of Cavalry," as it was known during the days of the Legion, were to be recognized further by green plumes. The disbanding of the Legion followed by 1802 congressional reductions spelled the temporary end of the light dragoons as part of the national martial force.

Front, side, rear, and interior views of the 1813 pattern enlisted infantry cap. Note the painted edging on the front piece in lieu of the earlier requirement to use white metal trim. FMNMAHS

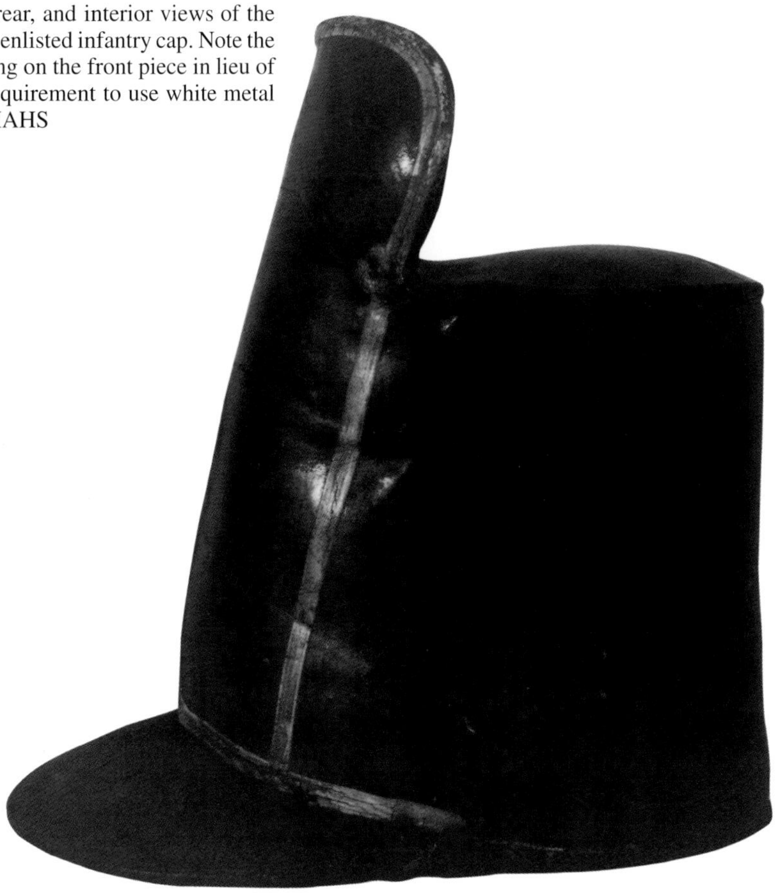

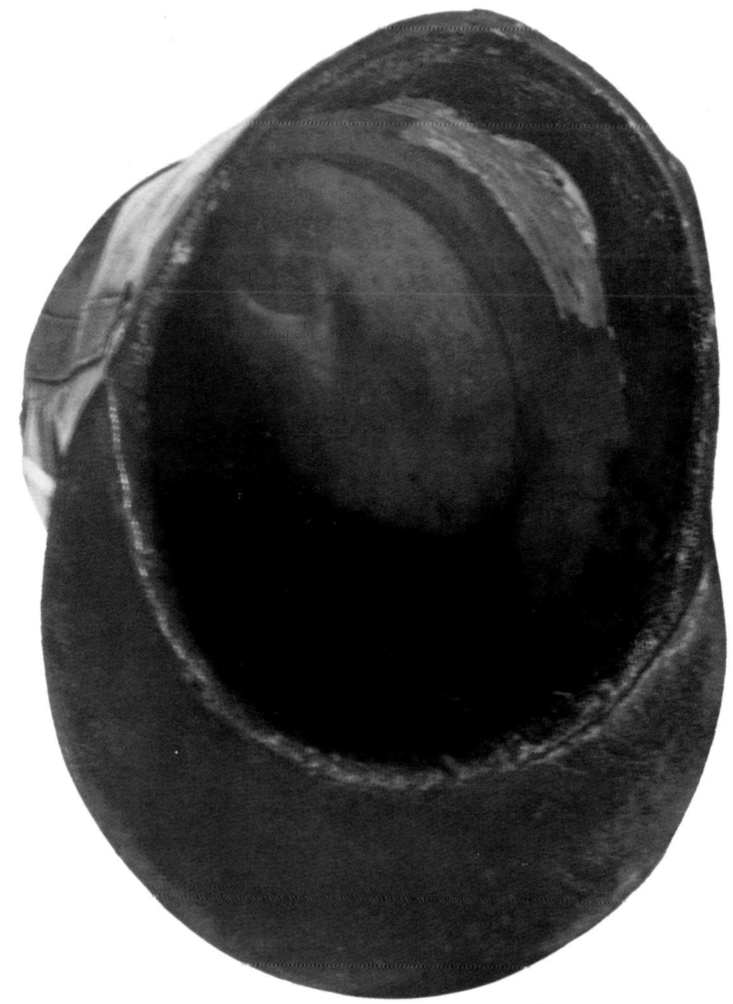

Front, rear, left side (with white worsted pompon), and right side of the second version of the 1813 pattern "tombstone" cap. Note the white cords are missing. JCN

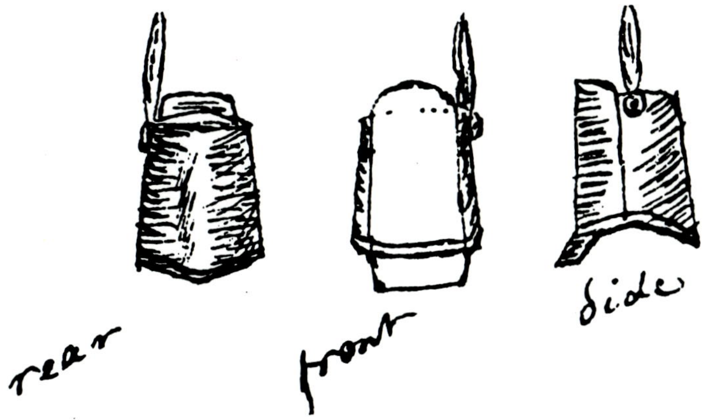

In May 1813, an anonymous officer serving at Ft. Niagara, NY, sent a letter to Callender Irvine in Washington, DC, suggesting an improvement to the 1813 pattern cap. The recommendation was based upon the observation that the leather used to form the cap's body was not sufficiently flexible to permit the piece of headgear to be seated on "the head without too uncomfortable pressure." The upright position of the front of the cap supposedly caused the headgear to be ungainly, and did not afford protection against the sun and the rain. Instead, the officer proposed "the angle" of the cap's front "should be very oblique...." Further, the position of the plume on the side was called in question, and a front placement was advocated. This sketch accompanied the letter, showing the cap's back, front, and left side as issued. NA

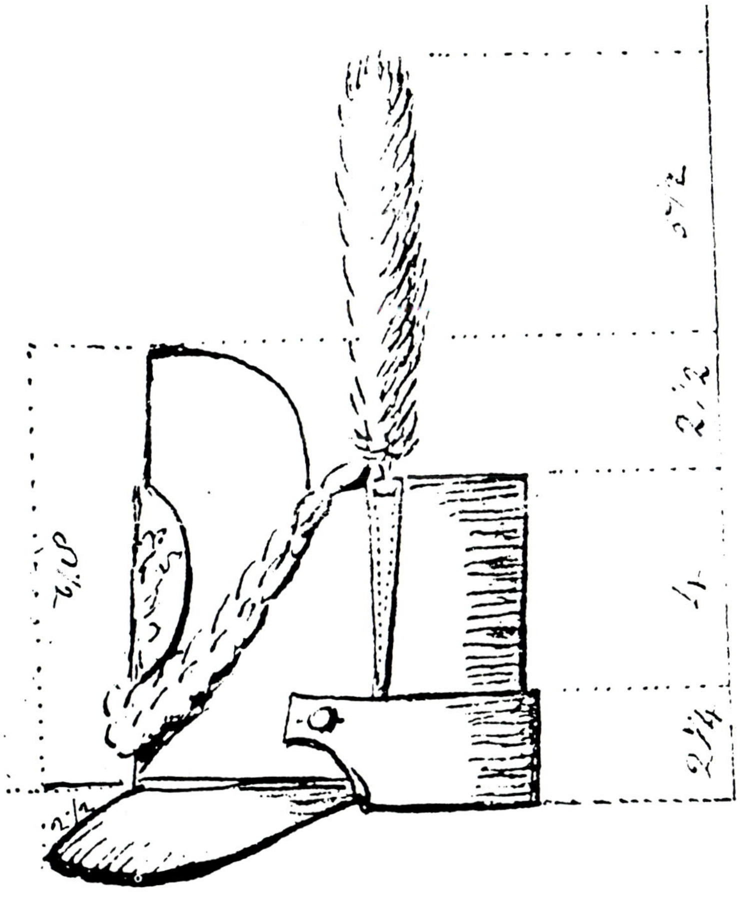

The military storekeeper at Baltimore, MD, Thomas B. Rutter, enclosed a drawing of the 1813 pattern infantry cap in a February 18, 1817, letter he sent to the commissary general of purchases detailing the state of the inventory of such headgear then on hand. The illustration included the flap that could be lowered to help protect the wearer's neck, as well as a tapered leather socket attached to the left side to hold the eight inch pompon. The cords appear to be double rather than triple woven, and festooned from right to left to form a semi-circle, rather than being attached at a high point on the right side then drooping down to the visor on the left side, which supposedly was the common position for the worsted bands. NA

The light dragoons were resurrected in 1808, when a regiment was to be raised after an incident at sea the previous year brought the United States and Great Britain to the brink of war.[12] These horsemen were to have a leather cap or helmet, ornamented with white tipped blue feathers, that for privates were not to measure more than 10 inches. The top of the helmet was to have bearskin attached. The former oval plate from the 1800 helmet was discontinued. The front of the cap now was to display the brass (subsequently changed to "white metal") letters "USLD," standing for the U.S. Light Dragoons.[13] Another change came in May 1808, with the substitution of leopard skin for the bearskin band previously specified! Evidently the cap also had a white horsehair crest.[14]

The 1808 expansion of the Jeffersonian army likewise included a Regiment of Light Artillery, consisting of ten companies of gunners who were to be mobile, often through the use of horses. One of the batteries was commanded by Captain George Peter, who along with his men did away with the cocked hat. Instead, Peter's company adopted a leather cap with "erect wings" on the rear and front, with a leather cockade attached to the latter. The cap had a "front piece" (visor) as well. A red plume with its stem resting on the lower edge of the crown was at first specified, but on May 21, 1808, Secretary of War Henry Dearborn wanted a "Blue feather, tipt with Red...the feathers of privates not to exceed ten inches in length" to be used. These were to be "real fathers, well made." Additionally, according to June instructions for contractors making the cap, the front was to have "USLA" in Roman letters of "good brass."[15] In most respects, then, this headgear type and its dragoon counterpart had a similar outline, the accessories probably being the basic distinguishing feature, although with no extant examples for comparison it is difficult to draw definite conclusions.

Yet a third unit spawned by the 1808 war scare, the Regiment of Riflemen, was to have a cap as well, the front of which was to bear brass

The variation of the front plate on this specimen of an 1813 pattern infantry cap may indicate that this piece was worn by an officer. SI

1 1/2-inch "in length" Roman letters "USRR."[16] These were to have brass tongues that allowed them to be attached to the front of the cap, which was to be of "jacked leather" and lined with linen. The prototype had yellow cloth binding in front, but the commissary general of the army allowed that one-inch brass trim could be employed instead. He also specified a green feather tipped in black measuring ten inches in height for privates. Finally a cockade was called for. With these elements decided upon, contracts were let in Washington, DC, and Philadelphia, in the latter case with George Green & Son and Samuel Dallam, Saddler, respectively to produce these "yeoman" crowned caps.[17]

A few years after the Rifle Regiment was outfitted in their special head dress a new cap was adopted for infantry rank and file (including company grade officers, while field grade officers retained their chapeaus). In 1811 orders were released that these foot soldiers would give up their cocked hats for black felt or beaver caps. These were described as standing from 6 7/8 to 7 1/4 inches in height with a 2 1/2 inch visor and having cords and tassels, along with a front plate that displayed an eagle, the regimental number, and branch designation (i.e., infantry).[18]

The following year, 1812, regulations published in February provided other details as to headgear for not only the infantry, but also the U.S. Army as a whole. To begin with, the light artillery cap was to be:

> Black, seven inches high, the crown eight & a half inches diameter; the visor two & a half inches broad, lined with stiff leather; a gold band & tassel falling from the crown of the cap on the right side; gilt plate in front; plume white, tipped with red, length 6 1/4 inches; cockade, black leather.[19]

Captain I.B. Crane of the Third U.S. Artillery indicated the artillerymen at Sackets Harbor in fact had adopted "the new leather caps which are raised in front, such as generally issued to the Infantry," but with "small plates," and "pompons white tip'd with red."[20]

An excavated specimen of an infantry cap plate for the 1813 pattern cap, in this case from Ft. Marks in the Florida Panhandle. Photograph by A.M. de Quesada. ADEQ

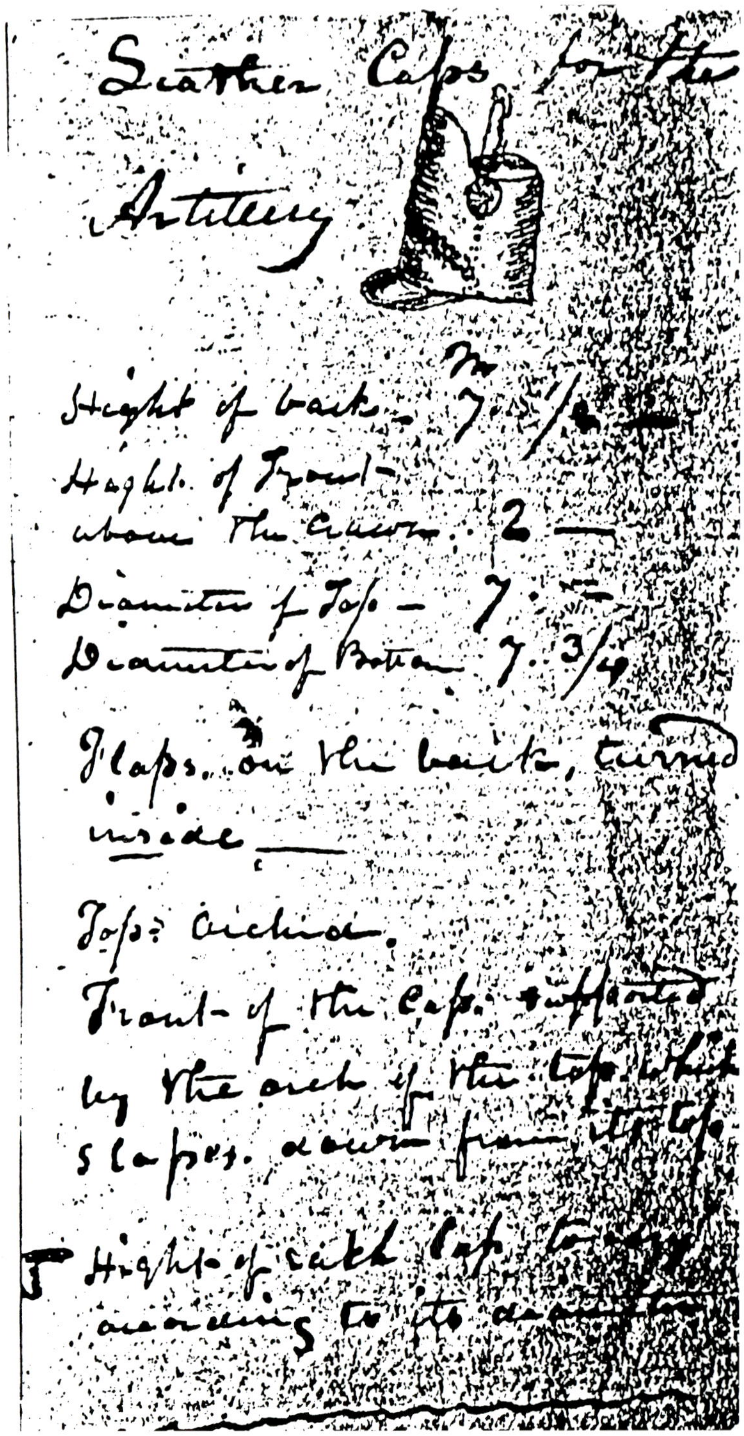

Leather Caps for the Artillery

Hight of back 7 1/4

Hight of Front above the crown 2 —

Diameter of Top — 7 —

Diameter of Bottom 7 3/4

Flaps on the back, turned inside —

Top arched

Front of the cap affected by the arch of the top which slopes down from the top

Hight of each cap [illegible] according to its [illegible]

Right: Captain William Gates of the Corps of Artillery communicated with the commissary general of purchases in a letter sent on January 16, 1816. He provided measurements and a profile of the cap worn by his gunners, which was the same style issued to infantrymen. DF

Infantry cap with a variant diamond-shaped plate similar to the 1812 pattern rifleman plate. A portion of the triple weave cord also is evident. JCN

Early in 1813 this beaver cap was to be phased out gradually by a leather model that drew its inspiration from a design adopted the previous year by Britain's troops, despite the fact that England and the United States were engaged in a war at the time![21] Unlike the felt caps, which were subject to damage from rain and other forms of moisture, the leather types theoretically could withstand the elements better. In late 1812 Callender Irvine, the commissary general of purchases for the U.S. Army at the time, summed up the reasons for this change in a letter to Secretary of War William Eustis, contending the leather cap for infantry, artillery, light artillery, and riflemen was "preferable as to appearance, comfort, durability, and on the score of economy...."[22]

Early the next year the secretary of war approved the new cap's design, but called for the rear hood that folded down to protect the neck to be held in place by buttons when not in use, rather than by hooks as originally proposed by Irvine.[23] At first, contracts all let in March 1813 called for "a molding 'round the Cap to be made of Block tin," and for a ring to be "affixed on each side of the said Cap, to place the band & Tassels...."[24] By the following month the metallic trim was replaced with a painted white edging.[25] Shortly thereafter the caps were available and issued to the troops.

The response was not always as desired. Although Irvine thought the design was neat and well proportioned, and the workmanship adequate, an officer stationed at Ft. Niagara, New York, found the style wanting. He made a number of suggestions to improve the caps. Subse-

Design of the 1814 pattern infantry cap plate. Courtesy of J. Duncan Campbell. NA

Front and back of an 1814 pattern Regiment of Riflemen cap plate. JCN

Side and interior view of the "Yeoman" style cap for members of the Regiment of Riflemen. Some artillery units were issued this pattern as well. JCN

A circa 1812 Second U.S. Artillery cap plate. DT

quently one of Irvine's subordinates, George Flomerfelt, acting under orders from his superior, inspected more than 7,000 of the caps in the inventory. Upon examination of the specimens, Flomerfelt found that nearly thirty percent of the articles did not conform to specifications. He also made it known that the varnish used to coat the leather bodies tended to crack. As a recourse he suggested painting the leather. By early 1814 some 15,000 more caps were ordered for infantrymen and 1,200 for artillerymen from the New York City firm of Robert Dingee, most of these being more closely in line with the model sought by government officials.[26]

The caps as adopted consisted of a nearly cylindrical leather body with a high front piece that rose above the crown by approximately three inches, the former element being attached separately. Inside sheep skin served as a sweatband. There also was a short linen lining with a drawstring.[27]

One contemporary illustration of infantrymen rendered by Charles Hamilton Smith, a British officer who painted a watercolor of four American soldiers and officers in 1816, depicted this cap with its accessories.[28] This included the simple cap plate at first referred to in 1811, but subsequently replaced by somewhat more substantial and ornate versions bearing an eagle, drum, and flag motif.[29] Thereafter several

Design of the 1817 pattern Regiment of Riflemen cap plate. Courtesy of J. Duncan Campbell. NA

Three U.S. artillery regiments received this type of cap plate in 1813. DT

Sketch of the yellow metal "second pattern" 1814 Light Artillery cap plate. Courtesy of J. Duncan Campbell

A leather U.S. Light Artillery cap with plate of the 1814 pattern. Photograph by Mark Sexton. ADA#103,346. PEI

variations on this ornamentation came into being. In some instances, no plate at all may have been attached.[30] The original plates were of white metal, but difficulty in obtaining items of this material and keeping them polished eventually led to the substitution of brass plates, as well as brass eagles on the black leather die cut cockades of the caps.

While variants of these accessories existed, the worsted pompons ultimately became more uniform. During the War of 1812 they evidently came in white for infantry, white tipped with red for artillery, and green for riflemen, but by 1818 "pompoms for all the caps" were to be white, and plumes were no longer to be used. Regardless of the color, these worsted pompons accented the left side, and at its base a black leather cockade with the eagle was called for.[31] A worsted band and tassel was prescribed to complete the cap. These either ran diagonally across the front, or in some instances were draped across the front and back, suspended from brass rings attached to the body by wires.[32]

The new "stovepipe" infantry cap and its accessories varied in quality and appearance, owing to the fact that stocks were obtained from

An example of the 1814 pattern Corps of Artillery cap plate. JCN

Right: Annotations on Smith's portrait of a major general and a staff officer in 1816 included an image of the latter individual's "Black bicorn with gold tassels at each end," while he noted the former officer had a "Black bicorn with gold lace, tassels, cockade loop and button. Black cockade with gold (?) eagle." By permission of the Harry Eakins Widener Collection. HL

Charles Hamilton Smith's painting of "United States Artillery" provided a glimpse of the black shako with yellow borer and cords, along with white plume prescribed in 1813. By permission of the Harry Eakins Widener Collection. HL

assorted makers and at different times. Variations included not only the cap bodies, but also as noted the plates and even pompons.[33]

Additionally, this pattern did not completely replace the previous "yeoman crown" cap, a pattern that had a top that was larger in diameter than the base. Indeed, the rifle regiments were authorized this type of headgear from 1812 through 1815, while certain infantry regiments and some artillerymen likewise evidently retained the pattern, at least for part of the war, despite the fact that Irvine indicated no more felt caps were being made by 1814. Some two years later Captain William Gates of the Corps of Artillery commented on the leather artillery cap, which by that time had been adopted for gunners.[34] As of February 1813, further clarification provided for field officers of the Rifle Regiment to retain the chapeau, while company officers would have the black cap with yellow band, tassels, and eagle and green plume, as would non-commissioned officers and the soldiers.[35]

Even as the cap for foot troops was evolving, so, too, does it appear that the dragoon helmet authorized in 1808 was in a state of flux. By 1812 orders simply described the piece as "According to pattern, blue feather with white top, feather nine inches long." This ornament may have been attached via a cockade and eagle on specimens issued early in the war. Evidently this leather helmet was again to bear a plate with a

Detail of the eagle, gold plaited bands, cockade, and button of an 1821 pattern "tar bucket"" for an officer of the Third U.S. Artillery. SI

A militia officer's form of the leather bell crown cap, which from the 1820s through 1832 was the primary headdress for company officers and enlisted men of the U.S. Army. The color of the pompon, the type of button in the cockade, and the chin scale color all indicated the wearer's branch and unit, in this case infantry. The cap is nearly identical to the regular army model. DT

Another example of the 1821-1832 regulation bell crown with white (pewter) metal chin scale, and eagle prescribed for the infantry. This example does not have the white worsted enlisted cords, the regimental numeral cut into the shield of the eagle, or the infantry button in the center of the cockade, thereby indicating that it is a militia piece of the era. In other respects, however, it conforms to the regular army style. CF

mounted dragoon in the act of charging in lieu of the brass letters previously applied to designate the horse soldier of the time, thereby returning to a similar plate called for in 1800. Specifications for the 1812 pattern did not mention leopard or bearskin trim.[36] Caps made around 1814 through 1815 have no indication of the feather ever being attached, although the white horsehair crest remained. Surviving examples may be part of a contract delivered by Henry Cressman of Philadelphia in May 1815, less than two months before Congress abolished the dragoons as part of the U.S. regular force.[37]

For nearly a decade, the patterns that came into being during the War of 1812 remained regulation, at least for the artillery and infantry. The dragoon helmet, however, was abandoned after horse soldiers disappeared from the rolls on June 15, 1815, as one of many economic moves to reduce the military.[38] Further, the chapeau was retained for generals, staff officers, and certain other officers throughout this period, and in various permutations continued to exist well into the twentieth century.[39]

In 1820, the status quo gave way with the introduction of a new leather "bellcrown." This particular nickname aptly described the item in that the top bells out, or is "scuttle-shaped," and is of a type which can be traced back to the Napoleonic era in Russia. Adopted in 1812, the *kiver* of Czar Alexander I's army soon caught the eye of other martial leaders.[40] This fashion ultimately spread to the Prussian, English, and other European forces, and subsequently made its way across the Atlantic.[41]

Infantry enlisted 1821 pattern leather cap for a soldier of the Fifth U.S. Infantry. FWSQ

An earlier photograph of the same Fifth U.S. Infantry 1821 pattern enlisted cap, taken in the 1870s, inexplicably depicted three tassels (not two) on the right side, but showed the correct original white pompon. MHS

U.S. Marine Corps company grade office's bell crown of the 1820s through 1830s. Photograph by A.M. de Quesada. USMCM

The version that came into being in the United States, while authorized in April 1820, was not available immediately. By the following year, however, the *General Regulations for the United States Army* described the model for company officers (second lieutenants through captains) and enlisted men as:

> ...of leather bell crown; gilt scales; yellow eagle, in front, three inches between the tips of the wings, with the number of the regiment cut in the shield; black leather cockade, one and one half inch in diameter, having a small yellow button in the centre, with an eagle impressed on it. Those of enlisted men will be leather, and of the same form as those prescribed for officers; brass scales.[42]

The regulation went on to state:

> Chapeau de bras will be worn by all officers, whether of line or staff, except company officers. Caps will be worn by all company officers when on duty with their companies....

To further set off officers of artillery, "yellow pompons five inches in length" were to be worn, while light artillery officers were to have white pompons with red tops, infantry officers white ones, light infantry officers yellow ones, and rifle company officers green ones. The men in each of these various units were to follow suit in terms of pompon colors.

The 1825-1832 forage cap, or "chako," with radiating worsted cords in white for infantry enlisted men. Infantry troops also had a "white metal" button at the top center of this cap. SI

Front and rear view of a c. 1825 chapeau. Staff officers and field grade officers of infantry traditionally wore the chapeau through much of the early nineteenth century. FAM

Tassels were another means to differentiate the wearer's branch, gold cord and bullion being called for the artillery and rifle officers, and silver cord and bullion for infantry officers. Enlisted artillerymen were to have "yellow worsted cords; those enlisted men of infantry...white worsted; and those of the enlisted men of the rifle corps...green worsted."

A year later, in 1822, a slight adjustment was made in that the chin scales and insignia for infantry was changed from yellow metal to white. Shortly thereafter pewter versions began to be produced and issued with the caps.[43]

Traditionally, promulgation of a new regulation issue item lagged behind its actual distribution to the troops. This was the case for the new cap, although by 1823 all enlisted men were to have them. One cap was provided for each five year enlistment. At the conclusion of this service, the cap was to be returned to the government, unlike other components of the soldier's uniform.[44]

One of the reasons for this close accountability was the cost. The cap was charged to the soldier at $1.50 plus an additional $1.51 for the pompon, tassel, bands, cockade, and insignia. This price likewise included either a foul weather painted linen cover or oilcloth cover made under contract by Benjamin Morange and Son or William Debraufre, respectively. In turn, officers laid out the princely sum of $8.50 to George Armitage for a complete cap, out of a base pay of $75 per month for company officers.[45]

In the case of officers, bands and tassels probably were made of silver or gold bullion, and evidently were plaited. Those for enlisted men, however, were of worsted in white for infantry and yellow for artillery, both styles being provided for by contracts, with John Gethem often receiving orders for these accessories at a cost of $.12 each. These cords were to be ten inches long with a 5/8 inch circumference, and were to end in two and one-half inch tassels that had a round head from which fringes emanated. The cord and tassels combined were to measure fifteen inches. These were attached to the right side of the cap from a brass ring, and seem to be the only adornment save the insignia, cockade with button, scales, and pompon.[46]

Thereafter, this cap first authorized in 1820 remained unchanged, except for pompons. For example, according to new uniform regulations adopted in 1825 the pompon for light artillery companies was to be yellow with a red tip, and for light infantry companies the color was to be white with a red top "should the President order one per regiment to take this designation."[47]

While the "tar bucket" was a thing of beauty to some, it was not an entirely practical item for all occasions. In fact, from time to time over the early years of its existence, the U.S. Army had provided its troops with various sorts of "foraging caps." In certain instances, old issue dress caps were to be dispensed for this purpose, which was the case in 1821 when the secretary of war approved a request to provide surplus 1813 "Waterloo" pattern leather caps to the troops, who could cut them down for fatigue wear.[48] A cheap gray cloth cap also was produced in that same year through the army's Schuylkill Arsenal in Philadelphia. It could be rolled to fit in the knapsack, and probably had some sort of flaps so the headpiece could be extended to protect the face and chin.[49]

This style was short-lived though, and in turn was replaced by a new forage cap approved in 1825, although the gray cap continued to be used for two or more years in some units. The 1825-pattern forage cap was to be of dark blue "sergeant's cloth," a fairly good grade of wool, to which a flat unbound leather "poke," or bill, was fastened. Worsted tape in branch colors (white was for infantry and yellow for artillery) encircled the base of enlisted caps, while company officers had silver or gold lace and displayed the regimental numeral on their *chakos*, as this item was called in the 1825 uniform regulations. Enlisted men, on the other hand, were to have company letter of white or yellow metal that

Side view of Thomas S. Jesup's c. 1825 chapeau de bras. Jesup served as quartermaster general of the United States Army from 1818 through 1860. WJS

Right: Detail of the cockade of Jesup's chapeau. WJS

The chapeau remained in use throughout most of the post-Napoleonic era, as evidenced by this example worn by William Jenkins Worth as a major of the Ordnance Department. Worth was promoted to this rank on May 30, 1832. This item dates from that period. FWS&HM

was pierced at several points so it could be sewn to the headbands. Once again the color depended on the branch, as did the cuff-sized branch button set into the center of the chako's top.[50] From this button twenty twisted 1/4 inch worsted cords radiated and ended at the top of the band. The color of these cords may have been dark blue, although on the existing specimens they are dark green, perhaps having changed to this color over a period of time from fading.

Only one chako was issued per each five year enlistment, at a cost of $1.70. The fact that this cap was worn more extensively than the bell crown led to some complaints about the fact that no foul weather cover was provided for it as protection against the elements. Despite this shortcoming, the cap was far more suitable for most martial functions than the "tar bucket."[51]

Perhaps the fact that no inclement weather accessories were made for the chako led to further consideration of the matter of headgear for field and fatigue duty. For this reason and others, the head of the army Clothing Bureau noted that a new type of cap was about to be selected as a replacement for the 1825 pattern. Adoption of this new style triggered the next round in the evolution of martial headgear.

Notes:

[1] Richard H. Kohn, *Eagle and Sword: The Beginnings of the Military Establishment in America* (New York: The Free Press, 1975), offers an overview of the traces the early years of what became the United States Army from the American Revolution to 1802, and thereby provides an in depth analysis lacking in the foregoing brief introduction.

[2] John Mollo, *Military Fashion* (New York: G.P. Putnam's Sons, 1972), 45.

[3] It should be noted that in January 1799, the War Office issued orders that the black cockade would bear a white metal eagle, in the case of non-commissioned officers, musicians, and privates of tin. J. Duncan Campbell and Edgar M. Howell, *American Military Insignia 1800-1851* (Washington, DC: Smithsonian Institution, 1963), 9.

[4] Howell and Kloster, *United States Military Headgear to 1854*, 2-3. According to John R. Elting, ed., *Military Uniforms in America: Volume II Years of Growth, 1796-1851* (San Rafael, CA: Presidio Press, 1977), 6, in 1802 the creation of the Corps of Artillerists and Engineers that were stationed at West Point had by that time adopted red plumes for the enlisted men.

[5] General Orders, Headquarters, Fort Adams [Mississippi], March 30, 1800, Record Group 94, Records of the Adjutant General's Officer, National Archives, Washington, DC (hereinafter referred to as RG94, AGO, NA).

[6] As noted by Earl J. Coates and James L. Kotchan, *Don Troiani's Soldiers in America, 1754-1865* (Mechanicsburg, PA: Stackpole Books, 1998), 117, this style was adopted in 1812, but "During the 120 years of wear, it underwent a series of changes both in form and trimmings."

[7] Howell and Kloster, *United States Military Headgear to 1854*, 3. Uniform Regulations, February 1812, General Orders and Orders, Southern Department, Vol. 677, RG98, U.S. Army Continental Commands, NA. The latter document called for the chapeau of infantry field officers to consist of a fan "not less than 9 1/2 inches, or more than 11 inches high & not less than 16 nor more than 18 in length, bound round the edge with a black ribbon, one half inch wide, with a white button, silver tassels and loop; black cockade 3 1/2 inches in diameter, with a silver eagle in the center. The cockade to rise about one inch above the brim; a white plume to rise 8 inches above the brim of the hat." This same February 1812 pronouncement likewise prescribed the same style for all artillery officers and enlisted men, except that the button and eagle would be of yellow metal and the plume would project only 6 inches above the head gear of enlisted personnel while it was to be 8 inches high for officers, while surgeons and surgeon mates were to have the chapeau as well with "a black cockade & eagle & black Ostrich feather."

[8] Howell and Kloster, *United States Army Headgear to 1854*, 9. For additional discussion of this subject see, William K. Emerson, "Cockades and Eagles," *Military Collector and Historian* XXXV No. 3 (Fall 1983): 104-112.

[9] Kloster and Howell, *United States Army Headgear to 1854*, 8-9.

[10] General Orders, Headquarters, Fort Adams [Mississippi], March 30, 1800, RG94, AGO, NA.

[11] Ibid. These plates were struck in thin brass and backfilled with lead. The oval device then was attached by a double wire fastener soldered to the back according to, Campbell and Howell, *American Military Insignia*, 7.

[12] During June 1807, after HMS *Leopard* "attacked and disabled the USS *Chesapeake* and impressed several members of the crew" caused a wave of anti-English sentiment to grow. This affair fueled national politics as "war hawks" clamored for retaliation. Maurice Matloff, ed., *American Military History* (Washington, DC: Office of the Chief of Military History United States Army, 1969), 122-3

[13] Howell and Kloster, *United States Army Headgear to 1854*, 9. That pewter letters were worn can be ascertained by correspondence from Colonel James Burns of the Second Light Dragoons, who in July 1812, requested letters for the caps of his regiment to be made of this material. Campbell and Howell, *American Military Insignia*, 11.

[14] Joseph M. Thatcher, "U.S. Light Dragoon Belt Plates and Helmets, 1808-1812," *Military Collector and Historian* XXVII No. 1 (Spring 1975): 16-18. Similar headgear to the regular army's light dragoon helmet was worn during and long after the War of 1812 era by some state troops. For some examples consult: Frederick P. Todd, "Uniforms in Connecticut, 1784-1820," *Military Collector and Historian* XXV No. 3 (Fall 1973): 126-39; Philip G. Maples, "Uniform of the 5th Regiment Cavalry Connecticut Militia ca. 1835," *Military Collector and Historian XXXIV No. 4 (Winter 1982):* 176-7; Charles Cureton and Fitzhugh McMaster, 4th Cavalry Regiment, South Carolina Militia, 1841," *Military Collector and Historian* XXXIII No. 3 (Fall 1981): 123; and Philip G. Maples and Anthony Gero, "Helmets of the Lockport Light Dragoons, 1856 To 1860," *Military Collector and Historian* XXXII No. 4 (Winter 1980): 155-6.

[15] Elting, *Military Uniforms in America*, Vol. II, 4.

[16] John T. Powell, "Regiment of Riflemen Cap Insignia, 1808-1812," XXVII *Military Collector and Historian* No. 4 (Winter 1975): 180, illustrates an excavated set of this insignia from a U.S. military site occupied between 1798 and 1810. See also, Campbell and Howell, *American Military Insignia*, 11.

[17] Marko Zlatich and Detmar Finke, "The Uniform of the United States Rifle Regiment, 1808-1810," *Military Collector and Historian* L No. 3 (Fall 1998): 123.

[18] Howell and Kloster, *United States Army Headgear to 1854*, 15.

[19] Uniform Regulations, February 1812, General Orders and Orders, Southern Department, Vol. 677, RG98, NA.

[20] I. Crane to C. Irvine, August 19, 1819, Consolidated Correspondence Files, Office of the Quartermaster General, "Uniforms," RG92, NA, hereinafter referred to as CCF, OQMG. The original plan was for the heavy and light artillery to have yeoman crowned caps, as were riflemen. C. Irvine to A. Stetson, August 5, 1813, LS, Book B, Commissary General of Purchases (CGP), OQMG, RG92, NA.

[21] See, Elting, *Military Uniforms in America*, II, 72, 76, and 80, for examples of the British progenitor of the cap, sometimes referred to various as the "Wellington," "tombstone," "Waterloo," or "Belgic" shako. Further, Robert H. Rankin, *Military Headdress: A Pictorial History of Military Headgear from 1660 to 1914* (London: Arms and Armour, 1976), 17-18, offers additional information as well as two photographs of specimens clearly depicting this item's influence on the U.S. model. For additional information consult, Alex R. Cattley, "The British Infantry Shako," *Journal of the Society for Army Historical Research* XV No. 60 (Winter 1936): 188-208. The British actually took their inspiration for this design from Napoleon's Legion Portuguese, but had modified the look to the degree that the Duke of Wellington wanted a side mounted plume rather tan a one in front. Cecil P. Lawson, *A History of Uniforms of the British Army* (London: Kaye & Ward, Ltd., 1967), 18-21.

[22] C. Irvine to W. Eustis, December 26, 1812, LS, Book B, 1813, CGP, OQMG, RG92, NA.

[23] W. Eustis to C. Irvine, January 23, 1813, LS, Microcopy No. 6, Roll 6, Vol. 6, Secretary of War, 1808-1889, RG107, NA.

[24] "Dallam," "Foering," and "Gilder" CCF, OQMG, RG92, NA. Each of these contracts called for the delivery of 1,000 caps, the dates being March 20, 1813, March 15, 1813, and March 10, 1813, respectively.

[25] "Primrose" and "Lukens" April 10, 1813, and April 12, 1813, ibid.

[26] Frederick C. Gaede and Stephen E. Osman, "Notes on the 1813 Infantry Cap" *Military Collector and Historian* LXII No. 3 (Fall 1991): 110. This article is highly informative and deserves to be read completely by those interested in the 1813-pattern cap.

[27] Gaede and Osman, "Notes on the 1813 Infantry Cap," 111. Also see, Coates and Kotchan, *Don Troiani's Soldiers in America*, 104, that provides a succinct discussion

of the "old plan" 1813-pattern infantry cap, in contrast to the more common form of the cap which "is believed to have been first introduced in 1814." This version is "distinguished by having the raised front made integral to the one-piece body, rather than being separately attached as on the 1813 contract caps."

28 For more on Smith read: René Chartrand, "The United States Forces of 1812-1816 as Drawn by Charles Hamilton Smith, Officer and Spy" *Military Collector and Historian* XXXV No. 4 (Winter 1983): 142-9.

29 Ibid., 104, notes that only one of the three 1813-pattern contract caps shows evidence of have a front plate. According to Elting, *Military Uniforms in America*, Vol. II, 44, the U.S. Corps of Artificers wore a similar cap, but this one was made of felt "bound with gold lace" on the front, with a leather visor attached. A yellow band and tassels, along with a brass colored metal plate, a black rose cockade with a gilt eagle, and a green plume completed this headdress.

30 Campbell, *American Military Insignia*, 12-16, illustrates a number of variations of the 1812-1814 period. Gaede and Osman, "Notes on the 1813 Infantry Cap": 111, indicates that some caps did not bear plates.

31 Ibid., 112, offers considerable details about plates, eagles, and cockades.

32 During the War of 1812 and onwards to about 1818 the cords were made in the main by Sebastian Salade of Philadelphia. These came in white cotton for infantry and yellow for artillery at a cost of $.08 per set. Sometimes white ones were dyed at the army's clothing facility at Schuykill Arsenal. Although worsted ones were called for in 1816, cotton evidently continued to be used instead. Stephen E. Osman, "Bands and Tassels on the 1812 Army Cap," *Military Collector and Historian* XLII No. 4 (Winter 1990): 147.

33 Stephen E. Osman, "Some Additional Notes on the 1813 Infantry Cap and Trimmings," *Military Collector and Historian* LXIV No. 3 (Fall 1992): 135.

34 See Elting, *Military Uniforms in America*, Vol. II, 26-29, 36-37, and 40-1; and Gaede and Osman, "Notes on the 1813 Infantry Cap": 111. For Captain Gates' complaints about the height of the leather cap see, Detmar H. Finke, "An Additional Note on the Leather Artillery Cap, 1815/16," *Military Collector and Historian* XLIII No. 3 (Fall 1991): 115. This article further notes that on February 2, 1817, joint orders from the Adjutant General and Inspector General's Offices required the infantry leather cap to be worn by all corps.

35 H.C. McBarron. "American Military Dress in the War of 1812," Pt. IV "Regular Riflemen" *Military Affairs* V (1940): 140.

36 Uniform Regulations, February 1812, General Orders and Orders, Southern Department, Vol. 677, RG98, NA.

37 Howell and Kloster, *United States Army Headgear to 1854*, 9-14.

38 According to Coates and Kochan, *Don Troiani's Soldiers in America*, 97, most of the dragoon caps from the 1814 contract "were delivered into stores and never issued, which accounts for their mint condition today."

39 See for example, Leonard E. Ball, "William M. Boyce, First U.S. Infantry, 1822-1836," *Military Collector and Historian* XXIV No. 2 (Summer 1972): 44-47, for an excellent example of a chapeau worn by a regular U.S. Army officer in the post-War of 1812 era, but prior to a new pattern being adopted in 1832.

40 John Mollo, *Military Fashion* (New York: G.P. Putnam's Sons, 1972), 112. Mollo indicates the piece was "probably designed by Alexander himself." as does Philip J. Haythornewaite, *Uniforms of the Napoleonic Wars in Color, 1796-1814* (New York: Hippocrene Books, Inc., 1973), 167. See also Philip J. Haythornewaite, *Uniforms of the Retreat from Moscow, 1812* (New York: Hippocrene Books, Inc., 1976), 153 and 158.

41 Mollo, *Military Fashion*, 131-132, and 140, illustrates Russian examples and a Prussian one. Rankin, *Military Headdress*, 22, likewise illustrates an other ranks shako for the Prussian *Landwehr* infantry c. 1815. Although the body in all instances of these European specimens are felt with a leather top and visor, the basic outline is that of a "bell-top." It should be noted that Howell and Kloster, United States Army Headgear to 1854, 19, states: "by 1830 almost every European army except the French" adopted the style."

42 U.S. War Department, *General Regulations of the Army; or, Military Institutes* (Philadelphia: M. Carey & Sons, 1821), 155. Unless otherwise stated, the same reference is the source for subsequent quotations concerning this item.

43 Howell and Kloster, *United States Army Headgear to 1854*, 19.

44 General Orders No. 53, Adjutant Generals Office, August 14, 1822. Hereinafter referred to as GO No., AGO, and date.

45 Howell and Kloster, *United States Military Headgear to 1854*, 20-21.

46 Osman, "Bands and Tassels of the 1821 Army Cap": 148.

47 War Department, *General Regulations for the Army; or, Military Institutes* (Washington, DC: Davis & Force, printers, 1825), 36 and 157.

48 Gaede and Osman, "Notes on the 1813 Infantry Cap": 113.

49 Howell and Kloster, *United States Army Headgear to 1854*, 22.

50 Stephen E. Osman, "Company Letters for Regular Army Forage Caps, 1825-1872," *Military Collector and Historian* XL No. 4 (Winter 1988): 157, illustrates several excavated examples of the early letters, which were first obtained from contract by George Armitage of Philadelphia. According to this article: "By 1831, forage caps were routinely requisitioned and issued to units 'with letters.'"

51 The above information was taken from, Howell and Kloster, *United States Army Head gear to 1854*, 22-25. Further, according to a "Comparative Statement of the cost of clothing for the United States army during the years 1827, 1828, and 1829" and a "Comparative Statement of the cost of clothing for the United States army during the years 1830, 1831, and 1832," forage caps were charged at $1.63, $1.61, and $1.29 in 1827, 1828, and 1829, respectively versus $1.49 in 1830 and $1.39 in both 1831 and 1832, for infantry and artillery. This was as compared to $1.35 in 1827 and 1828, and $1.31 in 1829, while from 1830 through 1832 the costs were $1.31, $1.30, and $1.37 1/2 for the leather cap, and additional sum of $.20 for pompons, and $.12 for bands and tassels during the same period. Cockades and eagle were to be $.06 in 1830, $.4 1/2 in 1831 and 1832, whereas cap balls (to hold the pompon?) were charged at $.05 in 1830 and at $.04 in the following two years. Additionally, cap plates for artillery were $.08 in 1830, and $.04 thereafter, as compared to sets of scales which ran $.45 in 1830 and $.30 for 1831 and 1832 in contrast to infantry plates that were $.08 in 1830, $.05 in 1831, and $.05 1/2 in 1832 with the scales being $.45 in 1830 and $.40 in 1831 through 1832. Finally, the oil cloth cover for these caps were to be issued at $.41 in 1830, and $.30 3/4 in 1831 and 1832. Microfilm Collections, Box 82, U.S. Army Military History Institute, Carlisle Barracks, PA, hereinafter referred to as USAMHI.

2

Expanding a Nation 1833-1860

During July 1832, a decision was made to adopt a leather forage cap. Nonetheless, some time passed before actual issue was permitted under General Order No. 38, Headquarters of the Army, May 2, 1833. Even then, this document authorized only West Point cadets and the troopers of the newly established Regiment of Dragoons to receive the cap.[1] All other troops, with a few exceptions, were to continue to receive the old chako until supplies were exhausted.[2]

When the leather caps eventually became available, there were distinct differences between those worn by troops in the field and those found at West Point. The former were to be of morocco leather and the latter of goatskin. Further, caps for dragoons were to have a slightly wider poke (visor) and a six inch folding flap in the rear that could be lowered to protect the back of the head from the elements. These differences accounted for the fact that in 1833 the dragoon pattern cost $.87 1/2, as opposed to the infantry and artillery version, which was priced at $.75 (versus the cadet model that ran $2.00 each to include a fee for the storekeeper at the military academy). Because this cap was considered impervious to moisture it did not require a cover, but an accessory for cold climates was provided consisting of a 2 1/2 inch wide black fur band that could be attached at the base to add some warmth around the ears and forehead, where it was to be tied.[3]

As for insignia, the company letter in yellow metal was prescribed "in all cases."[4] This meant both infantry and artillery troops were to employ devices of brass, but in reality evidence exists for both white and yellow metal being dispersed to differentiate the infantrymen (white) from artillerymen (yellow).[5]

This new forage cap was used for the next several years, being issued to troops during the campaign against the Seminoles in Florida and others until a replacement was proposed during the winter of 1838-39 by Major General Alexander Macomb, who was at that time in command of the U.S. Army. Inspired by the British 1825 pattern forage cap and by the popular use of civilian hunting and workmen's caps with

Front view of an 1833 pattern leather forage cap. A small flap in the rear, which could be lowered into position, was designed to help protect the neck from sun and rain. The button holding the chin strap in place is an incorrect 1884 pattern replacement, rather than the type originally issued with the cap. SI

The 1833 pattern forage cap, sometimes known as the "gig top," had the distinction of being able to be folded. Most other headgear of the Victorian era U.S. Army was rigid. SI

Front, back, side, interior, lining with maker's label (Luke Davies 102 Williams NY), and folded view of Captain Henry Dupont's 1833 pattern forage cap. Dupont served with the Fourth U.S. Artillery Regiment, as indicated by the number on the front of his cap. DHS

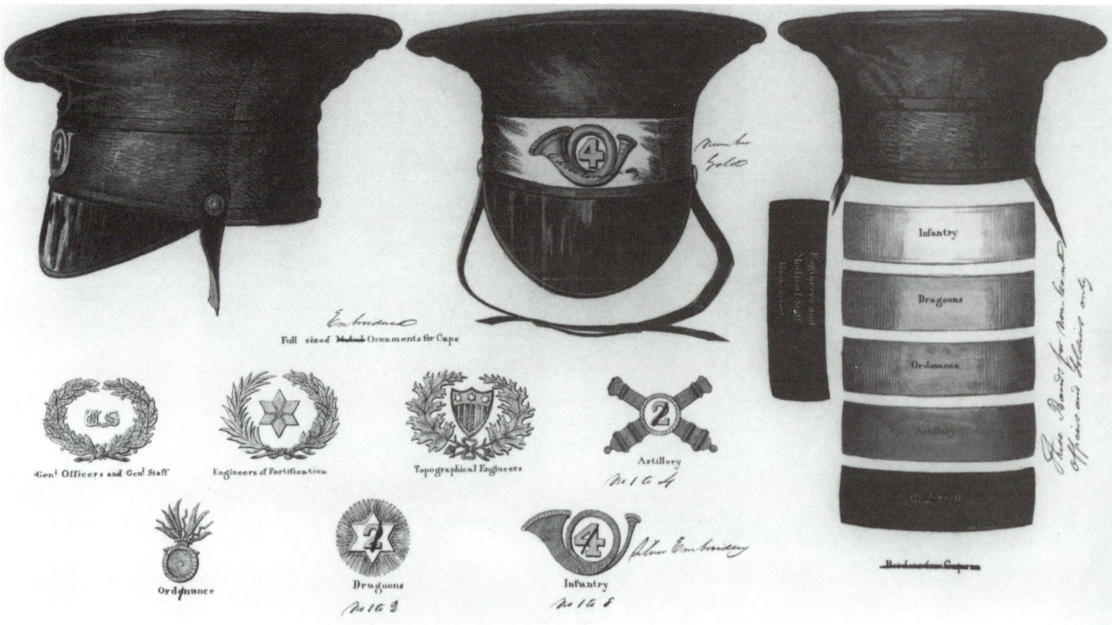

The preliminary concept for the 1839 pattern forage cap called for colored bands representing each branch, and on which an embroidered insignia was to be affixed in the case of officers, as shown here in a specification drawing that introduced the new cap. The provision for the band was discarded for the most part, while the use of insignia essentially would be optional when the cap finally was adopted. NA

leather visors and cloth tops, Macomb contacted the head of the Clothing Bureau in Washington, DC, to recommend a blue cloth model set off by color coordinated bands to distinguish the various branches. He provided a drawing of the concept and required prototypes for officers to be made up, the latter group having a version with patent leather chinstrap and silk oil cloth detachable covers for foul weather.

As work progressed, it was decided that both officers and men should have the colored bands around the crown, and also that officers would wear metallic insignia, such as the hunting horn for infantry, crossed cannons for artillery and the like, as opposed to the embroidered versions which Macomb had first envisioned. Additionally, the leader of the elite Corps of Topographical Engineers secured a cap with a black silk band with worsted lace that was adorned with oak leaves and acorns, as well as a shield encircled by oak leaves. Furthermore, cadets at the U.S. Military Academy obtained a black velvet band with a wreath enclosing the letters "USMA" all in embroidery, an adornment that remained regulation until dispensed with in 1843.

Several other minor details were finally attended to, including the decision that colored bands would be dropped for officers. With that, by 1840 efforts to secure new forage caps began for the rank and file, as well as for West Point cadets. Progress was slow, and those officials responsible for providing uniforms to the troops began to send out caps to seamstresses as piecework to enhance production, including some made of waterproofed fabric.[6]

Presumably the company letters continued to be made in white metal for infantry and yellow metal for artillery. Furthermore, the ornaments for officers were to be of gilt, yellow metal, white metal, silver, or plated, according to contracts let in 1839.[7] As an example of the variations that came to exist, in 1846 the regimental band of the First U.S. Dragoons were directed to wear a brass "1" on the front of their caps applied to a

This example of an 1839 pattern forage cap has the silver embroidery U.S. enclosed by a gold embroidered wreath, the insignia that ultimately came to be standard for general officers and staff officers, in this case for a member of the latter group, William W.S. "Perfect" Bliss, an assistant adjutant general and member of Zachary Taylor's staff during the Mexican War. He would marry Taylor's daughter. WC

Staff officer's removable blue wool band with silver embroidered device, the construction of which is evident on the backside of the cloth, for an 1839 pattern cap. This example was worn by Captain Samuel Gibbs French, an artillery officer during the war with Mexico who was wounded at Buena Vista. A native of New Jersey, Gibbs would later become a Confederate general. GHS

Front, side, and interior of Major General Zachary Taylor's 1839 pattern forage cap. WC

blue background, while a double row of yellow worsted tape ran around the crown.[8] During that year another piece of insignia was added: a stamped metal castle affixed to a black cotton velvet band for enlisted men of the newly created Company of Sappers, Miners, and Pontoniers.[9]

The cap as originally conceived was found wanting according to a uniform board that met in 1844. Recommendations to allow for one cap per year, rather than for one per every five years as prescribed by previous regulations, was suggested, or failing that an oil cloth cover was sought and three caps per every five year enlistment submitted as adequate under that scheme. These recommendations fell on deaf ears, and only one cap was doled out for every five year enlistment.[10] This may in part account for the relative rarity of surviving specimens.

Moreover, those few extant examples range in design and details. Most are hand made, but some that may be of manufacture from the 1850s have been at least partially machine sewn. The types of visors vary, and some caps are made without the colored bands, albeit the contemporary Mexican American War account by Samuel Chamberlain in his autobiographical *My Confession*, along with paintings based by an eyewitness artist, James Walker, depict colored bands.[11] Then, too, insignia is found on some caps for officers and enlisted personnel alike,

An officer's 1839 pattern forage cap worn by Lieutenant James Duncan, Second Artillery, was another of the many variations of this cap available between the time of its adoption and the final discontinuance of the cap in the 1850s. Michael McAfee Photograph. WPM

Another 1839 pattern forage cap exhibits the company letter. Those in brass or yellow metal typically were for artillerymen and dragoons, while those in pewter or white metal would be appropriate for infantrymen. This cap was made at the Schuylkill Arsenal, and has three black dots in the lining to indicate it is a size three. DT

Side, detail of chinstrap and sweatband, and rear of an 1839 pattern Schuykill Arsenal produced cap. Note the flap could be let down in the back to protect the neck. DT

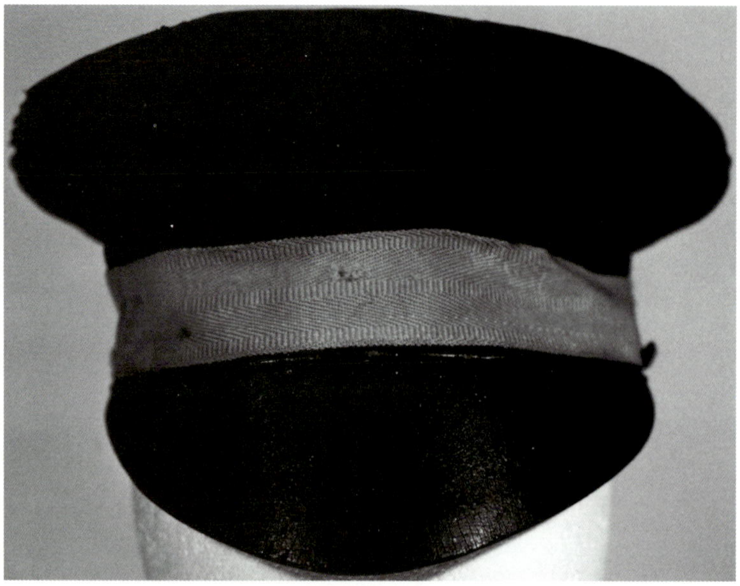

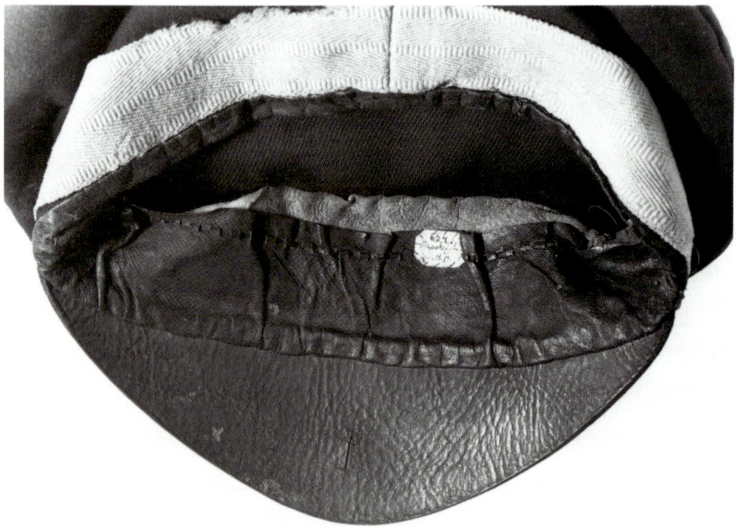

Front, rear, and interior view of an 1839 pattern Second Dragoons enlisted forage cap. Note the worsted yellow cap band that was a trademark of the regiment. Bandsmen of the First Regiment of Dragoons had a double row of yellow lace or facing that went around the base of the cap, and a regimental numeral in front. Tom Shaw Photograph. MNHS

Opposite: This sketch, rendered by a soldier in the First U.S. Dragoons, depicts Sergeant Lindner of Company D from the regiment as he appeared while stationed at Ft. Snelling, Minnesota, in the early 1850s. He wears the 1839 pattern forage cap with company letter. NA

The 1839 forage cap is referred to as "Type 1" by some sources, although this designation was not contemporary to the period when the style was manufactured or in use. The distinctive feature of this cap was its sharply pointed visor, which measured 2 1/2 inches at its widest. The padded crown had a 10 1/2 inch diameter. A 4 inch wide cape would be let down in the back, but when not in use was folded and kept in place by the black silk ribbons that were tied in the front. Two vest-size buttons held the patent leather chinstrap to the band. SI

The so-called "Type 2" 1839 pattern enlisted forage cap differed somewhat from the Type 1 in that its visor was more rounded and not applied in as steep an angle. Further, the crown was not padded. In many other respects, however, the cap resembled the Type 1, including the folded rear flap with ribbon ties, chin strap, and vest-size side buttons. Yet a third type was similar to the others, but had no chinstrap. Rather, the flap was held in place by black ties and a metal hook on each side toward the front of the crown that was inserted into a sewn thread eye. SI

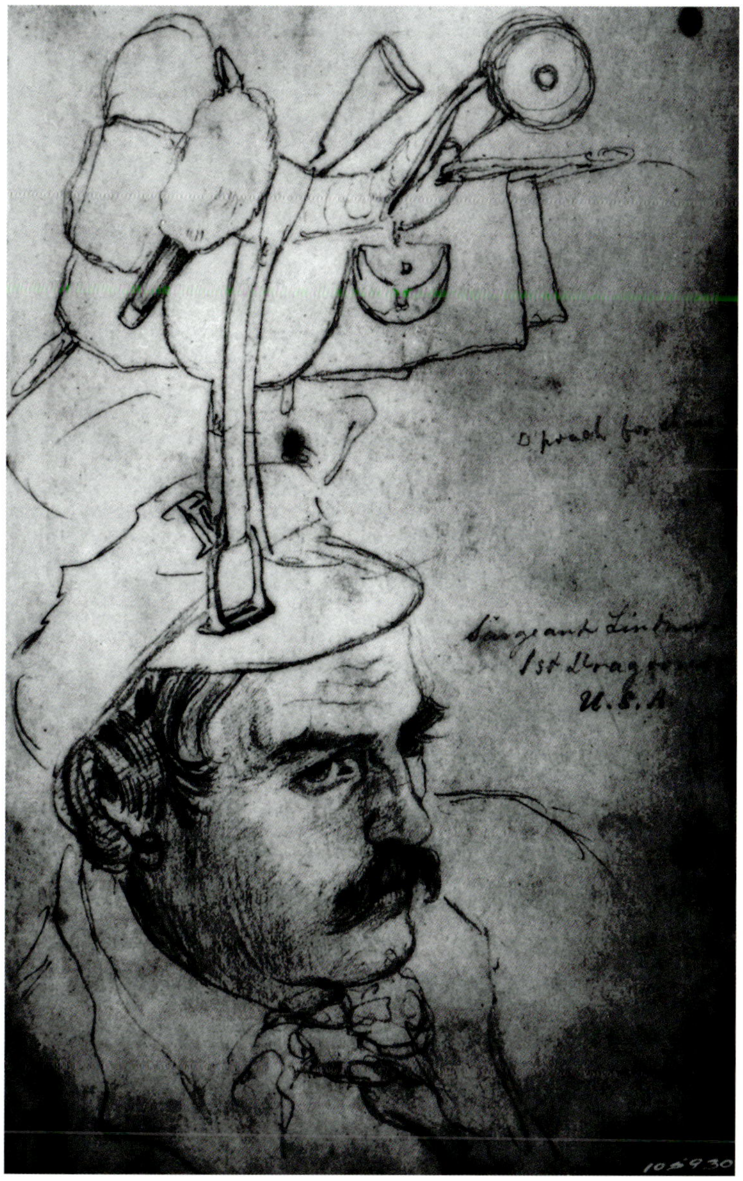

while it is absent on others. Variations aside, the cap seemed popular and saw widespread use well into the 1850s, despite the fact that it was supplanted officially early in the decade by another style.

The same situation applied to a somewhat lesser degree to the successor of the "tar bucket." As early as 1832 the head of the army clothing bureau, Major John Garland, asked the inspector general of the army, Brigadier General John Wool, for assistance. At that time Wool was on official travel abroad, and Garland requested the general send back specimens of the British kit with the tacit admission: "for I have perceived we have copied from the English in most of the changes which have been made [in the American uniform]."[12]

This correspondence was only the beginning of efforts to provide several items of new issue relative to the uniform, including the bell crown. An original attempt to provide artillery and infantry officers, regardless of their rank, with a cap was spelled out in 1832 by General Order No. 50, which published these specifications:

> ...of black beaver, six inches deep, with lacquered sunk tip, eleven inches in diameter, communicating by black leather stitched side straps, with a band of same, which was to encircle the bottom of the cap; patent leather peak [visor]; gilt eagle, number, and scales as at present worn.[13]

Scarlet eight inch cock feathers held by a gilt socket were to decorate artillery officer's caps, and white eight inch cock feathers were the mark of an infantry officer. In both instances, officers were to wear the caps when on duty, but regimental officers not serving with their units had the prerogative to "wear Cocked hats as prescribed for General staff officers, except that the loop will be of black silk: the eagle yellow, the tassels to conform to the colour of the button."

Conversely, General Order No. 50 went on to indicate those officers posted with their regiments were to obtain the new cap by July 1, 1833, and the class about to graduate from West Point, along with any other officers entering service after June 1832, were to procure the cap immediately upon commissioning. In like manner, enlisted men were to have the same cap, but with red upright hackles measuring eight inches for artillery, and white versions of the same height for all non-commissioned officers, musicians, and privates of infantry.

This scheme proved short-lived, however, because by 1833 a replacement for this head piece was approved. Soon contracts were let so that by later that year recruits would have been issued the cap, followed by most of the rank and file in 1834. In July, all remaining 1821 pattern caps were sold to the U.S. Marine Corps.[14] Even then, as an interim measure, pompons which presumably were on hand from the 1821 pattern bell crown were to be worn with the 1832 pattern cap in place of the feathers, or "hackles," that were set forth in the regulations for non-commissioned officers, musicians, and privates.[15] Eventually, the following scheme was to be in force: scarlet or white twelve inch long upright hackles would adorn those worn by artillery and infantry sergeants major respectively; hackles for regimental quartermaster sergeants were to be the same except in light blue; chief musicians would have white hackles. Ten inch white hackles were called for in the case of all other musicians, while sergeants, corporals, and privates were to have eight inch hackles in scarlet for artillery and white for infantry. Metal regimental numbers also were to be placed on the cap fronts to designate the wearer's unit.[16]

These were to be worn on caps that were identical to those set forth in the 1834 General Regulations of the Army for officers. This document specified that the hat for artillery officers was to be:

> ...black beaver, seven and a half inches deep, with lackered sunk tip seven and a half inches diameter with a band of black patent leather to encircle the bottom of the cap; black patent leather peak, gilt eagle and crossed cannons and number of the regiment as at present worn; a black strap of black patent leather, fastened on each side of the cap, to be worn under the chin. Plume—red cock-feathers, falling from an upright stem, eight inches long, with a gilt socket.[17]

This last mentioned item, the sheet brass plume holder, came to be known as a "tulip" because of its shape and was universal on all caps, although its design may have differed a bit from one maker to the next, and particularly among officers. Furthermore, infantry officers were to have the same cap, but wear white cock feathers and display a silver bugle on the front.[18]

Over the next few years, manufacturing problems evidently kept the cost of these caps high.[19] Nevertheless, the government let contracts for them and made two caps available to the soldier for each five-year

Second Lieutenant Bezaleel Wells Armstrong, West Point Class of 1845, was assigned to the First U.S. Dragoons in 1846. Although the dress uniform was to be worn with the tall cap and gold cords, Armstrong instead has opted for the 1839 pattern forage cap with the addition of a six-pointed star of the type that was sewn to the rear tails of the coatee. HP

Isaac Bowen, a company grade officer with the First U.S. Artillery from the early 1840s through the late 1850s, wears a pair of crossed cannon on his 1839 pattern forage cap to indicate his status as an artillery officer. Dragoon officers sometimes followed a similar practice, but instead their caps occasionally bore a six-pointed gold embroidered star of the type that was sewn to the rear of each tail of the coatee. Isaac Bowen Collection. USAMHI

enlistment.[20] Despite this fact, many troops seemed less than enamored with the caps, seldom wearing them "except for guard duty or on dress parade," according to inspector general Colonel George Croghan, who had considerable occasion to observe troops during the period.[21] The men must not have been impressed that they were outfitted in the height of European fashion, in this case most approximating the French cavalry headgear of the era.[22]

Adverse reactions to the contrary, the powers that be persisted on issuing the cap, albeit with a few additions over the years.[23] For one thing, in 1839 cadets at West Point were to don this cap in lieu of the old "tar bucket." Originally these gentlemen in gray were to have the artillery crossed cannon device, but between 1842 and 1843 a new castle insignia was adopted instead.[24]

Another 1839 change involved horse artillery officers, who were to substitute scarlet horsetail plumes for cock feathers. This trend continued. In 1845, enlisted men of light and horse artillery batteries were to follow suit.

Further, in 1841 enlisted personnel began to be added to the Ordnance Department, thereby requiring an outfit, including a cap. In this instance sergeants of ordnance were "to wear the uniform of the Ordnance Department, with the distinctive badges prescribed for the non-commissioned staff of regiments of artillery...."[25] This same use of the

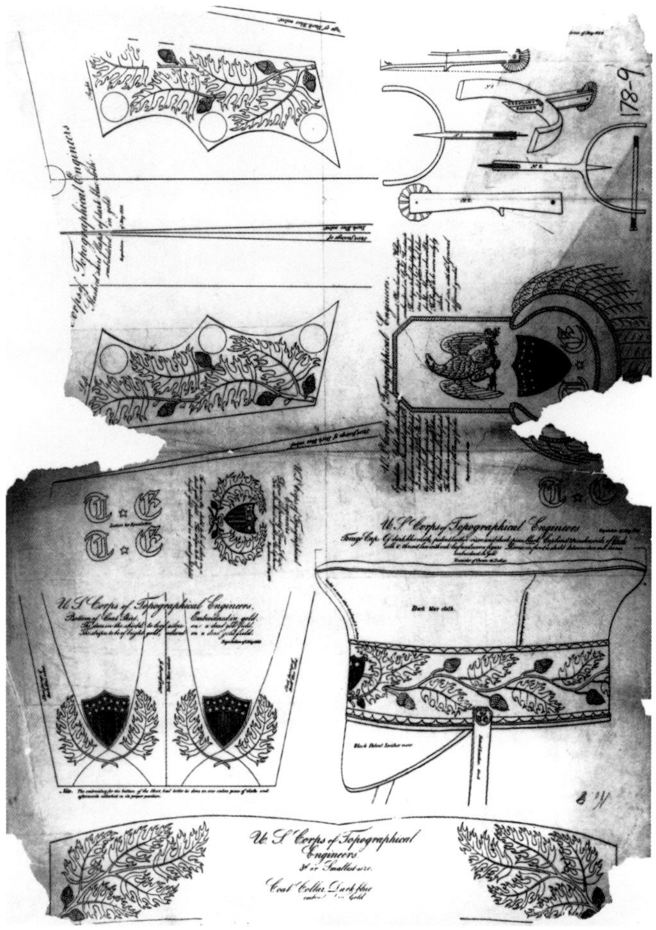

Right: An official drawing depicts the 1839 pattern forage cap for Topographical Engineers. These elite explorers had a black silk velvet band with embroidered oak leaves and acorns. The insignia on the front was to be a shield with oaks leaves, also of gold embroidery. NA

This artillery first lieutenant has elected to wear a plain 1839 pattern cap without insignia. WJS

Lieutenant Gordon Granger of the Regiment of Mounted Rifles exhibits a spread eagle device with an "R" in the center of a shield as the insignia for his 1839 pattern forage cap per regulations of the Mexican War era. WJS

basic artillery uniform also applied to the other "ordnance men," as enlisted personnel were termed in that department. Although there were several details which differentiated them from the artillery, as far as headgear was concerned, the cap was the same for both organizations.[26]

Then, as part of another expansion of the U.S. Army's enlisted force—this time during the Mexican War—the 1846 establishment of a Company of Sappers, Miners, and Pontoniers led to the adoption of the "Schako—same pattern as that of artillery bearing a yellow eagle over a castle like that worn by Cadets." A black 3 inch diameter spherical pompon topped the cap.[27]

Another new organization in the army, and one that predated engineer enlisted men was the Regiment of Dragoons formed in accordance with General Order No. 28, Headquarters of the Army, May 2, 1833. In general appearance the cap was akin to that prescribed for the artillery and infantry, but stood a slight bit taller at 8 1/4 inches. The body likewise tapered slightly toward the top, rather than being cylindrical. Further, a white horsehair plume was called for enlisted men and company officers, while field grade officers were to have a two tone plume of scarlet and white, in all cases held in position by a flaming grenade that was similar to the tulip. A gilt star with silver eagle and cap lines, being of gold cord for officers and yellow worsted for enlisted men, were the other prominent features of this cap.

Some three years after adoption, a recommendation to change the cap's body from fur felt to leather was made but not acted upon. In 1844 a design alteration to make the back of the cap lower than the front in order to have it seat better on the wearer's head was recommended by a uniform board, although evidently not carried out. Another suggestion of this board was implemented, however, because in 1845 light and

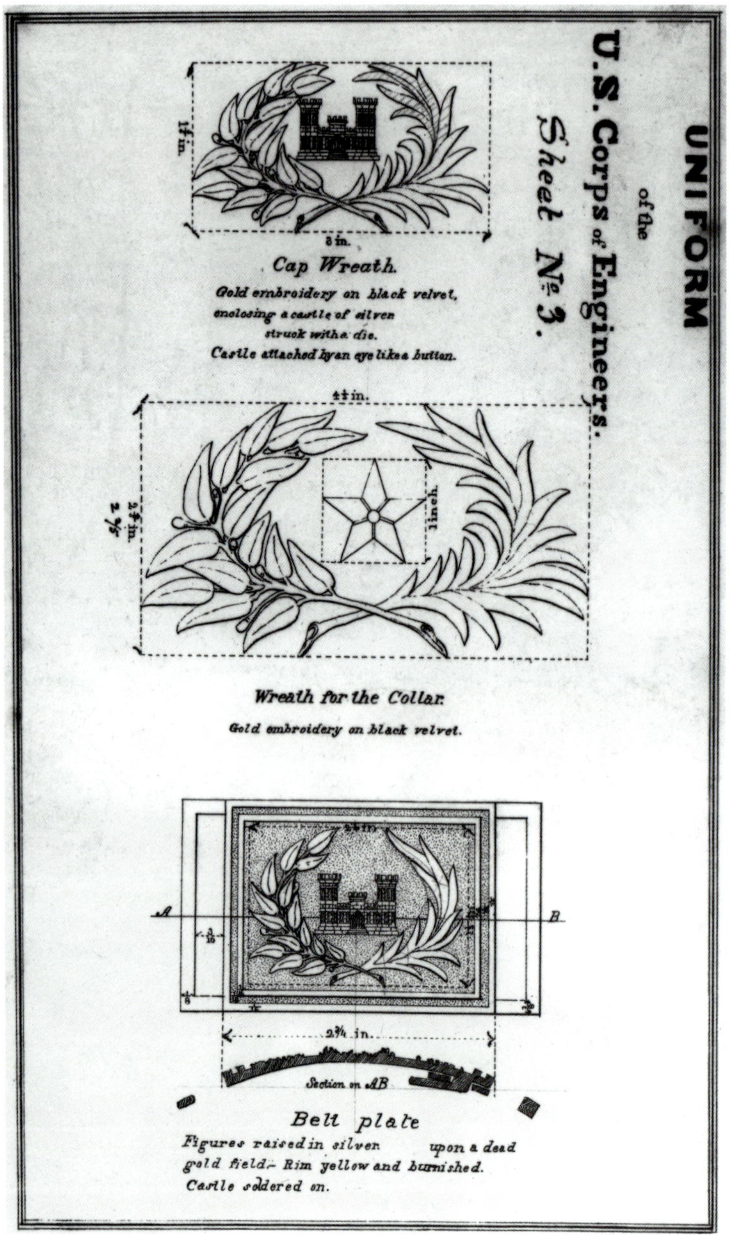

The official drawing depicting the Corps of Engineers cap device clearly shows the castle within the embroidered gold wreath was to be struck in silver and attached to the band with an eyelet. NA

The 1832-1851 infantry uniform cap had a sheet brass "tulip" mounted on the top that served to hold the white feather plume for officers, or a white eight inch worsted pompon for enlisted men, as seen here. DT

horse artillery caps were to have not only scarlet horsehair plumes, but also be ornamented with scarlet bands and tassels akin to the dragoon cap.[28]

The appearance of the cap for line troops in the early 1830s theoretically spelled the end of the chapeau for at least dragoon, infantry, and artillery officers. It should be noted, however, that General Order No. 50, Headquarters of the Army, June 11, 1832, gave colonels of artillery, dragoons, and infantry the prerogative when "not serving with their Regiments, nor doing duty in the line" the latitude to "wear cocked hats of the same description as those prescribed for General Staff officers, except that the loop will be of black silk: the eagle yellow, the tassels to conform to the colour of the button."[29] Some individuals may have welcomed this privilege, because there had been at least one occasion when an infantry colonel spoke out against losing his chapeau to the cap.[30]

Others, however, were less tradition bound, at least when it came to the chapeau. In fact, European military headgear models continued to influence U.S. Army styles in the post-Mexican War era, with English patterns persisting in popularity from the 1830s through 1850s when French dominance began to gain the upper hand.[31] Conversely, varied environmental conditions, especially for the majority of the army serving on "frontier duty," caused a grassroots reaction "for a more practical uniform for field wear...."[32] On February 13, 1850, Secretary of War George Crawford responded to adverse opinions about uniforms in general when he approved General Order No. 2. The first paragraph offered a rationale for issuing this directive, a candid explanation seldom found in orders. Crawford indicated:

> A large number of the Officers of the Army, probably more than half, have applied since the war with Mexico, to have a uniform less expensive, less difficult to procure, and better adapted to campaign and other service. Their opinions, reasons and wishes are entitled to attention and respect; and it is important that the garments and equipments shall protect the persons of the wearers, preserve their health and make them efficient....[33]

In this statement the secretary of war summed up the main arguments of those who placed purpose over appearance when it came to the uniform.[34] Among other features of General Order No. 2, unlike previous regulations that mandated one type of headgear for dress and another for field, one cap was adopted for both situations. Consequently a piece of headgear, which evidently was designed along the lines of the old 1833 pattern leather forage cap, but instead of dark blue wool, was to serve double-duty for enlisted men. This article was to be:

> ...of blue cloth, gig top shape; front and rear six inches high, rounded and stiffened with felt or other light material; visor of patent leather, 2 3/4 inches wide, reaching back to within half and inch of the tip of the ears, projecting nearly horizontal, but somewhat concave, so as to shade well the eyes and face; on the back flap—outside of cloth lined with thin japanned leather—height of the cap, when up, for protecting the neck from sunshine and rain; front ornaments metal, to be perma-

Not all officers found the 1839 pattern forage cap perfect for the field, as this artillery second lieutenant illustrates. A number of officers, including Major General Zachery Taylor, obtained a broad brimmed hat during the Mexican War. WJS

Right: This 1832 pattern infantry officer's cap lacks its white cock feathers. DT

nent, and to show the corps or arm; viz: Engineers, a castle; Ordnance, a shell and flame; Dragoons, two crossed sabers, (edges upwards;) with letter of the company in upper edge above, and number of the regiment below; Mounted Rifle Regiment, a trumpet, perpendicular, with the letter of the company above; Artillery, cross cannon, with the letter of the company in the angle above and number of the regiment below; Infantry, a horn bugle with sling, with the letter of the company above and number of the regiment within the sling; all yellow, except infantry, which will be white. For parades or full dress, the caps will contain a pompon of wool yarn, short fringe, spherical, three inches in diameter, on a bent stem without socket, and standing forward at an angle of 45 degrees: those of Engineer soldiers to be black; all others the color of the coat trimmings of their respective arms; those of company musicians will be a netted sphere 1 1/2 inches diameter, on a straight stem, without socket, and stiff horse-hair standing five inches high from upper side, and spreading gently; all of the color of their corps.

The same order described the proposed new cap for officers as something akin to the 1839 pattern forage cap, but with certain new insignia and bands around the crown to coincide with a color scheme adopted for each branch, something that had been proposed when the forage cap had been adopted but was not carried through systematically. Building on this prior concept, the 1850 pattern officer's cap was envisaged as:

> ...of the material and nearly the pattern of the present forage cap worn by officers; the band or body to be three inches high, the front of which to be thickened with felt or other light material on each side of the plume stem, so as to form a groove for its reception; the visor 2 3/4 inches broad, reaching back to within half an inch of the tip of the ears, projecting nearly horizontal, but somewhat concave, so as to shade well the eyes and face, with oil cloth cover or case, having a flap or cape from one point of the cap visor to the other, and made to fold, double, inside of the case when not wanted for protection of the neck. The cap to be worn without cover, in full dress, with plumes as now used, except those of the Dragoons will be orange color;

An infantry company grade officer's summer dress uniform complete with 1832 pattern cap topped with white cock feathers. WPM

This color plate from the *United Military Magazine* from 1840-41 clearly illustrates the outfit of an infantry captain in the 1832 pattern cap. JDC

and the Mounted Rifles, light green; those of mounted officers will rise four and those of foot officers six-inches above the cap; those of the Mounted or Field Artillery, Dragoons, and Mounted Rifles, of horse-hair, falling six inches. The front ornaments, as now worn in the staff, Staff Corps, Artillery, and Infantry, with the figure, for number of regiment (three quarters of an inch long) in the lower angle of the cross cannon for artillery, and within the bugle for infantry.

A British military periodical lauded the direction being advocated by the Americans, remarking that it was, "...good common sense in the article of dress, and a disposition to yield to the wishes of the soldiery in adapting their costume to their personal comfort."[35] Despite such an endorsement from a martial major power, and possibly similar responses from many observers in the U.S. Army, this relatively practical combat kit was not adopted for enlisted men at least, although some officers evidently procured the new outfit and were allowed to retain their purchases by General Orders No. 25, War Department, August 23, 1850. Conversely, the same order made it clear that enlisted men were not to adopt the new outfit after all, although in some respects the groundwork was laid in so far as branch colors and insignia were concerned for a new type of headgear in due course.

The reason this change was not adopted in 1850, however, was supposedly because "...so much clothing was on hand from the Mexican War there was no need to procure any additional stocks for some years."[36] In fact, the quartermaster general pointed out that more than a million dollars worth of clothing from the Mexican War remained in storage at Schuylkill Arsenal, the army's central clothing establishment

The regulation artillery officer's cap belonging to Lieutenant David E. Hale, West Point class of 1833 and commissioned in that year as an officer of the First U.S. Artillery, is the correct pattern for dress wear from 1832-1851, with scarlet cock feathers. Light artillery officers were to have scarlet horsehair plumes instead of feathers as of 1839. Enlisted men of light artillery batteries were given horsehair plumes in 1845, along with bands and cords similar to dragoon caps. Photograph by Michael J. McAfee. WPM

Another color plate from the *United Military Magazine* portrayed a captain of U.S. Artillery in the 1832 pattern cap. JDC

A second version of the 1832 pattern artillery officer's cap, this time for Edwin Rose, USMA Class of 1830, who was posted to the Third U.S. Artillery. Rose served with the regiment until 1837, when he resigned his commission. DT

in Philadelphia.[37] With ample supplies on hand and constant Congressional requirements to be frugal, the quartermaster general saw a new uniform as "injudicious and highly prejudicial to the interests of the Army."[38]

Nevertheless, momentum for change continued, leading to the formation of another uniform board to review the matter. Such boards were called into existence from time to time and became a common thread in the history of uniform development during the second half of the nineteenth century. This particular one convened pursuant to General Orders No. 40, War Department, December 31, 1850. Meeting early the following year, the group reviewed comments from the field, factoring this information into its deliberations. Moreover, it considered "...various collections of drawings exhibiting dress in use in Foreign Services, and having in view the character of the frontier service most likely to be required of American troops for many years to come."[39]

The board's report was the basis for General Orders No. 31, War Department, June 12, 1851. This directive inaugurated the use of a cap of dark blue cloth with a crown fashioned from four upright pieces that rose from 5 3/4 inches to 6 1/4 inches in front and from 7 1/4 inches to 7 3/4 inches in back. It was prescribed for all men, from privates to the most senior major general who commanded the army (although Winfield Scott clung to the chapeau despite this head piece's disappearance from mention in the 1851 regulations). Some of these early examples even had bodies made of gutta purcha, produced by a process patented by John Rider and John Murphy that allowed cloth to be vulcanized, thereby offering a potential weather resistant application for military clothing. Others would be made by a relatively new piece of technology in the manufacturing process—the sewing machine.[40] The new machine, however, soon would be employed for only non-critical portions of the cap, that is, the decorative band, and for producing chevrons, both of these articles not being subject to heavy wear, unlike coats, shirts, and trou-

Front and side views of an 1833 pattern dragoon officer's cap that belonged to Second Lieutenant James Clyman, who served from 1833-1835 in the Regiment of Dragoons. CSPRD

Captain Lucian Bonaparte Webster, Company C, First U.S. Artillery, in the 1832 pattern cap with scarlet cock feathers prescribed for artillery officers. USAMHI

The 1840-41 edition of *United States Military Magazine* also depicted a dragoon officer in the 1833 pattern cap for that branch. JDC

The 1833 pattern enlisted dragoon dress cap had yellow worsted cords. The cap began to be phased out after new regulations were adopted in 1851. SI

The enlisted 1833 pattern dragoon dress cap was to display a yellow metal starburst with a white metal eagle overlay that took its inspiration from French designs. Photograph by A.D. de Quesada. ADEQ

sers, which were ordered to be made by hand, this process then being deemed as producing more durable goods.[41]

Whether made by hand or machine, or with bodies of gutta purcha or felted cotton and rabbit fur, all caps were to have a black 2 1/4 inch visor and a leather adjustable chin strap with yellow metal buckle. Pompons were basic, too, those for generals being shaped like an acorn and made of gold embroidered net, 3 inches long. Officers and enlisted men had spherical worsted pompons that were color coded as follows: Adjutant General's Department—lower two-thirds buff, upper third white; Inspector General's Department—lower two-thirds buff, upper third scarlet; Judge Advocate—white; Quartermaster Department—lower two-thirds buff, upper third light or Saxony blue; Subsistence Department—lower two-thirds buff, upper third royal or ultramarine blue; Medical Department—lower two-thirds buff, upper third medium or emerald green; Pay Department—lower two-thirds buff, upper third olive green; Corps of Topographical Engineers and Corps of Engineers—lower two-

A sketch of a first sergeant of the First U.S. Dragoons at Ft. Snelling, Minnesota, circa 1851 demonstrates the 1833 pattern cap was worn into the early 1850s. NA

Side view of a dragoon sergeant wearing the 1833 pattern enlisted cap. SI

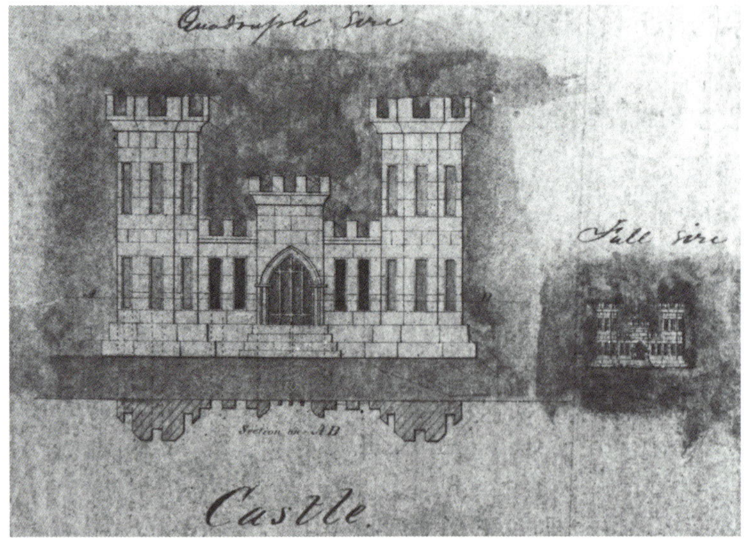

The original specification drawing for the 1846 pattern cap insignia for enlisted personnel of the U.S. Company of Sappers, Miners, and Pontoniers. The same stamped sheet brass cap insignia had been adopted for the headgear of cadets at the United States Military Academy several years earlier. NA

thirds buff, upper third black; Ordnance Department—lower two-thirds buff, upper third crimson; artillery—scarlet; infantry—light or Saxony blue; mounted riflemen—medium or emerald green; dragoons—orange; aides-de-camp—buff; adjutants of regiments—same as for Adjutant General's Department; and regimental quartermasters—same as for Quartermaster Department.

Enlisted men of artillery, dragoons, infantry, and rifles had the same color pompons as their officers, whereas enlisted engineers wore yellow, and ordnance enlisted personnel were assigned crimson. Furthermore, enlisted versions were attached to a yellow metal ring, 2/3 inch in diameter by 1/3 inch deep, with a yellow metal spread eagle 1 3/4 inches between the tips of the wings attached to this in order to hold the accessory on front of the cap. Officers had a gold net base ring permanently affixed to a gold embroidered spread eagle. Pompons always were to be worn when epaulets were used by officers. In turn, pompons could be removed when shoulder straps were substituted as a means of indicating officer's ranks. Conversely, enlisted men always were to have their pompons in place, in theory at least, unless the cap cover was being employed.

Samuel Ringold's "Flying Artillery" company also had a cap similar to that worn by dragoons, but rather than white horsehair plumes and yellow cords for enlisted men, the trim was scarlet. KC

The insignia for this headgear consisted of the silver embroidered script "T.E." in a gold embroidered wreath for topographical engineers, and a similar arrangement for officers of the engineers, excepting that a silver embroidered castle was placed in the center of the wreath instead of the script letters. Generals, adjutant generals, inspector generals, and officers of the Judge Advocate Corps, Pay, Quartermaster, Subsistence, and Medical Departments had the same type of gold wreath, but in the center appeared the letters "U.S." in old English characters. A gold embroidered flaming bomb was established for ordnance officers, while crossed sabers with a silver numeral above was assigned to dragoons, crossed cannons with the numeral above went to artillery, a perpendicular trumpet with numeral in the bend was the identifying element for mounted rifles, and a gold embroidered bugle (the "hunting horn" style) with silver regimental numeral in the bend was to be used by infantry officers. In turn, enlisted caps exhibited a stamped yellow metal turreted castle for engineers and a shell and flame for Ordnance Department personnel. The other branches simply had stamped sheet brass 1 inch high letters for their respective companies.[42]

An 1852 newspaper account noted the cap was "very nearly that of the French and some other European army regulations."[43] The one exception to those who were to be issued the new cap was at West Point, where the United States Military Academy's bandsmen were to retain the tall 1832 artillery type enlisted cap with a plume and cord.[44]

As with all items of uniforms, simply prescribing a new style did not mean that the pattern immediately appeared in the field. Consequently, some time elapsed before the 1851 pattern cap was in the hands of the troops, although officers, all of whom had to purchase their own uniform items, most likely obtained them quickly, as they were ordered to do so no later than January 1, 1852.

Once the 1851 pattern caps began to reach the rank and file, however, shortcomings became evident. For one thing, the facing cloth that trimmed the lower portion of the cap evidently tended to fade. It may have been for this reason, and to reduce the cost of materials to construct the hat that General Orders No. 1, Adjutant General's Department, War Department, January 20, 1854, called for a welt in the branch color, rather than the complete facings, to thereafter be used as trim on the cap.[45] Thus, the basic form of the 1851 pattern engineer and ordnance enlisted caps was extended to universal use for all soldiers, with the exception that now there was only one welt rather than the two that had been on engineer and ordnance headgear previously. This same order made one other change in that the buttons which held on the chinstrap also were to be one style for enlisted men. Prior to 1854 they were of brass with an eagle device that bore an "A" for artillery, "D" for dragoons, an "I" for infantry, and "R" for mounted rifles on the chest of the eagle. The new buttons retained the eagle, but the designating letters were discontinued.

Major General Edmund P. Gaines was shown in his chapeau in this plate from the 1840-41 edition of *United States Military Magazine*. JDC

Major General William Jenkins Worth's 1840 pattern chapeau was topped by a swan feather plume with black upper and white lower feathers in keeping with regulations for his rank. FWS&HM

The change to a welt may have resolved certain shortcomings of the 1851 pattern cap, but some other problems still remained. For instance, the pompon was fine for the parade ground, but not for routine wear or field operations. Fortunately this accessory could be removed. More to the point, however, the tall and stiff configuration of both the 1851 and 1854 pattern caps made them less practical for fatigue and combat purposes. For this reason, the issuance of stocks of the old 1839 pattern forage cap continued in some instances. Moreover, officers and men pressed privately purchased headgear into service in several cases.

Indeed, the army itself even made a short-lived attempt to address this situation during the early 1850s, albeit on a limited basis, by providing the so-called "Andrews hat," a type of headgear nicknamed for Colonel Timothy P. Andrews, the commanding officer of the Voltigeurs, a special unit that existed briefly during the Mexican War. Andrews had asked for permission to have "broad-brimmed soft felt" hats "of a pearl or stone color, capable of being looped up, but with a stiff brim when let down, and with an orifice for ventilation on each side of the crown that might be closed at pleasure...."[46] This forerunner of the drab campaign

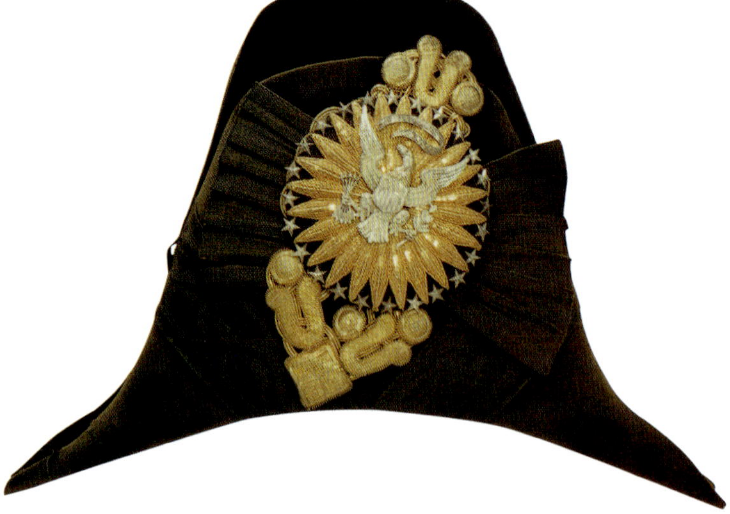

Side view, detail of the cockade, and case for a chapeau de bras belonging to Washington Hunt as a Topographical Engineer in the pre-Mexican War era. DT

hat seen decades later never reached Andrews' men, although 500 were made. The lion's share of these special pieces went to the Second Dragoons in Texas during 1851.[47]

Others who did not benefit from the Andrews hat took matters into their own hands, according to the early 1850s recollections of an enlisted man of Company B, First Dragoons. The diarist recorded that the men of his troop purchased "drab hats" as a substitute for issue caps.[48]

A second memoir of the era mentioned that some infantrymen in Texas who had been pressed into mounted service in 1853 secured "a broad brimmed slouched sombrero."[49] Similarly, by 1855 the Second Dragoons must have worn out their Andrews hats, but still favored a civilian "slouched hat" for field duty.[50] The next year, other troops in the Lone Star State, this time the Mounted Rifles, drilled "with blue flannel hunting shirts and felt hats."[51]

Following a similar inclination, in 1857 all the men in a strike force sent against the Cheyennes from Fort Leavenworth, Kansas, that included Companies E and K of the Sixth Infantry and Companies C, F, I, and K of the First Cavalry, wore "a broadbrimmed hat, each of a different color...."[52] This situation prompted the diarist to mention the assembled field force looked "more like Polish Scythemen than" they did U.S. Army regulars.[53]

Chapeau de bras of the type permitted in 1847 for colonels of line regiments. In this case, because of the silver braid the headpiece was for a commander of an infantry regiment. WC

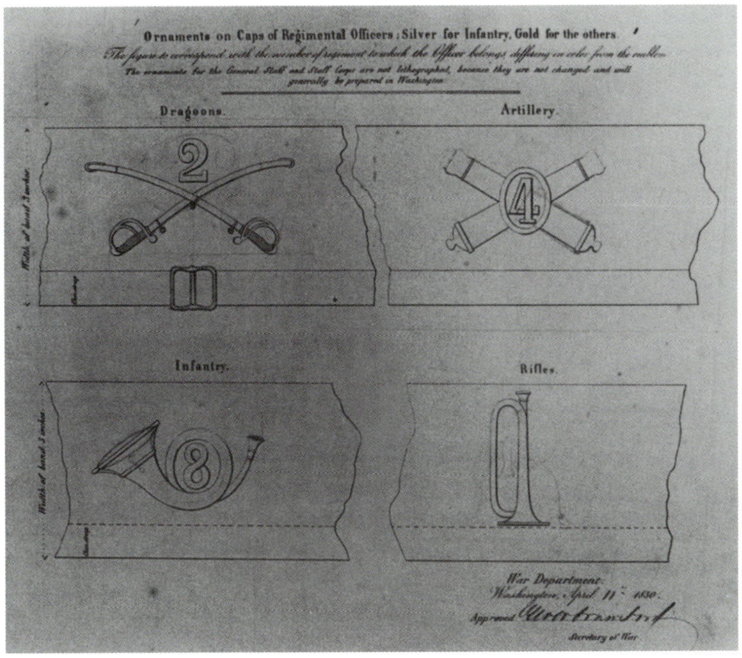

During 1850 preparations for new uniform regulations included reconsideration of cap insignia, including crossed sabers for dragoons, crossed cannons for artillery, a hunting horn for infantry, and a bugle for riflemen. The original concept was that the insignia were to be of gold embroidery for all branches with silver numbers for the regiment, with the exception of the infantry, where silver embroidery would form the horn, while gold embroidery would be used for the regimental number. The scheme was modified when the 1851-pattern officer's cap was adopted in final form to have all the branch devices in gold with the numerals in silver. NA

Such divergence from regulations also existed with another force gathered at Fort Leavenworth when President James Buchanan's administration decided to curtail what was perceived as a Mormon separatist movement in Utah Territory in 1857.[54] Among the 2,500 regulars was the Fifth Infantry regiment. The men of this unit apparently had the 1839 pattern forage caps.[55] In contrast, each company of the Tenth Infantry regiment in the expedition was allowed to wear non-regulation hats "provided they were all alike." Thus, most of the companies elected to fit themselves out with black hats, with the exception of one company of the regiment that opted for gray.[56] In an 1858 campaign, artillery and infantry officers in the Pacific Northwest once more found the slouch hat more to their liking than the issue cap.[57]

Such field expedients arose in part because of heightened military activities, especially in the West. Responding to these situations, the United States Congress deemed it necessary to add two new mounted regiments to the standing force on March 3, 1855.[58] These were the First and Second Cavalry regiments. Colonel Edwin V. Sumner assumed command of the First, while Colonel Albert Sidney Johnston took the reins of the Second Cavalry.[59]

One distinctive element of the dress for these two newly minted organizations was a black felt hat that looped up on the right side. The pattern had been favored by Colonel Sumner, who sat on the board that specified the cavalrymen's gear, and who had seen similar types of head wear in Belgium. He particularly liked the Belgian *chasseur à pied* headdress, which he described as, "a hat with a medium sized brim, turned up on the left side,...with a cockade, and a small black feather in full dress."[60]

Artist Henry A. Ogden depicted a first sergeant of artillery and a colonel of the same branch (center) wearing the 1851 pattern cap with scarlet accents that designated artillery. KC

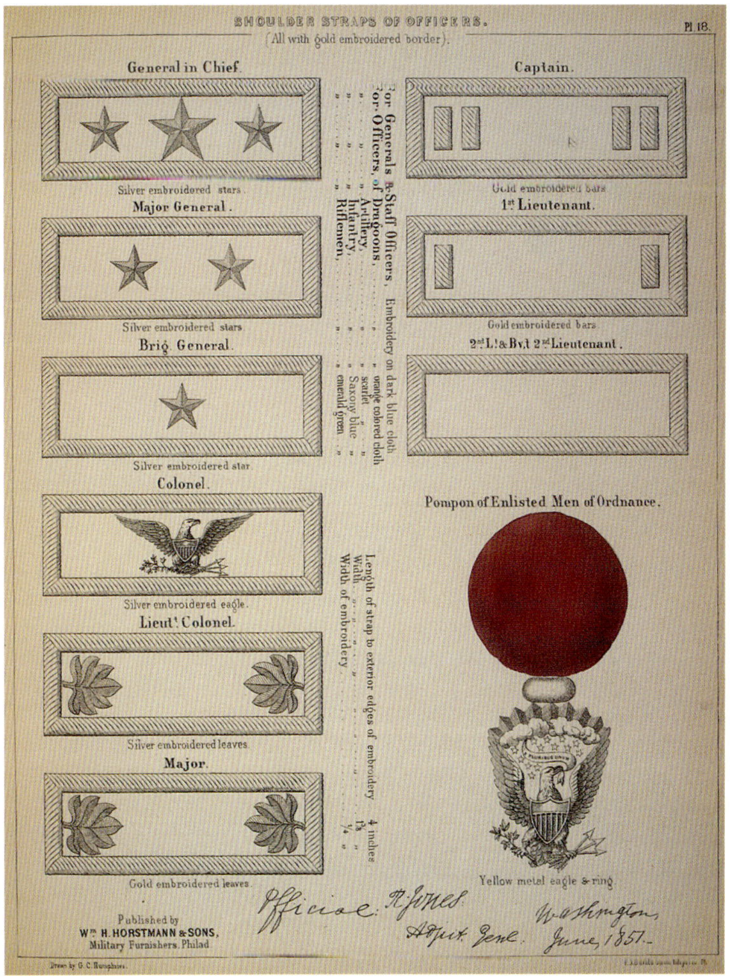

Depiction of the 1851 pattern pompon for ordnance enlisted men. Also shown are officers' shoulder straps of the period. GC

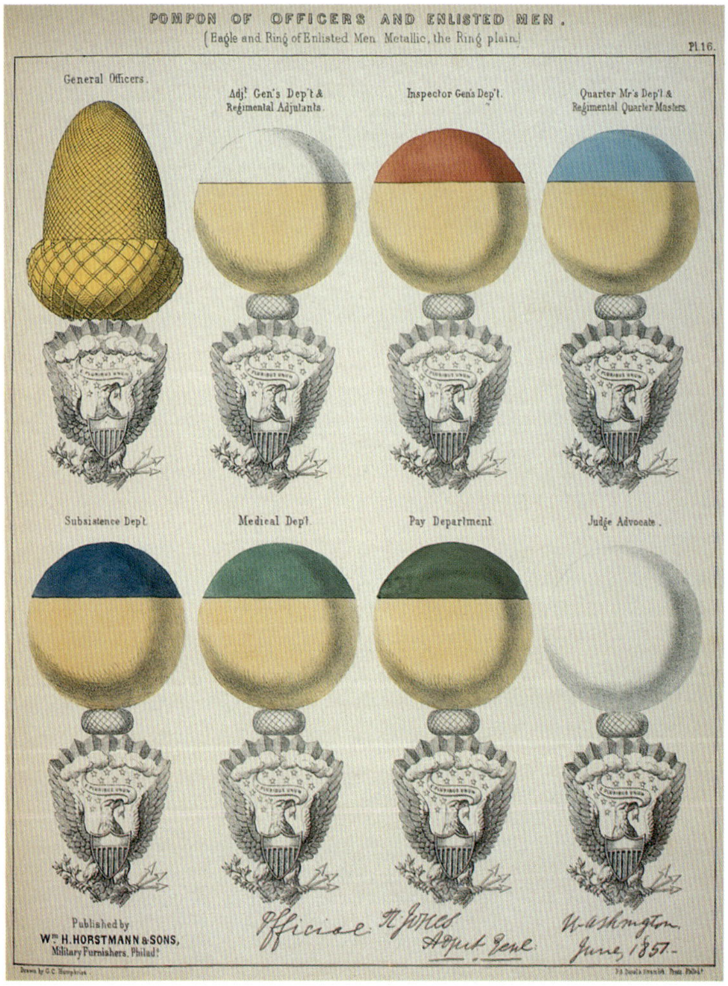

The pompons of all 1851 pattern caps worn by officers and enlisted men were spheres made of worsted and were color coded according to branch, except for generals, who were to wear a large gold net acorn, as illustrated in an Ogden print featuring mounted officers with a general as the central figure. GC

The 1851 pattern gold acorn pompon for general officers' caps. The material and shape were unique, as opposed to wool, round pompons for all other officers and enlisted men. EB

Left: Officer and enlisted pompons were color coded for the 1851 pattern cap, as seen in these illustrations that accompanied the uniform regulations of that period. GC

Although Inspector General J.K.F. Mansfield was a colonel, he appears in the uniform of his brevet rank of brigadier general, including the 1851 pattern cap for that rank with acorn pompon. NA

In fact, this hat was similar to the American cavalry hat that this group selected. The prescribed hat ultimately was adorned with a gold-wire festooned cord hanging from the top of the crown, and a second cord of the same material terminating in acorns for officers. This accessory was placed at the base of the crown. Enlisted men wore similar cords but of yellow worsted. Another difference that distinguished officers from rank and file entailed an embroidered eagle device (the U.S. Coat of Arms) to hold the right brim in place against the crown. Additionally, a spray of three ostrich feathers appeared on the left side of the hats worn by majors through colonels, while a pair of these feathers were prescribed for lieutenants and captains. Enlisted personnel had only one feather and a simple brass button with a stamped sheet brass eagle of the type that had been attached to the pompon on the 1851 and 1854 pattern caps, along with a strand of yellow worsted cord as a loop attachment. Issues for enlisted troopers also bore a large stamped sheet brass company numeral on the front, while officers wore a gilt embroidered regimental numeral. Leather chin straps completed the hat for both officers and men.[61]

The 1851 pattern enlisted infantry cap had a Saxony blue pompon and band. USACMH

Right: 1851 pattern artillery officer's cap. The regimental numeral was to be in silver, and the artillery crossed cannon insignia in gold embroidery or simulated embroidery of metal. All other officers had a similar cap, the differences being the color of the pompon and the insignia on the front. RB

Above and left: Front and side of an artillery 1851 pattern enlisted cap. Similar caps were issued to all other enlisted men, but the bands were to be in branch colors, except for engineers and ordnance men. RB

Enlisted engineer 1851 pattern caps had a yellow welt at the base and approximately midway around the body, which peaked at the center, such as this example. The pompon could be removed from the cap, as seen here. When in place, the Engineer Corps pompon was yellow. Ordnance enlisted men also had two welts of cloth—in their case crimson—rather than a band of facing material. SI

Left: Regiment of Mounted Rifles 1851 pattern enlisted cap. The pompon has faded from its original emerald green, which was to match the cap band. SI

Embroidered insignia for 1851 pattern officers' caps. GC

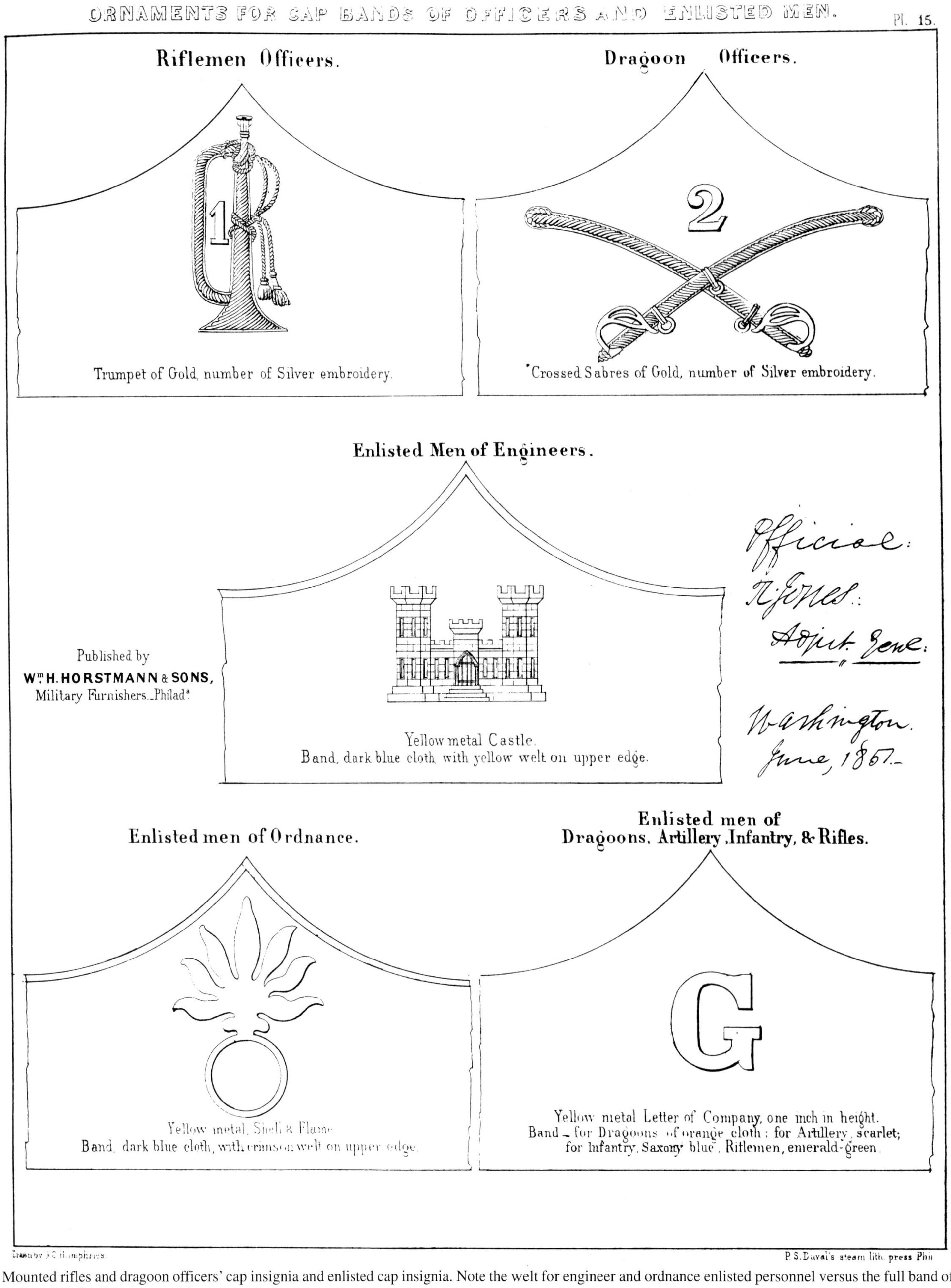

Mounted rifles and dragoon officers' cap insignia and enlisted cap insignia. Note the welt for engineer and ordnance enlisted personnel versus the full band of facing cloth for line troops. GC

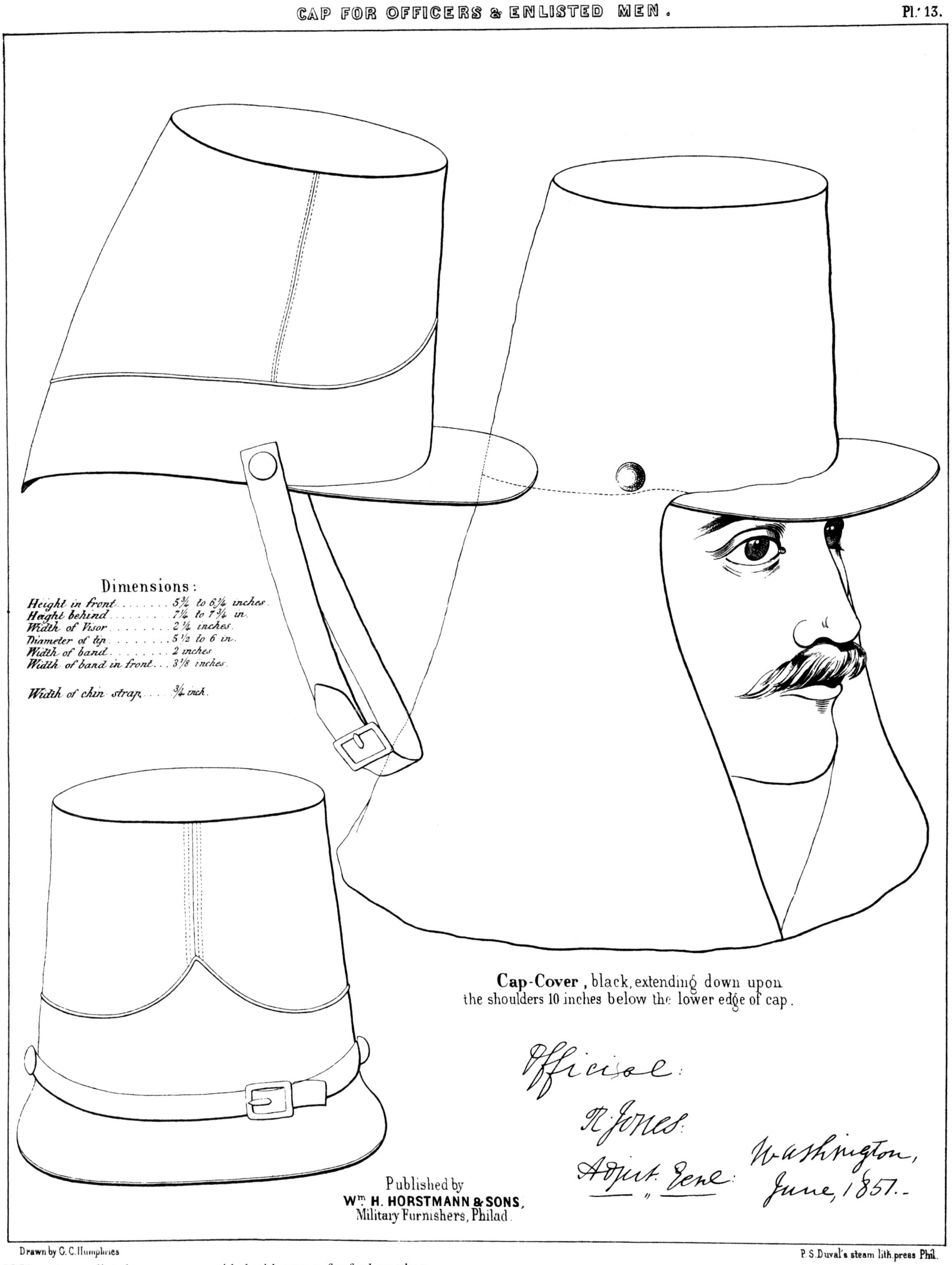

1851 pattern enlisted caps were provided with covers for foul weather.

The 1851 pattern officer's cap for infantry officers had a gold embroidered bugle with silver regimental number, in this case a "7" for the Seventh Infantry. SHSW

Right: A private of infantry or heavy artillery poses with his 1851 pattern cap, the only difference being the color of the band and pompon. EG

This hat was restricted to the cavalry, however, meaning that many soldiers, including some of the troopers of the new mounted regiments themselves, had to settle for the 1854 pattern cap. This fact was not without some advantage, though, in that men serving in some parts of the West found local Indians who agreed to trade for "old jackets and 'tar bucket' hats" (1854 pattern hats) in exchange "for buffalo robes, moccasins, and other articles..." that would provide warmth during the cold Western winters.[62]

Barter did not seem the best means to provide for the comfort of the troops in the estimation of some officers of the antebellum period. For one, George B. McClellan, a first lieutenant of engineers who was promoted to captain and transferred to the First U.S. Cavalry Regiment, had his own ideas about what sort of head dress Uncle Sam should furnish. While serving as a member of a U.S. military commission sent abroad to observe the Crimean War from 1854 to 1856, McClellan studied various European armies. He paid special attention to foreign equipment and uniforms.[63] Among McClellan's observations based on his European tour was the desirability of a less cumbersome cap that would be more in keeping with fatigue and field wear than the stiff 1854 pattern. He postulated that mounted troopers at least should have:

> ...a police cap, without visor, and of such a nature that it can be folded up and carried in the pouch [saddlebags], or wherever is convenient; the Scotch bonnet, Turkish fez, a Greek

Right: The 1851 pattern caps of paymasters and surgeons had pompons with buff on the lower two-thirds and dark olive green on the upper third for the former group, and emerald green on the upper third for medical officers. The individual seen here is Surgeon Robert Little Brodie. WJS

On the 1854 pattern enlisted cap the facing material bands of the previous 1851 pattern were replaced with a single welt in branch colors, much like those for engineers and ordnance men of the 1851 pattern. Red welts set off artillery enlisted personnel. SI

In 1854 the color was changed for infantry from Saxony to sky-blue, and thus the welt was to be in that shade on the cap. TC

cap of knit or woven wool, a flexible cap of the shape of the old forage-cap—any of these would answer.[64]

Additionally, McClellan mentioned the French forage cap with a conical top and large straight visor as another type of headgear that would serve this need. During the mid-1840s this *bonnet de police à visière* began to be issued to French troops, and in time became associated intimately with that nation's military as the *képi*.[65]

The year McClellan's report was published (1857), the engineer officer who commanded the Company of Sappers, Miners, and Pontoniers stationed at West Point asked that his organization be given a hat similar to the one the cavalry received in 1855, or that the 1839 pattern forage cap be reinstated, in either case for fatigue wear. By March 31, 1857, Secretary of War John B. Floyd looked favorably on this request for a fatigue cap, but sanctioned a sample cap of a new design to be made for consideration. In fact, two prototypes were constructed of the French *chasseur* pattern, one costing $1.00 with a high crown, and another that was priced at $.87 1/2 with a lower crown. The taller type was endorsed. As a result, the Schuylkill Arsenal produced a sufficient quantity of these for all enlisted engineers, the first seventy-four being issued to those men posted to Fort Leavenworth. There were also a like number of cap covers sent at the same time, although it is unknown what either the cap or the covers looked like exactly.[66] The idea was that the cap would be issued in alternating years over a soldier's five year enlistment, thereby reducing costs, as well as providing a more workman-like piece.

Later, in the summer of 1858, Brevet Major William H. French, the artillery officer who commanded Fort McHenry, Maryland, noted his

An 1851 pattern cap with the scarlet and buff pompon of an officer of the Inspector General's Department. Photograph by Michael O'Donnell. WPM

H.A. Ogden rendered this illustration of enlisted personnel in the 1854 pattern cap, including an artilleryman with scarlet welt, an infantryman with sky-blue welt, and a mounted rifleman with a green welt. GC

Front 1855 pattern cavalry enlisted hat. TC

Right side 1855 pattern cavalry enlisted hat. TC

Left side 1855 pattern cavalry enlisted hat. TC

1855 pattern cavalry officer's hat. SI

Rear 1855 pattern cavalry enlisted hat. TC

men removed the "stiffening" of their 1854 pattern caps "to wear them on fatigue." Although this apparently was not an uncommon expedient, the officer found the appearance unsightly. Because of this he advocated a "*light, comfortable, military*" cap that also was "cheap" to produce. To make his point he had four samples made, one each for artillery, cavalry, infantry, and staff, and sent these along to the adjutant general.[67] Despite the fact that this suggestion did not go through normal military channels of the time, it did reach the secretary of war, and from there went to the quartermaster general. Having made the rounds, approval for adoption came relatively soon with the promulgation of General Order No. 13, War Department, November 30, 1858, which read:

> For fatigue purposes, Forage caps, of pattern in the Quartermaster General's Office, will be issued, in addition to hats, at the rate of one per year. Dark blue cloth, with a cord or welt around the crown of the colors used to distinguish the several branches, and yellow metal letters in front to designate companies. For unassigned recruits dark blue cord or welt around the crown and without distinctive badge.[68]

General Order No. 13 also permitted officers to obtain such a cap "with dark welt and distinctive ornament, in front, of the corps and regiment." Evidently these insignia were to be of the type worn on the 1854 cap for officers, while it seems likely that a 1 inch high sheet brass regimental number of the type worn on the collar prior to 1857 for enlisted coats and jackets would have been affixed to the caps of the other ranks.

The 1858 pattern forage cap received mixed reviews, true to prior changes, but apparently it appealed to others, as indicated by the fact that officers at the Artillery School had petitioned for permission to obtain the head piece even before it was announced that it would be issued

Captain Thomas Wood of the First U.S. Cavalry retained the gold cords on his 1855 pattern hat, but has added the new gold embroidered crossed saber devices prescribed in 1858. Originally cavalry officers wore this insignia with edges downward per General Orders No. 3, Adjutant Generals Office, March 24, 1854. Woods wears his shoulder straps over his epaulets, a practice that began to be discontinued by the late 1850s. USAMHI

David Hunter was the colonel of the First Cavalry Regiment. He wears the regimental numeral in silver below his gold crossed saber devices on the 1858 pattern hat as was regulation for cavalry officers. Dragoon officers were to wear their regimental numerals above the sabers per General Orders No. 7, Adjutant General Office, June 24, 1858. USAMHI

Second Lieutenant Charles Bowman displays the numeral "1" in silver below his officer's hat insignia in keeping with the directive for cavalry officers to do so set forth in General Orders No. 7, Adjutant General Office, June 24, 1858. WPM

First Lieutenant Roger Jones of the Regiment of Mounted Rifles posed with his 1858 pattern officer's hat, with its distinctive perpendicular gold embroidered trumpet ornament. A silver numeral "1" appears in the loop of the trumpet, although there was no reason to designate the regiment with a numeral because it was the only regular army mounted rifle outfit in existence. USAMHI

throughout the army.[69] This same group also sought a means to address the problem of soaring temperatures and humidity at Fort Monroe, Virginia, where the Artillery School was located. As a consequence, attendees there would receive a special summer outfit that included a "round straw hat" for officers and enlisted men alike.[70] Later, a more detailed directive stated "a plain white straw hat with a black ribbon and without lining or facings on the rim" was to be worn.[71]

While such an initiative represented a way to deal with environmental or climatic conditions, not all the Quartermaster Department's efforts were so directed. In fact, three types of headgear of the 1850s further indicated the bent of some individuals toward show rather than practical concerns. Certainly the reappearance of the chapeau de bras for field officers and those of the general staff represented a purely fashion-oriented decision, and marked a reversion to pre-1851 fashion.[72]

In 1858 the new hat, which took its inspiration from a style issued to the First and Second Cavalry regiments three years earlier, was prescribed for all troops. This fur felt headpiece eventually was to looped on the left side for foot soldiers and on the right side for mounted troops (although considerable variation existed as seen in period photographs). Company letters were to be 1 inch high stamped sheet brass, and the regimental number 5/8 of an inch in stamped sheet brass, both of which were affixed to the front of the crown. Photograph by Kurt Cox. JML

This 1858 pattern cavalry officer's hat exhibits a rosette that holds the ostrich plumes in place. Binding along the edge of the brim also is evident, a characteristic found on officers' models of the period. EB

The 1858 pattern officer's hat was to have two black ostrich feathers for company grade officers and three for field grade officers, placed on the left side. The right side was to be looped up and held in position by an eagle device. Note the edge of the brim is trimmed in tape. SI

So, too, did a second head cover, one that evidently came into being because of a movement in 1857 among certain light artillery officers to return to the 1844 Ringgold cap. At first, the quartermaster general approved the use of the 1854 pattern cap with horsehair plume in scarlet for light artillery units that requested them according to letters of October 25, 1858, and January 25, 1859.[73] By February 12, the cap also was modified to have scarlet cords, much as they had in the 1840s. In fact, at first 1844 pattern Ringgold caps were provided because the head of the quartermaster depot in Philadelphia thought the 1854 pattern cap could not bear the weight of the plume. Soon thereafter, an artillery officer came up with a scheme to reinforce the newer cap, and thereafter that pattern was modified to be issued to those batteries requesting them, a practice confirmed by General Orders No. 20, War Department, August 6, 1860. Even then, commanders had the option of requisitioning the cap, or they could obtain a hat that was to be adopted by all branches of the army in 1858, thereby resulting in a mixture of two styles depending on the desire of the individual commanding officer.[74]

This second type of headgear took its inspiration from the former 1855 cavalry hat. Authorized by General Orders No. 3, Adjutant General's Office, March 24, 1858, several differences existed that distinguished the piece from the 1855 pattern cavalry issue, one change being the elimination of the festooned cord on the crown, and another the discontinuation of the leather chin strap. The acorn tips on enlisted hat cords likewise were replaced with small fringed tassels. These and other details were set forth in General Orders No. 3 as follows:

> *For Officers*: Of best black felt. The dimensions of medium size to be as follows:
> Width of brim, 3 1/4 inches,
> Height of crown, 6 1/4 inches,
> Oval of tip, 1/2 inch,
> Taper of crown, 3/4 inch,
> Curve of head, 3/8 inch,
> The binding to be 1/2 inch deep, of best black ribbed silk.
> *For Enlisted Men*. Of black felt, same shape and size as for officers, with double row of stitching, instead of binding, around the edge. To agree in quality with the pattern deposited in the clothing arsenal.

A black ostrich feather and worsted cords, which ended in tassels rather than acorns, also were prescribed for all enlisted men, in 1858, along with a sheet brass eagle device, which was used to hold the looped up side. The example shown here is for a mounted rifle trooper of Company G, as indicated by the green cords and brass insignia. The perpendicular trumpet insignia is one of two types extant from this period. It is unclear which of the styles was correct for this hat. Photograph by Gordon Chappell.

The 1858 pattern hat was to have worsted cords ending in tassels for enlisted men, with yellow ones being issued to cavalrymen and enlisted engineers. In turn, orange represented dragoon troopers and scarlet heavy artillery personnel. Crimson cords were provided to Ordnance Department soldiers. CF

The 1858 pattern black feather for enlisted 1858 pattern hats was to be inserted into a small black crocheted holder. NYSHS

Trimmings
For General Officers: Gold cord, with acorn-shaped ends. The brim of the hat looped up on the right side, and fastened with an eagle attached to the side of the hat; three black ostrich feathers on the left side; a gold embroidered wreath in front on black velvet ground, encircling the letters U.S. in silver, old English characters.
For Officers of the Adjutants General's, Inspector General's, Quartermaster's, Subsistence, Medical and Pay Departments, and the Judge Advocate, above the rank of Captain: The same as for General Officers, except the cord, which will be of black silk and gold.
For the same Departments, below the rank of Field Officers: The same as for Field Officers, except that there will be two feathers.
For Officers of the Corps of Engineers: The same as for the General Staff, except the ornament in front, which will be a gold embroidered wreath of laurel and palm, encircling a silver turreted castle on black velvet ground.
For Officers of the Topographical Engineers: The same as for the General Staff, except the ornament in front, which will be a gold embroidered wreath of oak leaves, encircling a gold embroidered shield, on black velvet.
For Officers of the Ordnance Department: The same as for the General Staff, except the ornament in front, which will be a gold embroidered shell and flame, on black velvet ground.
For Officers of Dragoons: The same as for the general Staff, except the ornament in front, which will be two gold embroidered sabres crossed, edges upward, on black velvet with the number of the regiment in silver in the upper angle.
For Officers of Cavalry: The same as for Dragoons, except the sabres will be reversed, with the number of the regiment in the lower angle.
For Officers of Mounted Rifles: The same as for General Staff, except the ornament in front, which will be a gold embroidered trumpet, perpendicular, on black velvet ground.
For Officers of Artillery: The same as General Staff, except the ornament in front, which will be gold embroidered cross-cannon, on black velvet ground, with the number of the regiment in silver at the intersection of the cross-cannon: The brim of the hat to be looped up on the left side, and the feathers to be worn on the right side.
For Officers of Infantry: The same as for Artillery except the ornament in front, which will be a gold embroidered bugle, on black velvet ground, with the number of the regiment in silver within the bend.
For Enlisted Men: The same as Officers of the respective corps; except that there will be but one feather, the cord will be of worsted, and the badges yellow metal, to be worn in front.
All the trimmings of the hat are to be made so that they can be detached; but the eagle, badge of corps, and letter of company, are to be always worn.[75]

This last requirement would be ignored more often than not over the passing years. Also in regard to insignia, cavalry officers and all enlisted men in the combat arms (artillery, cavalry, dragoons, infantry, and mounted rifles) previously had no hat insignia beyond either regimental numerals for officers or company letters for enlisted men for their 1851 or 1854 pattern caps, while the other officers and men did so

Hat Cords.

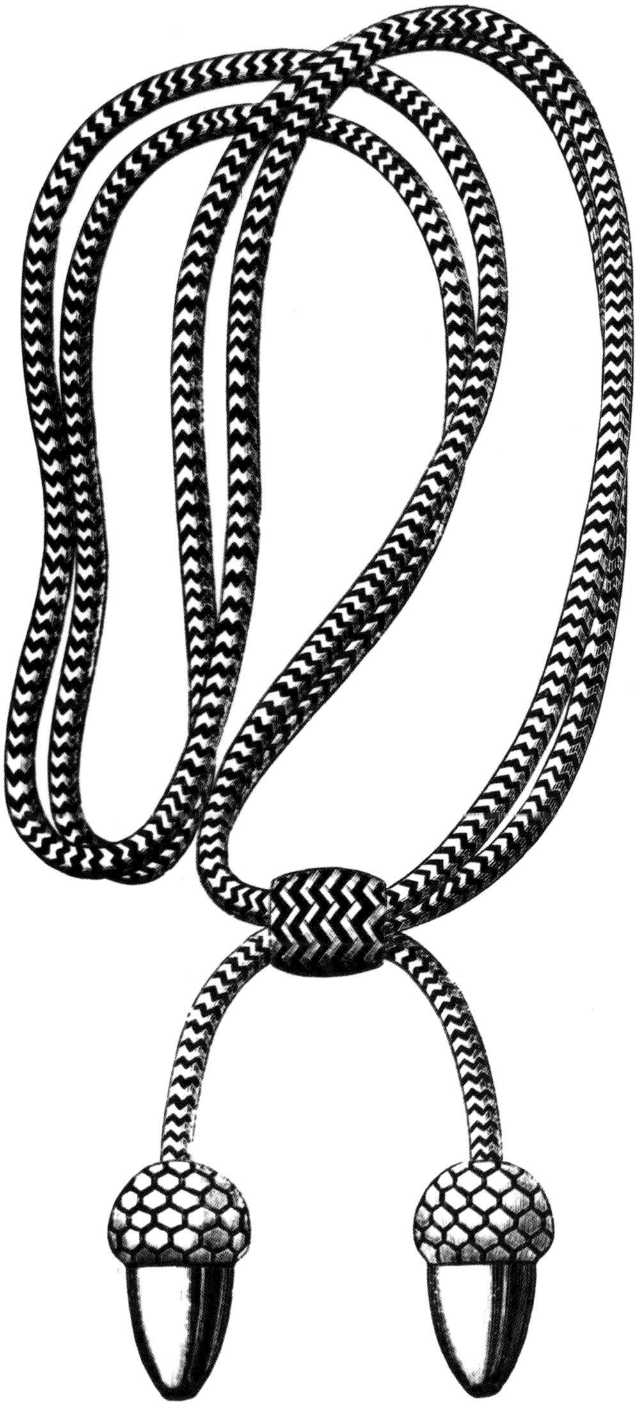

No. 63.

Gilt and Silk Machine Hat Cord.

No. 64.

Gilt and Silk Twisted Hat Cord.

The cords for the 1858 pattern hat for all officers except generals were to be gold and black mixed, while the thread was to be gold for general officers. KC

Hat and Cap Ornaments for Officers.

No. 125.—STAFF.

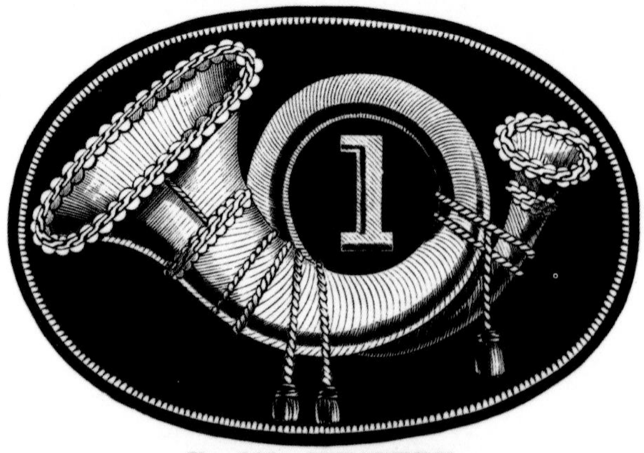

No. 129.—INFANTRY.

No. 126.

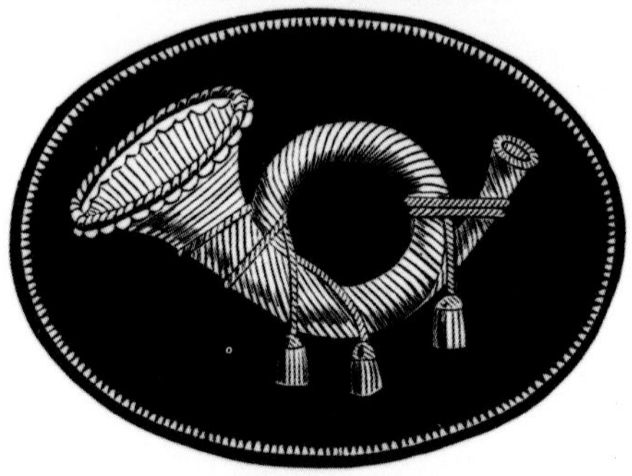

No. 130.

No. 127.—ARTILLERY.

No. 131.—CAVALRY.

No. 128.

No. 132.

Embroidered on Velvet for Hats, and on Cloth for Caps.—Ornaments in Gold, Letters & Numbers in Silver.
Nos. 125, 127, 129, and 131, U. S. Regulation Size. Nos. 126, 128, 130, and 132, Miniature Size.

Opposite: Officers' hat and cap insignia usually were embroidered gold devices with silver regimental numbers, the smaller ones being worn mainly on the forage cap or non-regulation slouch hats. There were metallic versions as well, which were inexpensive and more practical for field wear. Many officers purchased these less costly devices during the Civil War. KC

Second Lieutenant F.V. Farquhar of the Corps of Engineers wears the 1858 pattern hat appropriate to his branch, with two black ostrich feathers called for in regulations for company grade officers and the castle within a wreath for engineers. USAMHI

and continued to use the same scheme set forth in 1851.[76] This change placed everyone on the same footing. It likewise should be noted that hospital stewards received a further distinction with the adoption of the hat in that they were to have buff and green hat cords, the two colors combined making them unique among enlisted personnel. Moreover, the two hues closely approximated the half chevron these enlisted medical men had been provided since the early 1850s, although during that period they had no special headgear or insignia per se, except for the brass wreath with german silver "U.S." that was provided for by General Orders No. 2, War Department, February 28, 1857.

Additionally, General Orders No. 24, War Department June 24, 1858, made a further adjustment, perhaps for the sake of uniformity. This directive indicated that dragoons and cavalrymen would have the sabers worn with the edges placed upwards, rather than reversed from each other as in the past. The only difference would be that the regimental numeral would be located above the sabers for dragoons and below the sabers for cavalry.[77]

Above Left: Assistant Surgeon Thomas Williams in the 1858 pattern hat for staff officers, which included the Medical Department. NA

Left: In this 1860 image Major John Fulton Reynolds, commandant of cadets at the United States Military Academy, holds his 1858 pattern hat for field grade artillery officers. Again note the binding around the edge of the brim, an option found on a number of officers' hats. USAMHI

In this 1858 image, the commandant of Carlisle Barracks poses in the center of officers and ladies of the garrison wearing the ponderous hat adopted in that year, while the other officers in the group wear the forage cap of the period. USAMHI

Infantry bandsmen with the Utah Expedition depict the diversity of headgear worn in the field in the later 1850s, including what appears to be a number of 1854 pattern caps that have been compressed to provide a forage cap. The non-commissioned officer in the center has on an 1839 pattern forage cap and a triple row of buttons, probably indicating that he is the principal musician or chief trumpeter. USHS

The hat was not issued in large quantities until the following year. Soon thereafter one cavalry officer suggested that the chinstrap again be provided as with the 1855 pattern, a suggestion the quartermaster general sanctioned for cavalry and dragoons, at least for a limited time.[78]

Another cavalry officer reacted to the hat in less positive terms, writing "If the whole earth had been ransacked, it is difficult to tell where a more ungainly piece of furniture could have been found." He went on to indicate the 1858 hat was "somewhat more unwieldy" than its 1855 progenitor. It seemed "that the soldiers take great delight in seeing into what ludicrous shapes they can get their hat...." He concluded that the hat reminded the viewer of a stage costume piece worn by "Fra Diavolo," the title character to "one of the most frequently performed operas of the 19th century."[79]

Captain Jesse Gove, an officer serving in Utah, held a different opinion of the matter, recording: "We see by the papers that the uniform is to be changed. The cap or hat to be black and ostrich feathers. That will please you, but the other changes are disapproved by everyone here in the army."[80] During April 1858 Captain Gove's company was stationed in today's western Wyoming. His company was the only one in the regiment at that time to have received the "cavalry hat" as he called it, and he thought the men "looked splendidly."[81] He also underscored that the hat had a "black ostrich feather like Kossuth hats, turned up on the right side."[82] In a second instance, on May 27, 1858, Gove mentioned Kossuth hats were combined with worn uniforms, or interspersed with the old 1854 pattern cap.[83]

On yet another occasion, during February 1859 Captain Albert Tracy had a different experience. While on parade, a snowstorm covered the troops, some in the 1854 cap with pompons, others in "kepis," and still some in the felt hats, "with broad or looped up brims, and plumes of ostrich" that "were simply a mess, and shocking to behold" once drenched

The artillery troops at Ft. Monroe, Virginia, received the new forage cap in 1857, and the remainder of the army followed suit over the next few years, as this type of headgear ultimately became standard for the entire force. This picture of Corporal Davis Brurells was taken on February 20, 1858, and perhaps is the earliest image of the enlisted forage cap of this pattern. WJS

The enlisted forage cap of the late 1850s was to have a welt around the top (except for recruits, who had no welts) in scarlet for artillery, orange for dragoons, yellow for cavalry and engineers, crimson for ordnance, and emerald green for mounted riflemen, a practice that was discontinued by 1861. Here a dragoon of the 1858 era stands to horse at Ft. Leavenworth, Kansas, in the pre-1861 forage cap with the 1854 pattern mounted jacket trimmed in orange worsted lace. LC

In the late 1850s Second Lieutenant Kirby Smith of the elite Topographical Engineers (later to become a general officer in the Confederate Army) went to Utah with a major surveying expedition. An embroidered wreath with shield in the center indicates his branch on the front of the blue wool forage cap, a pattern of headgear that was unique to engineers from 1857-1858, when the secretary of war ordered that it be adopted for all branches and ranks. The transition was gradual, but by the Civil War this cap became the norm. NA

Colonel P.G.T. Beauregard, as superintendent of the U.S. Military Academy, obtained an engineer officer's forage cap of the 1858 pattern. This early model differs from later forage caps in that it seems to be a cross between the 1839 pattern and the "bummer's" cap of the Civil War. USAMHI

Sergeant Herman O. Renaldo wears the infantry forage cap of the 1858 pattern with a sky-blue welt around the crown, as does his unknown comrade. VJM

in the cold, moist flakes. Tracy concluded: "In the 5th Infantry, the loss and demoralization in brand new hats and plumes, is said to be something fearful. In our own regiment it was not light."[84]

The mixture of hats also was found in Nevada when a campaign was launched in 1860 against a local Indian group, the Piutes. Some of the forces sent there were men from Company H, Third Artillery, stationed in the San Francisco area, and a detachment from the Sixth U.S. Infantry dispatched from Benicia, California. According to a newspaper account the artillery wore "the regular army military hat, with letter II [sic], in gilt, on front, without pompoon [sic]" while the infantry company had "black Kossuth hats, with left brim turned up and fastened with a gilt *attache*, gilt bugle in front, and surrounded with blue cord and tassels...."[85]

In some respects this description could have pertained to a larger and better known conflict that was just around the corner. As 1860 drew to a close military leaders paid less attention to far off problems with American Indians in the West. The growing animosity between the North and South required their almost undivided attention.

In this circa 1860 image Lieutenant Charles Bowman wears an early version of the 1858 pattern forage cap. WPM

Notes:

1 Frederick P. Todd, "The Leather Forage Cap at West Point," *Military Collector and Historian* VI No 2 (June 1954): 38-40.

2 GO No. 53, HQA, July 26, 1834. The Seventh U.S. Infantry, however, was to be sent these caps during spring 1833, according to, Callender Irvine to Fayssoux, April 10, 1833, Commissary General of Purchases, Letters Sent, Record Group 92, National Archives, hereinafter referred to as LS, RG92, NA.

3 Howell and Kloster, *United States Army Headgear to 1854*, 38.

4 Howell and Kloster, *United States Army Headgear to 1854*, 38.

5 Osman, "Company Letters for Regular Army Forage Caps, 1825-1872": 157.

6 The above information was taken from Howell and Kloster, *United States Army Headgear to 1854*, 40-1.

7 Osman, "Company Letters for Regular Army Caps, 1825-1872": 157.

8 Order No. 26, HQ First Dragoons, Fort Leavenworth, Kansas Territory, December 31, 1846.

9 Howell and Kloster, *United States Army Headgear to 1854*, 45.

10 Howell and Kloster, *United States Army Headgear to 1854*, 45.

11 Samuel Chamberlain, *My Confession* (New York: Harper & Bros, 1956), and Martha A. Sandweiss, Rick Steward, and Ben W. Houseman, *Eyewitness to War: Prints and Daguerreotypes of the Mexican War, 1846-1848* (Ft. Worth: Amon Carter Museum, 1989), both offer information in text and visuals about the 1839-pattern cap, as well as other aspects of the uniform of the 1845-1848 period.

12 Major John Garland to Brigadier General John Wool, August 19, 1832, Clothing Bureau, LS, RG92, NA.

13 GO No. 50, HQA, June 11, 1832.

14 Howell and Kloster, *United States Army Headgear to 1854*, 26. Company officers as well as non-commissioned officers of the marines were to wear the hat according to a November 4, 1834 order issued by the commandant of the Corps. Entry 7, "Orders Received and Issued by the Commandant, 1803-1886," Vol. 3, 332, RG127, Records of the United States Marine Corps, 1798-1944, NA. A new bellcrown pattern was adopted in 1846, and replaced the old version shortly thereafter. Charles H. Cureton, *The United States Marine Corps* (London: Greenhill Books, 1997), 19.

15 GO No. 10, HQA, February 9, 1833. This directive noted: "In order to avoid any unnecessary expense to the public from the introduction of the new uniforms, the Secretary of War directs that so much of the old uniform, caps excepted, as may be on hand and in depots, shall be issued as far as it will serve to the lst, 3rd, and 7th Regiments of Infantry." From this language and from the decision to sell the surplus 1821-pattern bell crowns to the marines, the intent to see the new cap in use as soon as possible was clear.

16 For more on this cap and other elements of the uniform of the period consult, War Department, *General Regulations for the Army* (Washington, DC: Francis P. Blair, printer, 1834), 218-230.

17 Ibid.

18 Campbell and Howell, *American Military Insignia 1800-1851*, 26-28, describes and depicts the insignia for artillery, infantry, cadet, and engineer caps of the 1832-1851 period.

19 According to GO 100, HQ of the Army, November 7, 1833, the basic cap was to be charged at $2.72 for infantry and artillery troops, with an additional charge of $.37 1/2 for non-commissioned staff pompons, $.23 for artillery enlisted men, and $.20 for infantry enlisted men.

20 GO No. 67, HQ of the Army, July 31, 1832, stated: "2 Caps of felt, complete, with the brass ornaments and feather" were to be issued over a five year enlistment and but one forage cap.

21 Francis Paul Prucha, ed., *Army Life on the Western Frontier: Selections from the Official Reports Made Between 1826 and 1845 by Colonel George Croghan* (Norman: University of Oklahoma Press, 1958), 62.

22 Howell and Kloster, *United States Army Headgear to 1854*, 28.

23 Elting, Military Uniforms in America, Vol. II, 88-9; 94-5; and 118-9, offer descriptions of the artillery and infantry use of these caps.

24 Campbell and Howell, *American Military Insignia 1800-1851*, 27. The United States Military Academy's version of the cap was to be "seven inches high, or more, in proportion to the size of the Cadet, with a circular visor in front; black worsted pompon, eight inches long set in a yellow metal socket; cap-plate worn on front of the cap." Jacques Noel Jacobsen, Jr., comp. and ed., *Regulations and Notes for the Uniforms of the United States Army 1847* (Staten Island: Manor Publishing, 1977). This pompon is similar to the one worn on the cadet dress cap into the twenty-first century.

25 War Department, *General Regulations for the Army of the United States, 1841* (Washington, DC: J. and G.S. Gideon, printers, 1841), 78.

26 As noted in ibid., ordnance sergeants were to wear the uniform of a sergeant major of artillery, *sans* aiguillette, with a dark blue 1 1/2-inch stripe rather than the artillery's scarlet stripe on the outer seams of the "pantaloons." All other ordnance men were to be issued an identical outfit to their artillery counterparts, except that unlike artillerymen the ordnance personnel has a red welt let into the outer seams of their overalls. Elting, *Military Uniforms in America*, Vol. II, 116-117, depicts an ordnance sergeant in the proper garb, although the text states that apparently a brass "flaming grenade" insignia was worn on the front of the shako. The artillery crossed cannon actually seemed to be worn.

27 G.O. 18, HQ of the Army, June 4, 1846. See also, Elting, *Military Uniforms in America*, Vol, II, 128-9. Thus, the castle insignia approved in 1840 by the chief of engineers finally was to be employed for soldiers of that department, instead of just the cadets at West Point See, J.G. Totten, May 20, 1840, with an accompanying drawing of the engineer castle insignia dated January 8, 1840, File 77-F-178-8-2, NA.

28 Howell and Kloster, *United States Army Headgear to 1854*, 33.

29 GO No. 50, HQA, July 11, 1832.

30 John Garland to D. Baker, March 20, 1833, Clothing Bureau, LS, RG92, NA.

31 Frederick P. Todd, *American Military Equipage 1851-1872* (New York: Charles Scribner's Sons, 1980), 30-1; 45-50, discusses France's domination when it came to the U.S. Army uniform of the 1850s, whereas Edgar M. Howell and Donald E. Kloster, *United States Military Headgear to 1854 Catalog of United States Army Uniforms in the Collections of the Smithsonian Institution,* Vol. I (City of Washington: Smithsonian Institution Press, 1969), 26, points to England's influence in early times. In fact, the head of quartermaster clothing bureau even requested that an officer on tour of England in 1832 asked that patterns be sent back from that country for use in the United States. This letter included the tacit admission, "for I perceive we have copied the English in most of the changes which have been made..." in the uniform. J. Garland to J.E. Wool, August 10, 1832, LS, Clothing Bureau, OQMG, RG92, NA.

32 Howell and Kloster, *United States Army Headgear to 1854*, 56. The 1847-1851 garb is described in *Regulations for the Uniform of the United States Army 1847*. See Appendix A for a reprint of this regulation. Additional official correspondence concerning the uniform board of 1844 is located in Document File B 136, 1844, Box 150, AGO, RG94, NA. Additional correspondence related to the uniform from 1844 through 1854 can be found in LR, AGO, RG94, Microcopy 567, Roll 282, NA.

33 General Orders No. 2, War Department, February 13, 1850.

34 Howell and Kloster, *United States Army Headgear to 1854*, 56-7, indicates Colonel Sylvester Churchill, one of the two inspectors general of the period, reported that over fifty percent of the officers he spoke to about the uniform favored a more streamlined uniform that dispensed with the coatee and cap, these being replaced by frock coats and forage caps.

35 *United Service Gazette*, April 13, 1850.

36 Risch, *Quartermaster Support of the Army*, 302.

37 On April 2, 1794, an Act of Congress called for the establishment of four arsenals to provide for the needs of the American army. A few years later the first of these was founded on Gray's Ferry Road, and became Schuylkill Arsenal, so named because of the river on which it was located. At first both clothing and ordnance stores were provided by the facility, but after the War of 1812, with the building of Frankford Arsenal in New York, only quartermaster items were provided. L.C. Baird, "The Philadelphia Quartermaster Intermediate Depot," *Quartermaster Review* VI No. 6 (May-June 1927), 18-9.

38 Thomas Jesup to C.A. Waite, April 22, 1850, LS, Clothing & Equipment Branch, Vol. 12, OQMG, RG92, NA. Thomas Jesup to P. St. George Cooke, November 28, 1855, Vol. 14, ibid., reiterated why the 1850 change was halted writing, "when a former Secretary of War, on the recommendation of a few Officers of the Army, ordered a change of the uniform, there was a large war stock on hand of the old pattern sufficient for several years supply of the reduced Peace establishment." The quartermaster general went on to conclude: "The change was most injudicious at the time, and under the circumstances in which it was made—The great extension of our Territories had quadrupled the expenditures of the Military Establishment; Congress alarmed at these expenditures, was reducing the most necessary appropriations...." This reply was in response to Cooke's query why his regiment was still in old patterns. Jesup explained that he was required by Congress to issue existing stocks as long as sufficient service able items remained on hand. Not until the mid-1850s did clothing made for the Mexican War dwindle to a degree that new patterns could be obtained and issued on a widespread basis.

39 Brevet Lieutenant Colonel Joseph H. Eaton to Adjutant General, April 28, 1851; and Adjutant General to Major General Winfield Scott, May 22, 1851, AGO, RG94, NA.

40 Howell and Kloster, *United States Army Headgear to 1854*, 63 and 67.

41 Thomas Jesup to Nechard & Co., March 31, 1859, C&E Br., Vol. 17, OQMG, RG92, NA.

42 Howell and Kloster, *United States Army Headgear to 1854*, 40-53, offers more details about the 1851-cap.

43 "New Uniform for the U.S. Army," *Gleason's Pictorial Drawing-Room Companion* (March 22, 1852), 328. For depictions of the French version of the cap adopted in the 1840s see, Robert H. Rankin, *Military Headdress: A Pictorial History of Military Headgear From 1660 to 1914* (London: Arms and Armour Press, 1976), 32 and 34. It is interesting that the previous pattern of cap, which had been adopted in 1832 and subsequently issued to all but dragoons and mounted artillery also had French roots, as did its replacement of 1851 that, "was almost an exact copy of the form adopted by the French in 1844." Howell and Kloster, *United States Army Headgear to 1854*, 64.

44 From 1820 to 1850 the West Point band wore white uniforms trimmed in red, and the practice was revived from 1867 to 1873, according to Elting, *Military Uniform in America*, Vol. II, 94.

45 Howell and Kloster, *United States Army Headgear to 1854*, 66.

46 *A Medical Report upon the Uniform and Clothing of the Soldiers of the U.S. Army, 15 April 1868* (Washington, DC: Surgeon General's Office), CCF, Box 1171, OQMG, RG92, NA.

47 Howell and Kloster, *United States Army Headgear to 1854*, 54.

48 Percival G. Lowe, *Five Years A Dragoon And Other Adventures on the Great Plains* (Norman: University of Oklahoma Press, 1965), 83.

49 Teresa G. Viele, *Following the Drum: A Glimpse of Frontier Life* (Lincoln: University of Nebraska Press, 1984), 224-5.

50 Joseph H. Parks, *General Edmund Kirby Smith* (Baton Rouge: Louisiana State University Press, 1954), 90.

51 John Van Deusen Dubois, *Campaigns in the West, 1856-1851* (Tucson: Arizona Pioneers Historical Society, 1949), 114.

52 Ralph P. Bieber, ed., *Frontier Life in the Army* (Glendale, CA: Arthur H. Clark, 1932), 124.

53 Ibid., 140.

54 For background on this somewhat obscure phase of U.S.Army history read, Leroy R. Hafen, ed., *The Utah Expedition 1857-1858: A Documentary Account of the United States Military Movement Under Colonel Albert Sidney Johnston, and The Resistance by Brigham Young and the Mormon Nauvoo Legion* (Glendale, CA: The Arthur H. Clark Company, 1982).

55 Frederick P. Todd, *American Military Equipage, 1851-1872* (Providence, RI: The Company of Military Historians, 1977), II, 380 and 384.

56 Otis G. Hammond, ed., *The Utah Expedition, 1857-1858; Letters of Capt. Jesse A. Gove, 10th Inf., U.S.A., of Concord, N.H. to Mrs. Gove, and special correspondence of the New York Herald* (Concord: New Hampshire Historical Society, 1928), 15.

57 Lawrence Kip, *Army Life on the Pacific: A Journal of the Expedition Against the North Indians...in the Summer of 1858* (New York: Redfield, 1859), 122-3.

58 John F.Callan, *The Military Laws of the United States, Relating to the Army, Volunteers, Militia, and to Bounty Lands and Pensions from the Foundation of the Government to the Year 1863, To Which are Prefixed the Constitution of the United States. (With an Index Thereto,) and a Synopsis of the Military Legislation of Congress During the Revolutionary War* (Philadelphia: George W. Childs, 1863), 435-6.

59 George F. Price, *Across the Continent with the Fifth Cavalry* (New York: D. Van Nostrand, Publisher, 1883), 11-22, gives an overview of the formation of these regiment with an emphasis on the Second Cavalry that would be redesignated the Fifth in 1861.

60 Sumner's Report on Trip to Europe, microfilm, LR, M-567, Roll 506, AGO, RG 94, NA. According E.V. Sumner, A.S. Johnson, J.E. Johnston, and W.J. Hardee to Jefferson Davis, July 19, 1855, LR, Ordnance, RG156, NA, the enlisted hat was to have an eagle device, although the only known surviving specimen does not.

61 Howell, *United States Army Headgear 1855-1902*, 1-5, offers further details on this piece of headgear.

62 Harold Langley, ed., *To Utah With The Dragoons (Salt Lake: University of Utah, 1974)*, 39.

63 For a reprint of McClellan's letter on this subject and a description of the 1859 model of the saddle and horse equipments consult, Randy Steffen, *The Horse Soldier 1776-1943*, Vol. II (Norman: University of Oklahoma Press, 1978), 53 and 58-63.

64 *Report of the Secretary of War, Communicating the Report of Captain George B. McClellan*, 248.

65 Howell, *United States Army Headgear, 1855-1902*, 13.

66 Ibid., 12-13

67 Brevet Major William H. French to Colonel Samuel Cooper, August 11, 1858, LR, File 102-F-1858, AGO, RG94, NA.

68 A december 1, 1858 Circular from the Adjutant General's Office went on to underscore that recruits were to be issued only the forage cap and four-button sack coat, and not until they joined their regiments would they obtain the mounted jacket or foot soldier's coat and the dress hat.

69 Petition dated October 13, 1858, File 349B, 1858, ibid. A circular dated December 1, 1858, from the Adjutant General's Office, indicated that form that date "the coat and hat are only to be issued to permanent parties at depots and rendezvous" while the "forage cap and sack" were to "be issued, instead, to all unassigned recruits. They will then receive the dress uniform now on joining their regiments." Microfilm Collections, Box 82, USAMHI.

70 GO No. 5, WD, May 19, 1858.

71 GO No. 77, Headquarters of the Artillery School, June 7, 1858, Post Returns of Ft. Monroe Artillery School and Post General Orders, September 12, 1854-July 18, 1860, RG98, NA.

72 GO No. 31, HQA, June 12, 1855, allowed general officers and field grade officers who had held brevets as general officers to wear the chapeau they had been authorized in 1847, so long as it was on ceremonial occasions when not serving with troops. GO No. 3, WD, March 24, 1858, extended this practice to all field officers for general wear and to staff officers. Finally, GO No. 27, WD, December 22, 1859, modified the earlier order permitting, "all officers of the General Staff, and Staff Corps, to wear, at their option, a light French chapeau, either stiff crown or flat...." Officers below the field rank would have two feathers and those of field rank would have three.

73 Howell, *United States Army Headgear 1855-1902*, 23, and 96-7. Evidently old white horsetail plumes remaining from the 1833-pattern dragoon enlisted cap still were in stock and were dyed scarlet, the proper color for artillery. Todd, *American Military Equipage*, 378.

74 Ibid., 23.

75 The feather also could be removed, but when worn was intened to be attached to the hat by means of a crocheted black wool worsted socket at least for enlisted men. How widespread the use of this small appendage was is not known, but as late as two years after the Civil War over 12,000 of the feathers and their sockets were included in a listing of "damaged and irregular clothing and equipage ordered to be sold at public auction." *Annual Report of the Secretary of War*, 1867, Vol. I, 542-3.

76 GO No. 2, WD, February 13, 1850, had called for insignia for enlisted men, but this directive was rescinded before it could take effect. According to, Campbell and Howell, *American Military Insignia*, 31, the trumpet for the 1858-pattern mounted rifles en listed hat insignia was that proposed in 1850, but Gordon Chappell, "Dress Hat of the First Regiment of Mounted Rifles, 1858-1861," *Military Collector and Historian* XXII No. 2 (Summer 1970): 58-9, disagrees.

77 F.C. Townsend and Frederick P. Todd, "Branch Insignia of the Regular Cavalry, 1833-1872," *Military Collector and Historian* VIII No. 1 (Spring 1956): 1-5, traces changes in the cavalry and dragoon insignia.

78 Howell, *United States Army Headgear 1855-1902*, 7.

79 Albert G. Brackett, *History of the U.S. Cavalry* (New York: Harper and Brothers, 1865), 160-1. Fra Diavolo was a brigand chief (tenor) in an *opéra comique* production of the same name by Daniel-Francois-Esprit Auber and Eugène Scribe. First performed in Paris on January 28, 1830, by 1907 this opera had played in Paris no less than 900 times. In addition, within two years after its premier, it was performed abroad and formed part of the repertory of many houses including in New York. The inspiration came from a French play that made its debut in 1808 as *Fra Diavolo, chef des brig-ands dans les Alpes*. Stanley Sadies, ed., *The New Grove's Dictionary of Opera*, Vol. II (New York: Grove's Dictionary of Music Inc., 1992), 268-9.

80 Hammond, *The Utah Expedition*, 164.

81 Ibid., 150.

82 The reference to the style of the hat was derived from Louis Kossuth, who had achieved considerable international fame in his efforts to free Hungary from Austrian rule, and who achieved a certain popularity among Americans after a visit to the United States. Kossuth's image was that of a democratic freedom fighter, complete with dashing broad brimmed hat. In more recent times this headgear has been referred to as the "Jeff Davis" or "Hardee" hat, the latter after William J. Hardee, who also cast his lot with the Confederacy, although no contemporary references can be found using this terminology. Evidently these nicknames are of more recent origin, perhaps being invented by collectors and militaria dealers.

83 Hammond, *The Utah Expedition*, 278.

84 Alter, *The Utah Journal of Captain Albert Tracy*, 55-6. This is one of the earliest uses of the term "kepi." Presumably it referred to the forage cap adopted in the late 1850s. According to Brinckerhoff, *Military Headgear in the Southwest*, 8, the term was a "French word of German origin to describe a military hat."

85 "Movement of Troops," Sacramento *Daily Union*, May 29, 1860.

3

Preserving a Nation 1861-1865

More than 2 million men left civilian life to serve in the Union Army. As this chapter shows, they brought with them a spirit of independence that was reflected in their approach to army regulations, particularly when it came to what they wore on their heads. In this image, two stalwart troopers, posing with Colt Revolving Muskets, illustrate some of the diversity that resulted from this sense of freedom. One wears the regulation cap while the other has obtained a soft felt hat, quickly favored by the rank and file as a more practical and comfortable piece of headgear. CPL

Although America's Civil War had been looming for years, when the firing on Fort Sumter in the harbor of Charleston, South Carolina, finally ignited hostilities the Federal government found itself woefully unprepared for the coming fight. At the outset on April 12, 1861, the regular army consisted of only 14,663 men scattered in posts across the continent. The nation was not only in desperate need of troops but also just about everything else military.

To answer the crisis, President Abraham Lincoln quickly issued a call for 75,000 volunteers to serve for three months. With diverse motives, and even more diverse uniform styles, eager volunteers rallied around the Stars and Stripes and the states scrambled to clothe them. Uniforms and equipment sometimes varied from company to company in those first high-spirited months, as small militia units expanded or banded together to form regiments and were inducted into U.S. service. Some marched off in attire that was locally designed and sewn by neighborhood tailors. Others wore clothing supplied on a state level according to the state's own particular regulations or depending on whatever that state was able to purchase. As a result, units might be seen in European-inspired outfits that included towering Napoleonic bearskins, French kepis, feathered Italian *bersaglieri*, Scottish tams, and Zouave fezes.[1] Even the old shako was seen on the heads of more than a few erstwhile heroes.[2]

As war fever spread, *Yankee ingenuity* combined with the industrial revolution to create some very singular items of headgear. One oddball covering that actually saw limited service was a hat/havelock combination patented in July, 1861, by J. F. Whipple. While Whipple owned the patent, it seems the hat was originally created by James M. Loomis, a Chicago hatter. Loomis had headgear of his design manufactured in New York for an independent Illinois infantry company, the Sturges Rifles, in the summer of 1861and received orders to outfit more units from that state with them. In a June 3, 1861, front page article, The Chicago Tribune described the gray felt hats as "resembling an ordinary felt hat, the rim dishing deeply, turned downwards behind and cut away from side to side in front where a neat leather visor is substituted. Thus the neck and head are well protected, leaving the front clear and unobstructed." A button on each side of the crown allowed the brim to be fastened up.

While the Tribune article proclaimed the hat "the best now in use," the rank and file felt differently. Writing home, a soldier of the 10th Illinois Vols. called the invention "ugly as the devil" and most of his comrades seemed to agree.[3] A diary entry by a soldier of the 11th Illinois on Oct. 11, 1861, simply stated "Drew new hats. We don't like them." Thirteen days later the same soldier said "we bought red caps to wear" in place of their new havelock/hats.[4] Apparently Loomis never patented his design and it was taken, with slight modifications, by Whipple who received a patent on it. [5] Whipple, a New York City hatter, seems to have had some connection with the Seamless Clothing Manufacturing Company that made the headwear and many of Whipple's patent were sold to New England troops. Whether this was a mutually agreeable business arrangement in which Loomis received compensation, or a simple pirating of an unprotected idea is unknown at this time.

Another similar hat was patented that December by Philadelphia hatter Charles L. Pascal and was issued to some Pennsylvania cavalry units in the early part of the conflict. The body of Pascal's hat resembled the 1858 Army Hat and featured a unique brass locking device to fasten the brim up or down.

Options and variations seemed to defy cataloging.[6] While these creations were no doubt avowed to be healthy, comfortable, and superior to the regulation headgear, they proved impractical and were short lived. Other inventive geniuses created inserts, ventilators and miscellaneous devices to "improve" upon any shortcomings of the government issue material and at the same time line their pockets with some greenbacks.

All these products catered to an army of very self-reliant citizen-soldiers who exercised their own judgement when it came to what they wore on their heads, just as they had conscientiously done as civilians. After all, to men in Victorian America a hat was a statement of style and status. The result was perhaps the most colorful array of military headwear ever seen in the U.S. Army and higher authorities were only marginally successful in regulating it. Though they may have become Federal troops, the volunteers retained their independent civilian spirit to the end and their headgear reflected that fact.

Perhaps the first widespread "enhancement" in headwear to afflict soldiers was the havelock (named after its designer, Sir Henry Havelock, a British general whose troops used the device during the India Mutiny just a few years earlier).[7] This accessory was essentially a cap

The first volunteers marched off to war in militia finery that usually included obsolete headgear. Just before leaving Hanover, Pa., 21-year-old David Schull posed in uniform for this ambrotype beneath his shako ornamented by a tall cascade of colored feathers. His service to the Union was brief as he "died from an attack of pneumonia brought on by the exposure consequently attending camp life;" his hometown's first casualty of war. CPL

The shako, inspired by those worn by the U. S. Army in the previous decade, was still popular with many militia units at the outbreak of the war. This example was worn by Pvt. Smith W. Anderson of the famed Seventh New York Militia when it was mustered into U.S. service for three months in April 1861. CPL

With its wide, deep visor and tall crown this early cap by Kunz and Reinger of Erie, Pa., tries to emulate the 1858 pattern cap but remains almost shako-like in appearance. It probably adorned a member of a local militia company during the first months of the conflict. WM

cover of lightweight white cloth with a neckpiece that extended downwards in the back. The intent of the design was to reflect the rays of the sun away from the cap and the bare neck of the wearer and allow air to circulate underneath. But, as a United States Sanitary Commission report revealed, the American version of the havelock seldom worked as intended:

> The havelocks as generally made, are of little use. The articles worn by Indian troops, pictures of which probably suggested that termed in America the havelock, is quilted and stiff, rested on the shoulders, and thus kept open, clear of the ears, allowing free circulation of air beneath.[8]

Captain William B, Parisen of Co. E, 4th New York Volunteer Infantry, purchased this elegant chasseur cap no doubt when he entered service in April, 1861. Its chin strap is fastened with buttons that bear the coat of arms of the State of New York and it features the nickname of the unit, *Scott Life Guard*, embroidered on a medium blue velvet band. Such expensive embellishments underline the early volunteers' esprit d'corps along with the importance of headwear to men in Victorian America. DT

Existing specimens, however, reveal that the American interpretations were not stiffened to allow air to flow beneath them and so draped limply, unsoldierly, and uncomfortably upon the wearer. The Commission's July, 1861, report went on to say the havelock made the soldier's cap "excessively conspicuous—quite unfit for scouting and skirmishing duty. It interferes with hearing, and through common neglect of duty of volunteer officers, it is allowed to be worn without uniformity, and becomes very untidy."

Nonetheless, there were havelocks aplenty for the first volunteers. They were usually hastily made by zealous, patriotic sewing circles or loved ones at home, none of whom, as the Sanitary Commission report pointed out, could guess the proper qualities of a true havelock from the engravings they saw in the illustrated magazines of the day. They looked easy to make and, after all, appeared to be urgently needed lest the Union warriors be struck down by the hot Dixie sun in the oncoming summer.

"Havelocks were turned out by the thousands, of all patterns and sizes, and of every conceivable material," recalled one woman after the war.[9] The wife of General Charles Collis remembered afterward they were "the ruling mania of the hour. The sewing societies made nothing but havelocks; the shop windows were full of them, and the poor fellows in the army were so inundated with them that those who had the fewest relatives and sweethearts were much the best off."[10] While a Boston newspaper reporter could comment on the dashing look of the 12th Mass. Volunteers when they arrived in the city "in their snow white havelocks, and neatly arranged knapsacks and blankets," the soldiers themselves were far from enthusiastic about these omnipresent bags.[11] The Sanitary Commission observed they "were worn or dispensed with according to the caprice of individuals."[12] Another noted "They were worn in every imaginable fashion,—as nightcaps, turbans, sunbonnets, bandages, sunshades—and the fate of the Havelock was sealed. No more time nor money was wasted in their useless manufacture."[13] After the first few months of active service, the havelock rapidly disappeared from the Union Army. Its Confederate adversary was, however, slower to catch on and as late as January, 1862, was calling for its troops to wear "a white duck or linen cover, known as a havelock" in hot weather.[14]

As the war got underway in earnest and the volunteers' first uniforms began to wear out, Federal regulation garb slowly replaced any militia or state-supplied items the soldiers might have had. It was at this

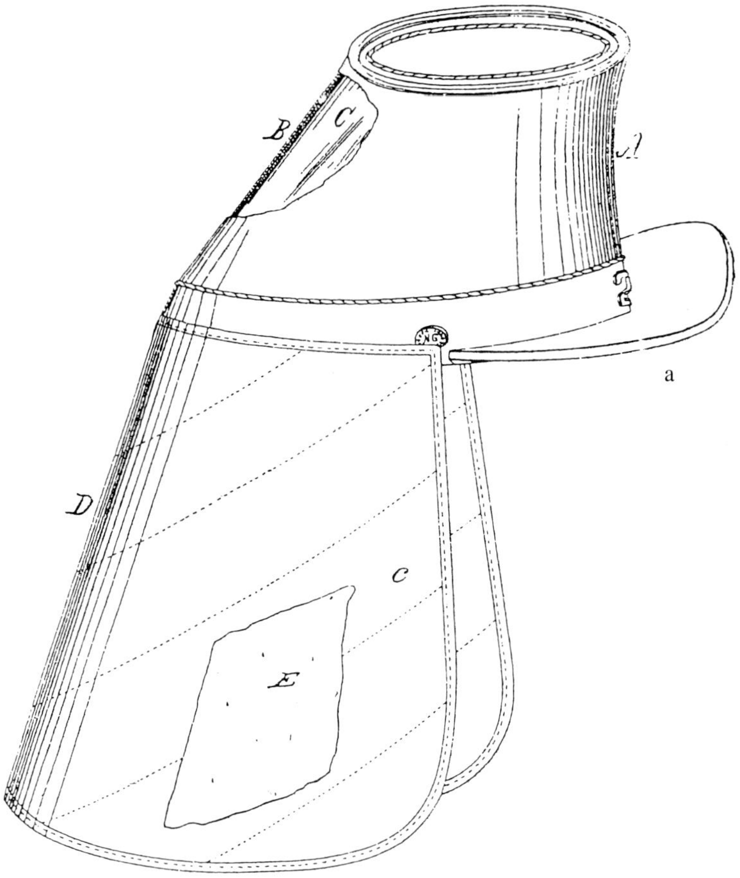

a

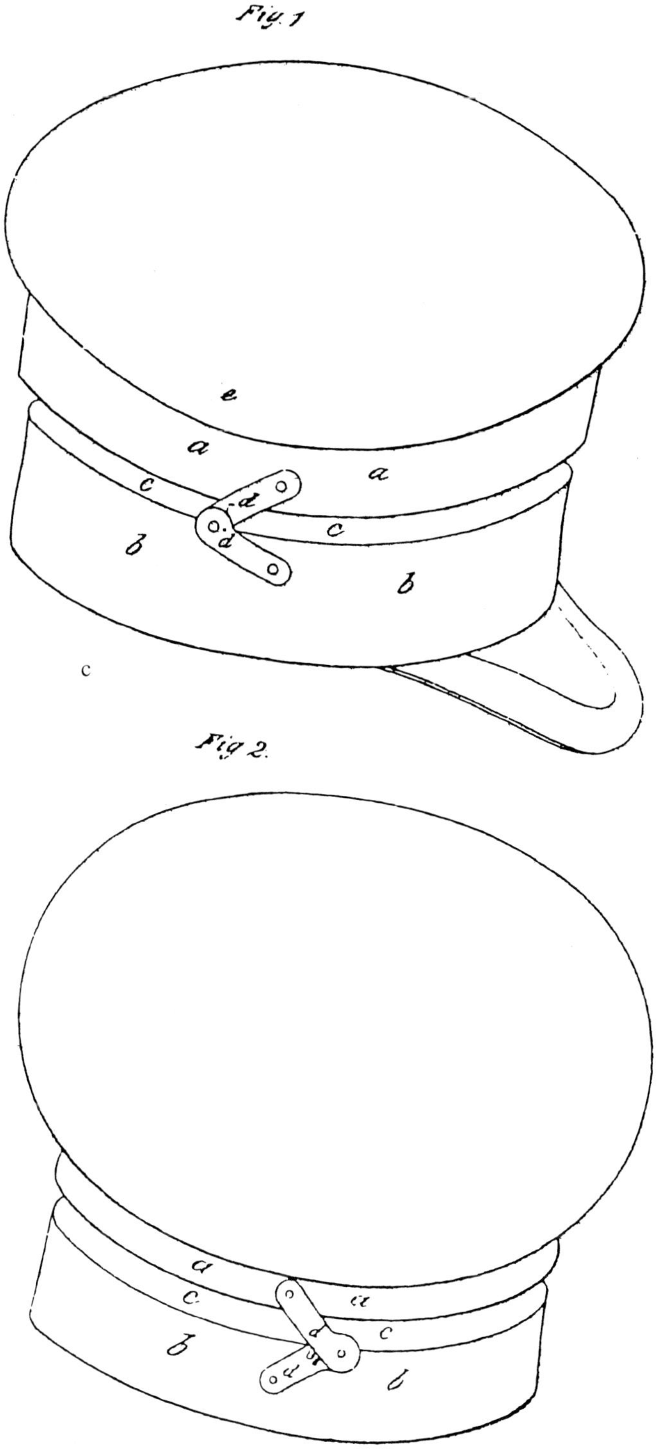

c

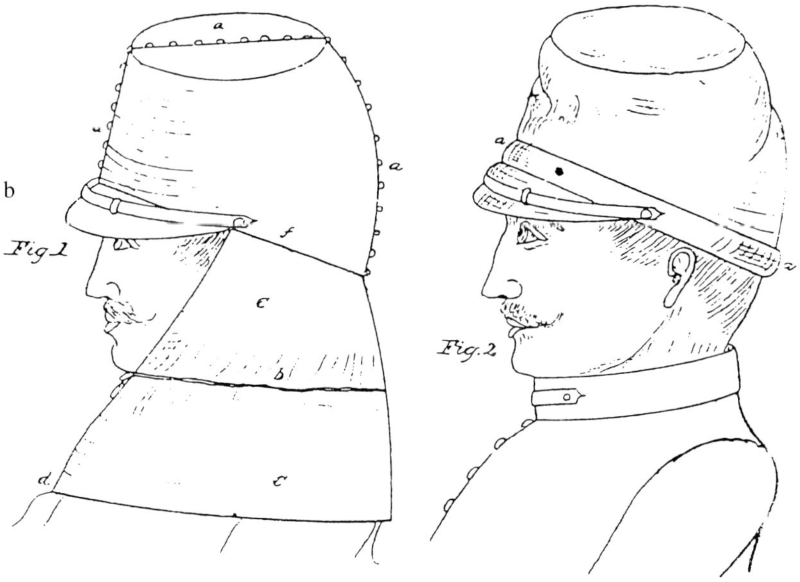

b

At the outbreak of the Civil War, fertile minds produced—at least on paper—a number of "new and useful" additions to America's military headgear. Many were aimed at improving ventilation and increasing protection from the elements. (a) J. K. Gittens of Green Point, N.Y. patented a cork-lined cap with a detachable cork-lined havelock in October, 1861. (b) In July, 1862, Sarah Mossman of Cleveland, Ohio, patented a waterproof covering which could be stored inside the forage cap and a matching cape which could be rolled up around the base of the cap when not in use. (c) John O. Blythe of Philadelphia, Pa, received a patent in August, 1861, for a cap capable of having its upper section lifted by means of hinges to allow air to flow freely underneath. (d) A wire mesh cap with "guard bars" for "protection against sword cuts" was patented in September, 1862, by southerner James W. Bryant of Welaka, Florida (being careful to note that his "assignor" for the rights to the patent was "Lewis A. Osborne of Newark, New Jersey"). Whether Bryant was a loyal Union man or just hedging his bets against the war's outcome is unknown.

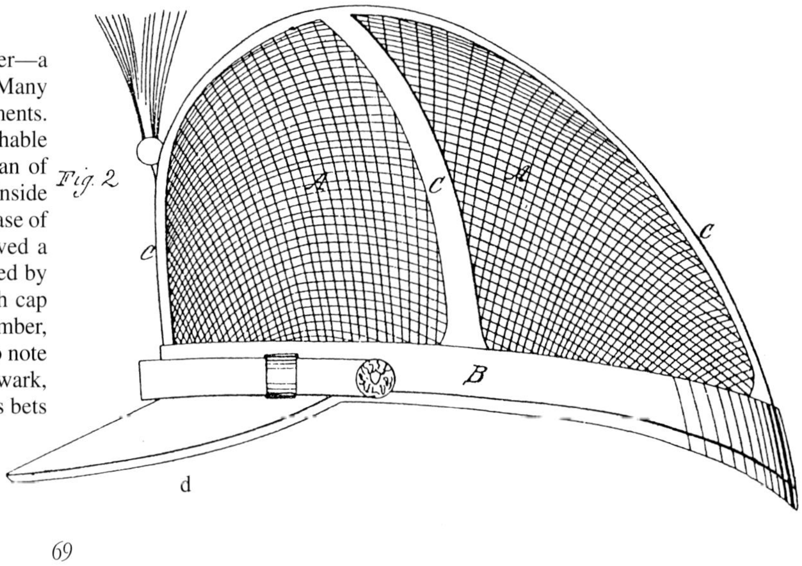

d

a

(a) Members of the Seventh New York Militia, two wearing their white linen havelocks, relax in camp in April 1861. Patriotic citizens flooded the army with these nearly-useless cap covers in the first months of the conflict. NA (b-c) Pvt. Charles A. R. Dimon of Co. I, 8th Mass. Vol. Inf. ("Salem Zouaves"), wore this light linen havelock. His name, carefully embroidered beneath the visor cover, suggests this was a gift from a loved one. CPL (d-e) Havelocks were considered worthless by the time the 44th Mass. Vol. Inf. was organized in September, 1862, yet some members, like Frank Fitz of Co. C, obviously received a supply of them from the City of Boston, as indicated by the stampings on the neck piece. DT (f) The fact that this havelock was one of three found with the effects of Capt. John D. Ottiwell, who served with Co. D, 12th N.Y. Vol. Inf. from May to August, 1861, testifies to the quantity distributed to the troops as the war got underway. LB As in the 1860s, havelocks are easy to make and follow no specific pattern. Individuals and institutions are encouraged to be cautious in acquiring examples of them, paying strict attention to the item's provenance.

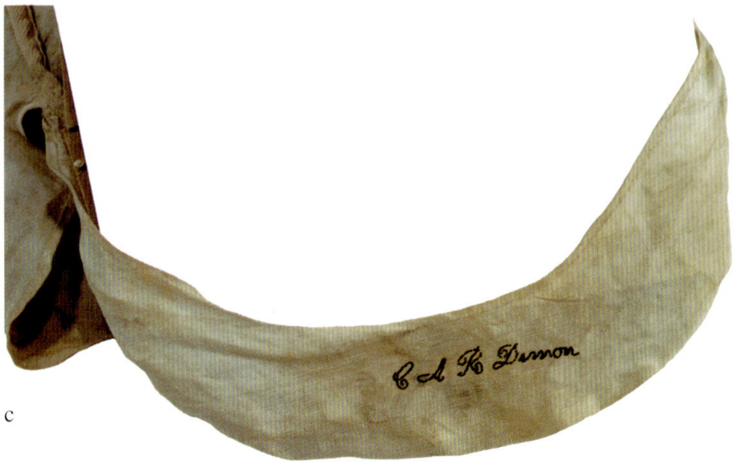

c

b

d

e

f

point that the majority of volunteers began to encounter the two basic items of headgear the army had adopted just a few years earlier (introduced in the last chapter): the hat and the cap.

For dress occasions, there was the army's sturdy and imposing 1858-pattern Army Hat. The tall, stiff crowns, brass insignia, plumes and distinctive wide brims moved a soldier of the 19th Maine to say they were "too gaudy to describe."[15] Here again, the Sanitary Commission presented thoughts on the subject finding that "The regulation hat, as it now stands, is better than any other military headdress to be seen now in Washington. Yet its heavy and inelegant character might, it is hoped, be somewhat modified without lessening its essential value."[16]

Slight changes were made in the original regulations concerning the hat and it continued in service throughout the war. For one thing, War Department General Order No 4 (February 26, 1861) rescinded the previous practice established by General Orders No. 3 (March 24, 1858) that singled out infantry and artillery officers as the only ones to loop their hats on the left side and wear their ostrich plumes on the right. Thereafter, even the cavalry would loop their hats on the right; this change perhaps resulting from the fact that when the "carry arms" was executed from the saber drill the hat brim would interfere with the blade.

Shortly thereafter, General Orders No. 6 (March 13, 1861) retained this scheme for officers but directed that from that point forward enlisted men in dismounted units were to have their brim hooked on the left, while hats for mounted troops would turn up the right. Additionally, the same order specified that enlisted insignia would include the branch devices above which went a 1-inch brass company letter surmounting a 5/8-inch regimental number where applicable. However, the order retained the differentiation of dragoon officers from cavalry instituted earlier, in that the regimental silver numeral went above the crossed sabers in the former instance and below them in the latter.

No matter how the insignia was placed or on what side the brim was looped up, the hat was almost universally disliked by the volunteers, as it had been by many in the regular army when it was first introduced. No wonder. It was awkward, hot, adorned with a fragile ostrich plume and made the wearer look like one of the "pilgrim fathers landing on plymouth."[17] Although a soldier from the 45th Mass. Volunteers recalled the hat with fondness, saying " the gorgeous brass eagle and looped up side gave the hat a jaunty and picturesque appearance," few of his comrades seemed to agree.[18] A more typical recollection was that of a veteran of the 13th Massachusetts: "The hats were neither useful nor ornamental. They were made of black felt, high-crowned, with a wide rim turned up on one side, and fastened to the crown by a brass shield representing an eagle with extended wings, apparently screaming with holy horror at so base an employment.[19]" The historian of the 63rd Pennsylvania remembered the "considerable grumbling" caused by the issuance of the army hat. "They were high, stiff affairs, and had enough brass fixings about them to make a preserving kettle. We only drew them once and were glad that they never asked us to wear them again."[20] A veteran of the 40th New York recalled that when the feathers for the hats were issued "the men destroyed them."[21] The diarist of the Thirteenth Massachusetts was able to report that within six weeks of being issued their hats they had become a source of entertainment for the men ("the comical shapes into which some of them are turned excites a good deal of amusement") and were quietly "disappearing."[22] The men of the

Philadelphia hatter Charles L. Pascal received a patent on a hat/havelock combination on December 10, 1861, and with partner James Sullender sold several thousand to Pennsylvania for use by a number of cavalry regiments (including the Second, Sixth and Fifteenth). Its distinctive feature was a brim that could be lowered "as to afford protection to the wearer's neck from both the heat of the sun and the effect of storms" and to "present a neat and ornamental appearance" when raised, according to the patent. The first known contract was in November, 1861, for 100 pieces for the "Anderson Body Guard," also called the "Anderson Troop," which would later become the nucleus of the 15th Pennsylvania Cavalry. Clockwise from above left: (a) Colonel Richard H. Rush, commander of the Sixth Pennsylvania, is depicted wearing Pascal's creation on this patriotic envelope. (b) An unidentified horseman posed beneath one for the photographer, holding a prop musket to appear as warlike as possible. CPL (c) Armed to the teeth, Pvt. Andrew Sullenberger, Co. D, 2nd Pa. Vol. Cav. looks particularly fierce under his hat. RP

Left: Mounted on his horse, Pvt. Andrew Sullenberger, Co. D, 2nd Pa. Vol. Cav., holds the company guidon on the way to war and provides a rare look at Pascal's patent cap "in the field." RP

This example of what today is called the "Pennsylvania Cavalry Hat" belonged to William Spencer, originally a 1st Lt. in the independent "Anderson Troop" of cavalry. The 100-member unit was raised in the fall of 1861 to act as the headquarter guard of Brig. Gen. Robert Anderson. It served as the core upon which the 15th Pennsylvania Cavalry was organized in 1862, at which time Spencer was promoted Lt. Col. He resigned in February, 1863. Both the members of the Anderson Troop and the 15th Cavalry were among the units that received C. L. Pascal's distinctive hats. The 1861-62 Quartermaster's Contract Book in the Pennsylvania State Archives indicates they were manufactured by the Philadelphia firm of Sullender and Pascal and sold to the state "full trimmed and mounted" for $4.60 each. The hats were made of black felt and featured a brim, bound along the edge, that could be folded down to protect the neck, with a unique brass catch that "locked" it in either the up or down position. This specimen appears to have a Third Division, I Corps, badge on the front of the hat that seems to be original to the piece. The presence of this is unexplained, as neither the Anderson Troop nor 15th Cavalry were ever part of that organization. Any other meaning that insignia might have has been lost, so far, to time. CCHS

111th Pennsylvania, however, were more demonstrative about their "unmilitary and unpopular black dress hats." As the unit was *en route* to active service with the army, their train halted on a bridge over the Shenandoah River and the men "saluted the historic stream by pitching these hated tiles into it, and so were rid of them forever. From that time they wore the regulation cap."[23]

A noteworthy exception to this was the First Division, I Corps; better known as the Iron Brigade. This group of courageous Western regiments was commanded by General John Gibbon, a West Point graduate and no-nonsense regular who, in 1862, ordered his men to wear the army hats to instill some *esprit* and give the volunteers a more soldierly appearance. It worked. The men embraced the tall felt hat and it became their mark of distinction. A member of the Sixth Wisconsin Vols. wrote that "they look gay. It makes our Regt. look better that it did" and an Indiana officer told his father proudly that they were "the finest looking Brigade in the great army of the Potomac."[24] Since most of the soldiers in that Army of the Potomac had abandoned the army hat, they surely made these men from Michigan, Wisconsin and Indiana stand out in battle and branded them among their admiring comrades as hard fighters. A veteran of Berdan's Sharpshooters remembered seeing them "looking like giants" as they crossed the Rappahannock, "their big black hats and feathers conspicuous."[25]

At least one state, Rhode Island, provided its early volunteers with a local adaptation of the army hat. Although it looked like the government issue headwear at first glance, photos suggest the Rhode Island version had a bigger crown and a curled edge to the brim. The initial

Private Thomas Riddle, Co. K, 8th Ill. Vols. is ready for action in his gray state issue uniform complete with the headgear designed by Chicago hatter James M. Loomis. The gray havelock/hat featured a brim which could be either buttoned up or let down for protection against the elements and was issued to many Illinois troops in 1861. Riddle has buttoned one side up and left the other down for a particularly rakish look. Note the button affixed to the side with the brim down. ISHL

In 1861, Col. Hiram Berdan's First and Second U.S. Sharp Shooters were issued a gray version of the havelock/hat, along with a gray felt overcoat bound in green also made by the Seamless Clothing Company. According to the unit historian, the hats were worn "principally on outpost duty or in bad weather" and were "good enough around Washington…but after out first appearance before the enemy…they were discarded as endangering a fire from the rear." Pvt. Leonard A. Small, Co. D, 2nd U.S.S.S. wore this example, seen in a side and rear view. It is unknown who the contractor was, but the slits in the brim may have at one time allowed the sides to be buttoned up to the crown as per the design of J. M. Loomis. Pvt. Small has used them to run his chinstrap through. JG

a

c

b

d

New York City hatter Jonathan F. Whipple patented a havelock/hat combination on July 16, 1861, a few months before Charles Pascal's version of a similar concept. Unlike Pascal's invention, and unlike the hat designed by James M. Loomis which Whipple appears to have copied, Whipple's hat apparently had no method to fasten the brim up. Photographs show that two models were produced: one made of cloth and the other of stiff felt. (a-b) The felt model was produced by the Seamless Clothing Manufacturing Company in New York City and bears the company's name in gold, stamped into the front of the sweatband (the only item of Civil War headgear known to have the maker's name embossed on the band). DT Whipple's cap also enjoyed some initial popularity with New England troops, particularly those from New Hampshire. Like Pascal's Pennsylvania Cavalry Hat, it probably proved too expensive and bulky for service once the war commenced in earnest. (c-d) This example of the hat was worn by Lt. George W. Taylor of the Fourth Battery, Mass. Light Artillery. Taylor has added a small, stippled brass "4" to the front beneath a black inked "Mass. BATTERY," along with two rows of ventilation holes. CPL Opposite: Examples of the soft, cloth Whipple cap can be seen on Private Albert Gilman of Co. G, Third New Hampshire Vols. (left) and a well armed New England NCO. Judging by their construction, it is doubtful that the Seamless Clothing Manufacturing Company produced these variants. CPL

order of hats were destined for the 1st Regiment of Rhode Island Detached Militia and were purchased on April 18, 1861, from Providence military outfitters Bowen and Pabodie along with the regulation brass eagles to loop up the brim and distinctive silver letters.[26] Photographs also indicate that Illinois issued its first regiments a variant on the army hat as well, but made of gray felt.

But, it was the humble forage cap that gained ascendancy as the war progressed, offering some measure of conformity and defining forever afterwards the *look* of the Civil War soldier. It was essentially the tall model first prescribed in 1858, but with one change dictated by War Department General Order No 4 (February 26, 1861) which discontinued the colored welt for enlisted forage caps, resulting in the all blue, ubiquitous "bummer's cap." Period photographs attest that this simple cap and its variations maintained a measure of predominance among the volunteers until the end of the conflict.

It received mixed reviews from wearers. Some thought it was "useful and even natty," having "room for a wet sponge, green leaves, a handkerchief, or protection against the sun in the top," while its "...slanting visor fits easily against the forehead."[27] Others countered it was a "waste of cloth, too baggy, and caught the wind."[28] Soldier-author John Billings in his classic *Hard Tack and Coffee* described it as "coarse and unfashionable to the eye."[29] A private from Massachusetts remembered it as "an ungainly bag with pasteboard top and leather visor."[30] One newspaperman quite accurately reported that the cap "in addition to being of itself very hot to the head, does not suffice to ward the heat

Opposite: Due to profiteering and the haste to uniform a flood of volunteers, the quality of the military goods manufactured at the war's outset varied. One major complaint was the fading of uniforms that were not properly dyed with indigo but rather with cheaper substitutes. Such was the case with this cap worn at First Manassas by Pvt. Edward N. Whittier, Co. C, 1st Rhode Island Vols. Once dark blue, the cap soon faded to a brownish-purple. DT In December, 1861, A letter from "An Observer" in the December 23, 1861, Boston Journal called attention to the "wretched purple caps" worn by troopers in a cavalry unit he had seen. "Many will be surprised to know that these caps were a handsome blue when bought." He went on to say the fading was "simply owing to caps being made of cloth not dyed with indigo blue" and suggested "dealers who sell such caps to soldiers ought to be made to repent by a loss of patronage..."

The overwhelmingly Italian 39th N. Y. Vols., also known as the Garibaldi Guard, wore a distinctive broad brimmed hat, or *Bersaglieri*, with their Italian-inspired uniform. One observer called the headgear "as comfortable as they were picturesque." However, the colorful hats lost their beauty after some hard service in the field, as suggested by the two soldiers in the back of the camp scene above. NA

from any of those portions of the face and neck which it ought properly to protect."[31] The Sanitary Commission called it "pert, unsubstantial, ungraceful, uncomfortable, and dangerous.[32]

The earliest known detailed description of the forage cap is found in the 1865 Quartermaster Manual which states the caps are to be:

> ...of six sizes; the bodies to be made of dark blue forage cap, or facing cloth. A cap of medium size is 15 inches in circumference at base; height in front, 4 3/8 inches; in rear, measured from base to crown, 5 inches; the body to be stiffened around the base by a piece of buckram, 2 1/2 inches wide; a single row of machine stitches, 16 to the inch, sewed through the buckram and body of the cap, with black silk or linen thread, commencing at a point in the center of the front, 1 1/2 inches below the crown, and extending each way, by curved lines, around the sides of the body to a point in center of rear, 1 1/2 inches above th base of the cap; the crown to be stiffened by a stout circular sheet of pasteboard, and the cap lined throughout, inside, with good black silesia; a sweat leather, of good black goatskin morocco, 2 inches wide, to be strongly sewed to the base of the cap and through the cloth buckram and lining; a visor of stiff glazed leather, best quality, black above and green below, in form of a crescent, the outer curved edge 13 inches long, and the interior edge 9 inches long, 2 inches wide in the middle, to be strongly sewed on the front of the base of the

One of many units to wear distinctive headgear was the 3rd New Jersey Cavalry, also styled the "1st U.S. Hussars." As seen in the image of Pvt. Lewis Goble of Co. B (Left), the regiment wore a short jacket decorated with rows of yellow braid and something that resembled a visorless forage cap worn with the "tilt" sideways. CPL, SI

cap; a chin strap, of best quality soft and pliable black glazed leather, composed of two pieces 5/8 inch wide, each piece 9 1/2 inches long, and having sewed on one end of each, a black leather loop of same width and material, and on the other end a vest button of brass, strongly sewed to the cap at the extreme points of the visor; on one of these pieces is to be attached a slide, of No. 19 sheet brass, 7/8 of an inch wide, made with a bar in the center, over which the strap passes and fastens at the middle of the chin-straps in front of the cap; at the base, over the visor and around the crown, a welt of the blue cloth covering is inserted; weight of cap, 4 2/3 ounces."[33]

The forage cap bore no markings inside except occasionally for a small paper label glued to the crown by the contractor. On this was printed sometimes nothing more than the maker's initials and perhaps the cap's size. An additional marking can be found in the caps that were examined by Edward Wheeler, an "inspector of hats and caps" assigned to the government clothing depot in New York City. Wheeler was active there from September 26, 1862, until he left the service on June 30, 1864. He then was rehired shortly afterward to continue his work until July 15, 1865. A small, two-line stamping "E. Wheeler/Inspector N.Y."

Colonel Lewis Merrill ordered royal blue forage caps with an orange welt for the men of his 2nd Mo. Cavalry from a maker in St. Louis. Before the war he had been a captain in the 2nd U.S. Cavalry, where he might have first seen forage caps with colored welts. This one was owned by Pvt. Darius Seely of Company H. DT

Although it was far more practical than its predecessor, the 1858 Army Hat was still a cumbersome and hot affair made from black felt stiffened with a shellac/ alcohol solution, the brim reinforced by two rows of stitching. They were not popular with the men of the regular army and some volunteer regiments even refused to draw them. By 1864, Quartermaster General Montgomery C. Meigs reported there was "scarcely any demand" for the hat. The 1861 Uniform Regulations called for it to be looped up on the right by mounted men and the left by foot soldiers, and fastened by a "brass eagle, having a hook attached to the bottom to secure the brim." Enlisted insignia was of "yellow metal" following the pattern that began with the 1851 uniform regulations. A worsted cord "the same color as that of the facing of the corps" and a single ostrich feather completed the trimmings. CPL

The stamped brass eagle device for the Army Hat included a bent wire hook to hold up one side of the brim. CPL

has been found impressed into the sweatband of several examples, the only inspector marking ever observed in the forage cap.[34]

As with much of the material provided by contractors in the war's first stages, the forage cap faced problems with quality control. Even in 1862, the assistant quartermaster stationed at Detroit, Captain George Lee, was moved to write to Colonel George H. Crosman, who then was in charge of the Philadelphia Clothing Depot, complaining the caps being furnished were of "a very inferior quality" as to material and color, "being what the men call rotten. They come to pieces very soon and the color of a portion is...that known as Logwood...which when exposed to rain and sun turns a dingy reddish brown."[35]

Yet, despite negative comments and shoddy construction, the forage cap was to become forever identified with the Union forces. Perhaps for its slight weight and portability; perhaps for its capacity to be adorned and altered, the Northern soldier appeared to grudgingly accept the style. Indeed, there were at least two commercially produced variations on the theme that were purchased individually by the men from sutlers or military outfitters. One such cap had a distinctive downward sloping, crescent visor and sometimes a slight "hump" in the back that gave the crown a particularly rakish tilt. Known then and now as the "McDowell" pattern after being made popular at the war's start by Gen. Irwin McDowell and his staff, it was nearly identical to a fatigue cap worn at the time by the much-admired Austrian army where it was known as a *lager mutze* (literally "camp cap"). This was no doubt the inspiration for McDowell and others to copy that style for themselves. Possibly reflecting on it after the war, a writer remembered that "it looked like an Esquimaux canoe on his head, wrong side up."[36]

During the conflict the McDowell Cap enjoyed widespread popularity, even among Western troops, as verified in the letters of Capt. William Mitchell, Co. D, 1st Wisconsin Vols. On August 3, 1863, he instructed his father to have "36 caps made for the company of the

Two warlike troopers stand ready for the fight. The cavalryman to the right has adjusted his Army Hat for the most dashing look possible. CPL

Clockwise from above: (a) Here Lt. A. J. Shippley and Pvt. Judson Armor of Co. E, 105th Pa. Vols., pose for posterity. Shippley has chosen to wear a forage cap while his comrade is in his fully trimmed Army Hat. (b) These two have paused in camp to display the Army Hat's notorious "Pilgrim" effect when not looped up. (c) This angry New Englander has discovered an artful way to wear the hat's worsted cords, which should be resting flat on the brim according to regulations. CPL Within a few months after these images were taken, these soldiers had most likely bid farewell to their Army Hats for the duration of their service.

McDowell pattern-the same as the small one I wore home," adding to be careful "and not get the McClellan style." The cost of the caps, about $1 each, was covered by each man and on September 6 Mitchell wrote home that "the caps arrived alright and suit us all." He later noted that such caps would cost $3 or more from the sutlers. The company no doubt wore their new McDowell Caps into action 13 days later at Chickamauga, at which time Captain Mitchell was killed by a musket ball that struck his neck.[37] When the war ended and the volunteers mustered out, America's copy of Austria's *lager mutze* also disappeared, except for a version with a much lower crown that Boston's Bent and Bush and others continued to make almost into the 20th Century and which was worn by some New England national guard units.

The other variant was an upgraded forage cap that featured a quilted lining, better chin strap, and thicker visor that was bound on the edge. The number of existing specimens indicates this was a widely popular option among both officers and enlisted men. The rank and file seemed more than willing to purchase their own caps if only to get one that fit properly, underlining both the importance of a head covering to the 19th

Some enlisted men found ways to lose their Army Hats quickly. Others, liking the protection of a broad brimmed hat that cost them nothing, altered their hats for comfort and wore them in the field. Sgt. Jason Lewis of Co. A, 46th Mass. Vols., wore the specimen on the left. Note the small, flat silver letter and numerals used for the unit designation. JCG An unidentified member of the Fourth U. S. Cavalry lowered the crown and personalized his army hat with brass lettering, a plume held by a rosette, and officers' hat cords. DT

Veterans of Co. E., 78th Pa. Vols, pose at Lookout Mountain, TN, wearing broad brimmed hats for protection and comfort. Like the Western units brigaded with them, many of these Army of the Cumberland soldiers appear to be wearing altered versions of the Army Hat. RP

The men of the Iron Brigade, the First Division, I Corps, embraced the bulky Army Hat and made it a badge of distinction. This battle battered example was worn by Sgt. Philander Wright, Co. C, 2nd Wisconsin Vols. Wright was wounded while carrying the regimental colors at Gettysburg. WVM

(a) Looking at this image of Sgt. John Prescott, Co. G, 33rd New Jersey Vols., it is evident why the rank and file thought the forage cap was "an ungainly bag with pasteboard top and leather visor." CPL (b-c) In a three-year enlistment, soldiers were authorized to draw two caps the first year, one the second, and two the third. Millions were made by a variety of contractors and they became forever associated with the Union soldier, like this example made by the New York City firm of Murphy and Griswold. CPL

During the war, most contractors of the 1858 Army Cap marked their products with a small, simple paper label in the crown, sometimes giving the cap size in either standard and/or "government" terms (sizes 1-4, with 4 being the largest). Here are examples of the labels of (Left column) Matthew Brooks, Phila., DT George Hoff, Phila., CPL, and Thomas Murphy and William C. Griswold, New York City, CPL; (Right column) Lewis J. and Issac Phillips, New York City, CPL, M. F. Thompson, and Charles Goodrich, Cincinnati. JML, Unknown manufactuer, possibly under contract with New York state. DT

Century man and the government's notorious reputation of issuing garments that were the wrong sizes. Such stories were legion during the war and became part of the folklore afterwards, like that told by the historian of the 118th Pennsylvania Vols. as he recalled the unit's issue of "the shapeless mass of cloth" that was their first uniform. "One, to whose lot fell a forage cap that covered his ears, was assured it would shrink to proper proportions in the first rain storm, while another, whose cap sat nattily upon the very tip of his crown…was consoled with the assurance that the August sun would soon expand it to suit his comfort and convenience."[38] Naturally, some of the Army brass did not approve of anything that wasn't *government issue,* as Private Alfred Bellard, serving with the Veteran Reserve Corps in Washington D.C., found as he encountered his major when going into the city on a pass. "He ordered me back…to take off my fancy cap and store boots…At the next parade I had no army cap and the one the Lieut. got for me was some two sizes too large and came down over my ears. I made it answer by pinning it up."[39]

The lower profile "chasseur" pattern *kepi* drawn directly from the French was considered quite fashionable and found favor with many officers, notwithstanding it was ridiculed as "tiny and useless" by a writer for the Chicago Tribune.[40] This was the style originally advocated by then-Captain George B. McClellan after his service with a military commission observing the Crimean War from 1854-56. Indeed, McClellan himself wore one during the Civil War and the style became known to some as the "McClellan Cap" or took the name "cadet cap" after its adoption by the U. S. Military Academy in 1857.[41] In addition, photographic evidence and specimens in private collections indicate the enlisted men of a number of units seem to have also been supplied with chasseur caps, despite regulations calling for forage caps. Even before the war, kepis had become part of the standard uniform of certain militia units, such as the famed Seventh New York. Examples show great variation in elevation, from moderately tall to almost pancake flat, seeming to get lower as the war progressed. After the war, in 1872, the army would at last designate the chasseur pattern as the official forage cap for its troops.

As the soldiers gained experience in the field, they soon realized the shortcomings of government issued headwear, particularly the lack of ventilation and protection from the sun. Some tried to alleviate the former problem by cutting air holes in their hats and caps or buying patent ventilators and other devices. But to remedy the lack of protection, nothing but a broad-brimmed soft hat would do and many soldiers obtained their own to wear on active service. Some simply "altered" the army hat by crushing and shaping it to their satisfaction, and wearing it with little or no insignia; trends that seemed especially prevalent in the war's Western theater. Such was the case in one Ohio unit whose commander actually ordered his men to modify their issued hats for their own comfort and wear them in place of the forage cap.[42]

The private purchase of headgear in the Civil War was pervasive. On occasion, a "company fund" might be pressed into service, as happened with a company from the 2nd Mass. Vol. Cav. whose Captain first purchased 100 caps for his men when their original issue forage caps became soiled and "were only fit for stable use." With active campaigning underway, he later used the fund to buy his men slouch hats.[43]

Others bought slouch hats from sutlers, or, like Pvt. Samuel Tomlinson of the 12th New Jersey, had them sent from home. In May, 1863, he complained in a letter to his parents that "We have had orders not to wear a hat of any kind, nothing but caps we are allowed to wear. It seems rather hard for these caps are very warm and not fit to wear in warm weather." Despite the ban, in early June Tomlinson asked his parents to send him a "light colored" hat as soon as possible, adding "these caps are not fit for summer and I get a headache easy." By the time his hat arrived in camp it was August and Tomlinson was in a Newark, N.J., army hospital convalescing from a wound received at Gettysburg. His Lieutenant sold it to another officer in the regiment and gave Tomlinson the money. "(He) thought that I would not want it and I shall not now."[44] Bugler Charles W. Reed of the 9th Mass. Light Battery likewise grumbled to his mother how his face was "burning smartly" under the Southern

These samples of brass letters and numerals for the 1858 Army Hat and 1858 Cap were submitted to Pennsylvania's Quartermaster General R. C. Hale by Warner and Harper of Philadelphia on May 29, 1861. By June 5, they had sold the state more than ten thousand "Company letters A to K" at two cents each. These were affixed to forage caps that were then sent to Keystone State regiments already in the field. The same company was also supplying letters and numbers to the U.S. Government's clothing depot at Philadelphia's Schuylkill Arsenal. CPL

The forage cap, according to the 1861 Uniform Regulations, was to have only "yellow metal letters in front" to designate companies. In reality, the cap was personalized far beyond regulations; sometimes on a regimental basis, sometimes on individual whim. Above left an unknown trooper has decorated his with company letter, regimental number, and the brass eagle intended to loop up the brim of the Army Hat. CPL Pvt. Samuel K. Miller, Co. E, 167th Pa. Vol. Inf., above right, has added a militia hat eagle to his array of forage cap brass. CPL Right: The companies of Californians who fought as part of the Second Mass. Vol. Cav. were well known for both their state pride and their personalized headgear. Here Pvt. Jacob Walther of Company E has used the regulation brass letters to spell out "California." Regimental commander Charles R. Lowell, Jr., a non-Californian, was not pleased with the inventiveness of his men from the other coast. Lowell's General Orders No. 8 of May 23, 1863, ordered that "Company commanders will see that their men wear on the forage cap only the insignia of the corp, and the number and the letter all made by regulations all other letters must be removed before the next parade or inspection, and not again worn either in or out of camp." WS

This young warrior (above left) has arranged his brass to show some unit pride: "3 MICH." Likewise, the private (above right) has spelled "MASS." Seventeen-year-old Pvt. John Hoffman, Co. B, 5th Ohio Vol. Cav. (above) has added an "O.V.C." beneath his crossed sabers. CPL

Opposite: The 1861 Revised U.S. Army Regulations called for the forage cap to have only "yellow metal letters in front to designate companies." But since so many of the rank and file had abandoned their hated army hats, many times some or all the available brass insignia was placed on the forage cap instead. And, as photographs and existing examples show, the application was made in a great variety of ways; sometimes at the direction of regimental commanders and sometimes at the whim of the individual. Just a few of the countless variations are shown here. (a) Wagoner Leveritt Lynn, Co. B, 24th Connecticut Vols. used his infantry hunting horn, regimental numbers, and company letter on the crown of his cap as it would have been affixed to the front of his army hat, "the number of the regiment, five-eighths of an inch long,…and letter of company, one inch." DT (b) In 1863, Pvt. J. K. Hundecker, Co. C, 179th Pa. Militia affixed his brass in a similar manner. JCG (c) Capt. Benjamin F. Winger, Battery D, Second Pa. Heavy Artillery, wore this government issue cap which he decorated with the battery letter and "P.V" for Pennsylvania Volunteers in the five-eighths inch "scroll" style, and the regimental number in a one inch figure over his branch of service designation. CPL (d) An unknown soldier chose to place the brass insignia on his chinstrap, leaving only a patent brass ventilator on top. DT (e) The 44th Mass. Vols. appears to have used silver letters and numerals on its caps as seen in this example worn by Pvt. William H. Hawley of Co. C. The devices are essentially identical to those worn on caps issued by the State of New Hampshire (see page 133). RR (f) By the close of the war, many Pennsylvania units used small, stippled, three-eighths inch brass letters and numbers, as seen in this example worn by a member of the 177th Pa. Vols. CWLM

a

b

c

d

e

f

Buckles on the chinstraps of most Civil War headgear fall into three catagories. Type 1: the common "slide, of No. 19 sheet brass, 7/8 of an inch wide" called for by the Quartermaster Department on the regulation 1858 Cap (left). Type 2: A thicker, beveled-edge version found generally on commercially produced forage caps (center). Type 3: a cheaper, thinner slide of stamped brass, hollow in back, often encountered in pre-war militia and early war caps (right). CPL

sun. In a letter home in May, 1863, he instructed her to buy a felt hat for him from the Boston firm of Palmer, Batchelders and Co., being sure it had a fashionable low crown and not "one of those great high crowns."[45]

Eventually, most soldiers came to prefer a wide brimmed, soft felt hat for campaigning. It was relatively light, sheltering and very portable. As early as 1861, a Boston newspaper praised the version worn by the uniquely dressed Garibaldi Guard (39th New York), saying when looped up at the side "they were as comfortable as they were picturesque." The paper also felt it had another advantage, namely that it was "inaccessible to the Confederate army! The rebels have neither the material nor the manufactories requisite for making this hat."[46]

As the enlisted men sought out comfortable headgear for themselves, they came to realize that not every commander appreciated such individual initiative. When the Colonel of the 33rd Wisconsin returned from leave in December, 1863, he found light colored, privately purchased hats were appearing throughout his unit, which like many in the Western campaign, already wore the black 1858-pattern hat as a matter of course. He responded with a Special Order stating that:

> White or light colored hats are out of place in the line. A single white hat upon "Dress Parade" destroys in a measure the beauty and uniformity of the whole line. It is therefore ordered that Non-Commissioned Officers or soldiers shall not be permitted to wear upon "Dress Parade" or upon other occasions of duty any other but the regulation hat. No light colored hats of recent purchase will be permitted to be brought into camp and if brought in will be excluded from it.[47]

The major of the 16th New York no doubt thought he had solved the problems of heat, exposure, and uniformity. On June 13, 1862, while the regiment was on campaign in Virginia, he presented each man "a nice straw hat, with a ribbon around it, on which is printed the number of the regiment in gilt letters and figures. The officer's hats are bound with black, the others have no binding."[48] The unit saw considerable action starting just days later in the grueling Seven Days Battles, no doubt comfortable and conspicuous to Confederate marksmen under their new straw hats. Most likely the unusual and fragile coverings had disappeared by the close of the campaign.

The 1861 uniform regulations already allowed officers to wear a hat "of best black felt." This, of course, was supposed to be a more elegant version of the 1858-pattern hat. But the officer corps also disliked the unwieldy headgear and so interpreted the regulation more broadly, buying for themselves what we are familiar with today as the

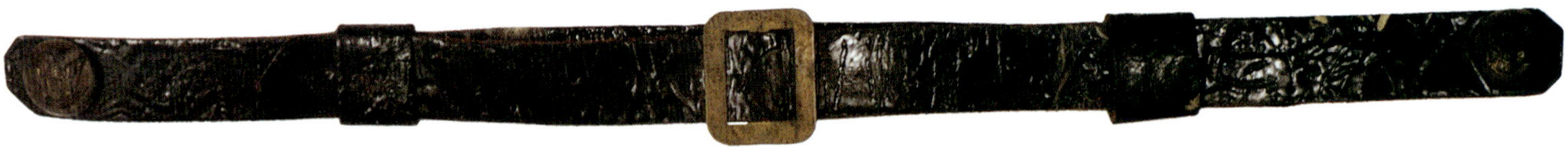

The forage cap's chin strap, made "of best quality, soft and pliable black glazed leather" with a loop at each end was fastened to the cap with the general service "vest button of brass, strongly sewed to the cap near the extreme points of the visor." Some privately purchased forage caps included a slash at the button to permit removal of the strap. CPL

Buckram, a coarse material made from hemp, had been used as a stiffener in the lining of clothing for centuries. A strip 2 1/2 inches wide was used for that purpose in the base of forage caps, behind the sweat band.

"slouch hat."[49] It was ornamented in a variety of ways. Sometimes all the regulation embroidered insignia of the 1858 hat, including the plume, was affixed to create what was called the "Burnside Pattern" hat.

Into this already stunning mix we must add non-regulation headwear that was sanctioned and sometimes provided by the Federal government.[50] This includes a variety of fezes with colored tassels, produced under government contract by firms such as Adolph and Keen of Philadelphia.[51] Such exotic caps were part of the uniform issued to the 155th Pennsylvania Vols. in January, 1864. Describing the outfit, a veteran wrote "the greatest and most impressive part of the uniform was the turban, after the Turkish plan. It was composed of a sash of white flannel about a foot wide and ten feet long, which would be nicely wound, so as to set or fit on a red skull cap, to which was attached a blue tassel. This turban was seldom worn except on dress-parade or dress-occasions; but the red fez cap with tassel was always worn on fatigue or other duties."[52] Indeed, a turban was probably something the American volunteer found quite mystical. The rather pompous British journalist William Howard Russell observed the negative effect the incorrect use of the turban could have when he visited the camp of Duryea's Zouaves in July, 1861. "But for the ridiculous effect of their costume the regiment would have looked well enough; but riding down on the rear of the ranks the discolored napkins tied round their heads, without any fez cap beneath, so that the hair sometimes stuck up through the folds, the ill-made jackets, the loose bags of red calico hanging from their loins...made them appear such military scarecrows, I could scarcely refrain from laughing outright."[53] If the photographic record is any indication, the compact and eccentric fez became a favorite thing to wear as a "smoking cap" or to relax in when off duty; and many non-zouaves can still be seen posing in tintypes and cartes d'visite for loved ones at home in these privately purchased tassled bonnets. John Billings of the 10th Mass. Light Battery remembered "They did very well to lie around camp in, and in a degree marked their owner as a somewhat conspicuous man among his fellows, but they were not tolerated on the line; few of them ever survived the first three months campaigning."[54]

The Union also provided several units with complete French Chasseurs-a-Pied uniforms. Ten thousand sets were ordered from Goddilot of Paris in early 1861 and delivered by December, complete with all the necessary accoutrements, knapsacks, tents, etc. There were

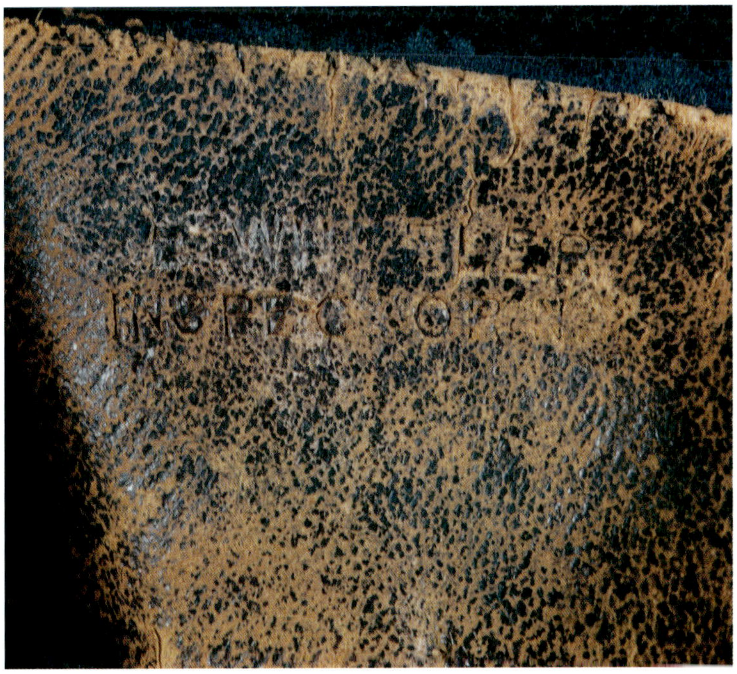

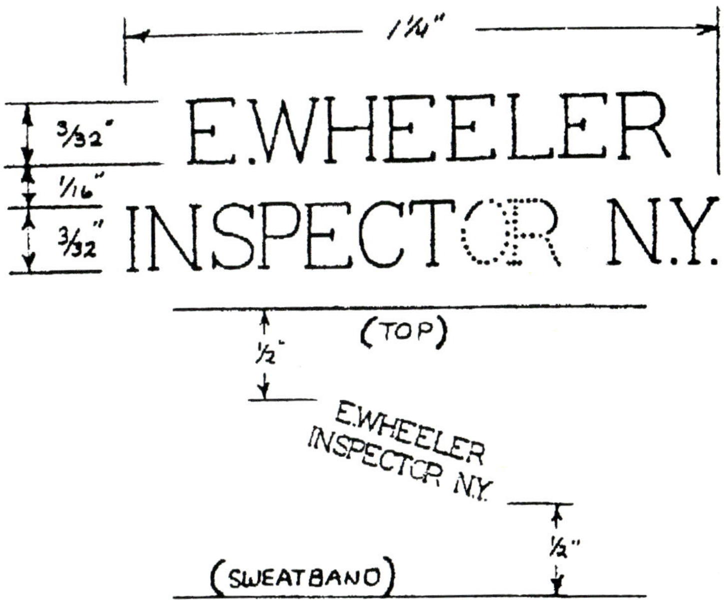

Edward Wheeler was one of the government's clothing inspectors in New York City. Unique to Wheeler, his name appears stamped into the sweatband of the caps he examined, as on the cap made by L. J. and I Phillips, left. CPL A detail of the Wheeler imprint found on another cap, rendered by R. Bryce Workman, is seen at right.

Manufacturers sometimes used wool substitutes for uniforms as illustrated by these forage caps made of satinette, a material that could be finished like an all wool fabric but which actually consisted of cotton warps with woolen filling. Fading on the crown of the unusually tall cap to the left indicates it once had the brass insignia of the 31st Maine Vols. CPL The commercially produced cap on the right more closely follows those produced by government contractors. The paper III Corps badge on the crown indicates it was worn by Pvt. Samuel E. Radcliff, Co. E, 6th New Jersey Vols. CHS

a

b

c

The government also supplied Col. Hiram Berdan's 1st and 2nd Regiments of U.S. Sharp Shooters with their distinctive green uniforms, including forage caps. (a) This specimen, in the collection of the Milwaukee Public Museum, bears a III Corps badge on the top and was worn Sgt. John T. Schemerhorn, Co. H, 1st U.S.S.S. HM (b) Pvt. Leonard A. Small, Co. D, 2nd U.S.S.S. placed a small silvered metal eagle on the crown of his cap, along with insignia denoting his company and regiment. JG (c) Aside from its color, the sealed pattern of the Berdan's cap in the collection of the Smithsonian Institution is made like other government contract caps and has the label of Philadelphia contractor George Hoff in the crown. As on the coats issued to Berdan's units, the buttons on the cap are hard rubber, chosen because they reflected sunlight less than brass. SI

two pieces of headgear with the uniform: the French Model 1860 leather infantry shako (with a distinctive "American" frontplate worn beneath a red/white/blue metal rosette) and a fatigue cap similar to the folding overseas caps used by GIs in the next century, trimmed in light yellow with a matching tassel and infantry bugle insignia in the front. The soldiers of the few units who received them all seemed to be very proud of their eye catching garb and Frank Leslie's Illustrated News reported them to be "commodious and comfortable, as well as soldierly."[55] In addition to the frontplates, the French provided the shakos with a plume of black rooster feathers for "dress" occasions and a green pompon for daily wear. However, it seems that the pompons were never actually issued. Photographs suggest the first troops to receive the shakos—the 62nd and 83rd Pa. Vols. and the 18th Mass. Vols.—received them with the plume but without the frontplate. However, some units of New York's Excelsior Brigade later received the shakos with the plates, judging by an illustration in a September, 1862, *Frank Leslie's Illustrated News* and specimens unearthed at some of the brigade's campsites. Unfortunately, about a third of the imported uniforms could not be issued as the soldiers of France were a bit smaller than their American counterparts and thus the "small" sizes of their uniform were too little for the smallest Yankee. Most of these were sold by the government at auction around 1864, along with 6507 surplus shakos, 6233 plumes, 6576 front plates, and other parts of the imported uniform considered "entirely useless for any purpose connected with the manufacture of clothing and Equipage for our troops." Some of the surplus shakos found their way into military bands and photographs show them being worn by musicians in the Veteran Reserve Corps.[56]

In the mad effort to uniform the overwhelming tide of volunteers, at least some regulation headwear was ignored after the opening salvos of the war. Most notably, the artillery cap that had been adopted with scarlet plume and cords in the 1850s saw very limited issuance, although given the small number of mounted batteries prior to the Civil War, this cap was always in the minority. In fact, even before the war and during its early phases some light batteries opted for the 1858 hat in lieu of this

Above: After a few months in the field, soldiers came to favor a light colored, broad brimmed, soft felt hat and obtained them from home or from sutlers. Here, Pvt. Charles H. Rhoads, Co. K, 129th Pa. Vols., is ready for a hard campaign in this view "taken in camp near Fredericksburg, Feb. 22, 1863." CPL

Right: Obviously influenced by input from the rank and file, the uniform of the Landis Independent Battery of Pa. Light Artillery included a light colored slouch hat. RP

cap.[57] Regardless of the pre-war regulations, the small stock of artillery caps on hand was almost ignored once the North and South had faced off.

However, as the fall of 1863 approached, these tall and ungainly caps were reborn as an item of issue, mostly because certain light batteries had by then been assigned to garrison duty or as occupation forces "at established posts."[58] The first hapless group of Yankees to get them was the 23rd New York Battery stationed in New Bern, N.C., around September. Despite the fact that a number of the caps were already on hand, in January, 1864, the quartermaster department let a contract for 1,452 additional caps with the Philadelphia firm of W. C. Dare. William Horstmann Brothers provided the plumes and other trappings. These caps cost $2.89 each as opposed to the previous $1.06. The increase in price may have stemmed from inflation, given rising costs during the war. Although the reasons for the higher price cannot be determined with certainty, the physical appearance of the cap is not a matter of speculation because of the rather detailed description provided by the 1865 quartermaster manual and the presence of numerous existing specimens.[59]

> *Uniforms caps for light artillery*—of six sizes; the following are specifications for caps, No. 3 medium size, viz: body of cap made of stiffened felt, so as to preserve its form; made on sample block, and covered with dark blue forage cap cloth; diameter at base, 7 1/2 inches; at crown, 5 3/4 inches; covered at top with stiff glazed leather, of best quality, extending over body 3/4 of an inch; sewed strongly at 4 points,—front, rear, and sides, with 5 stitches each, and depressed in the crown 5/16 inch; and a band of thin glazed leather, best quality, 1 1/8 inches wide encircling base; height of cap in front, 5 3/4 inches; in rear, curved, 7 3/8 inches; circular vizor of stiff glazed leather, 11 3/4 inches long, inside edge, and 19 inches on outside edge, breadth in the middle, 2 3/4 inches, strongly sewed on body with 20 stitches; sweat leather of black morocco of best quality 3/4 of an inch wide, sewed on exterior of base of ca, and folded inside; a small piece of morocco, 1 1/2 inches long and 1 inch wide, sewed inside body of cap, 1 1/2 inches from the top, with ten stitches, leaving a loop to receive the whalebone stick of hair-plume; two chin straps of glazed leather, best quality, 5/8 inch wide, one of which to be 8 inches long, having sewed at one end a strong 7/8 inch buckle, of No. 19 brass; at the other end a yellow vest button, with a piece of No. 18 iron wire, 2 1/2 inches long, looped in the eye of the button, with which to fasten the end of the strap to the cap, and having a glazed leather slide attached to the strap, through which to pass the other end of the strap after it has been buckled; the other chin strap of soft glazed leather, of same quality and width of short chin strap and 12 1/2 inches long, and having 4 holes, punched at equal distances, to receive the tongue of buckle when on the cap; the other end of this strap is fastened to the hat by a yellow vest button, with wire, similar in all respects to

This soldier and bandsman of the 4th Rhode Island Vols. wear their state's version of the army hat, issued to its early regiments and using the Federal regulations as a broad guideline. The Providence firm of Bowen and Pabodie supplied the hats in April, 1861, along with the special silver letters and numerals seen here. CPL, NA

that described above for fastening the other end of the strap to hat.

Brass crossed cannon,—stamped on thin sheet brass, No. 28, representing 2 cannon crossing each other at the trunnions, muzzles upwards; length 3 1/2 inches; breadth at breech of cannon, 5/8 inch; breadth at muzzle, 1/2 inch provided with 4 brass wire loops, 3/8 inch long, strongly soldered on the back to fasten them on hat.

Brass bugles,—stamped on a thin sheet of brass, No. 28, length, 3 1/2 inches; height across a crook, 1 1/2 inches; provided with 2 iron wire loops, one of which is 3/8 inch and the other 1/2 inch long, strongly soldered on back of bugles to fasten them to hat. [Why the infantry enlisted insignia was described here is unknown because the cap supposedly was restricted to light artillerymen. No period version of this cap with original infantry insignia is known to the authors.]

Above left: Officers of the widely imitated Austrian Army, like this Hussar pictured in an 1850s uniform guide, wore a fatigue cap or *lager mutze* that was probably the inspiration for a similar cap among the American volunteers called the McDowell Cap. Here (above right) Capt. Gerard Reynolds, Co. M, 11th Pa. Vol. Cav., and (left) 1st Lt. John R. Goodman, Co. A, 58th Pa. Vols., hold their versions of the same cap which appear nearly identical to the Austrian version except for the insignia. CPL

(Above left) The classic Civil War "McDowell Cap" sometimes featured a "hump" in the back along with its distinctive tall crown and angled crescent visor. CPL (Above right) Captain J. Henry Sleeper, Boston socialite and gallant commander of the 10th Battery of Mass. Light Artillery, wore this cap with richly embroidered artillery insignia on the front that has the regimental designation in silver metal in the center. Note that the hatter apparently was out of the figure "1" and substituted the letter "I" in its place. CPL (Below) Two views of a particularly tall McDowell Cap, with a notably small "US" staff insignia, made by the Washington firm of James Y. Davis, a prolific supplier of military clothing. DT.

Horse-hair plumes,—of bright scarlet, fast color, length 15 inches; circumference at the base, where it is encircled by a brass ring, 3 1/2 inches; height; diameter of brass wire wing 1/8 inch; securely plaited and fastened for a distance of 4 inches on a square piece of whalebone, 8 inches long and 1/2 inch square; the plume to be secured at its lower end, around the whalebone, by a piece of red morocco 3/4 inch wide, sewed around it.

Tulip, for horse-hair plume,—A thin sheet brass, No. 28, tulip of 4 leaves, strongly soldered to shell and flame of same metal; length from bottom of shell to top of tulip leaf, 3 1/2 inches; length of tulip proper 2 1/2 inches; diameter measured across top of tulip leaves, 1 inch, opening at top to receive the plume; at button of tulip proper a round opening, 1/2 inch in diameter; a strong loop of brass wire, 1-16 [1/16] inch diameter, 3/4 inch long, forming a rectangle, and strongly soldered to inside of shell, so as to pass through the cap and hold the tulip and plume.

Eagle, for light artillery cap,—of thin sheet brass, No. 28, holding in the left talon 3 arrows, and in dexter talon and olive branch, and with beak turned to the right; height from talons to beak, 2 inches; breadth, from tip to tip of wings, 3 inches; breadth, from arrow points to tip of olive branch, 2 inches; a strong brass wire loop 1/2 inch long and 3/8 inch broad, securely soldered on back of eagle, to pass through the cap and hold the lower end of plume stick.

Cord and tassel for light artillery caps,—to be made of scarlet worsted braided cord, (with cotton filling inside of cord,) and braided on a carrier machine, about guage [sic] 5 or 3-16 [3/16] inch thick; two plaits, with about 2 1/2 inch cord between them; the one for the front of cap 14 inches long, and the one for back of cap 17 inches long; from each plait is 6 feet of cord, with round plaque, 2 5/8 inches in diameter, (made of 3 gimps,) and a tassel, attached to the end of each cord; these two cords pass through a tassel and two small slides, and about 4 inches about the plaques; to have a small loop netted on, by which to attach and suspend the plaques from a button on the breast of the coat. The tassels (three in number,) are to be of solid worsted, with a netted head, about 2 1/2 inches long, including head; the skirt or fringe of tassels, composed of from 809 to 90 ends of bullions; the cord and tassels to weigh about 3 1/2 ounces.

Scroll and ring, for light artillery caps,—The scroll to be made a circle, sheet brass, No. 28, 1 inch in diameter, corrugated, convex 1/2 inch; a hole in the centre in which is inserted a double loop of brass wire 3/4 inch long, projecting 1/2 inch on

(Above left) Capt. Charles Burton, Co. K, 7th Conn. Vols. used a brass, faux embroidered infantry bugle on the front with an unusual silver "7" within the bend. DT (Above right) Enlisted men, too, liked the look of the McDowell, as evidenced by this example worn by Sgt. George Turner of Battery A, 3rd Rhode Island Heavy Artillery. CPL

Two officers strike a pose for this ambrotype, one wearing a commercially produced forage cap (left), the other in an Austrian or "McDowell" Cap. CPL

Commercially produced forage caps, sold by military outfitters and sutlers, were superior in quality to those made by government contractors and widely popular with both officers and enlisted men. (Top left) This classic privately purchased cap, made by Laing and Co. of Philadelphia, was worn by Gen. John W. Geary when he commanded the 28th Pa. Vols. PHMC (Top right) Like Geary's, this example, worn by Major D. R. Hastings of the 12th Maine Vols., also has embroidered infantry insignia on the front. Note the false embroidered number "1" was inserted upside down. PHMC (Center left) This example, made by Lamberti of Philadelphia and worn by an unknown Pennsylvania cavalry officer, has the insignia embroidered directly onto the material. CWLM (Center right) Capt. Charles P. Pierce wore this cap when he served on the staff of General Henry M. Judah. It is by the Washington D.C. firm of M.H. Stevens. CPL (Above left) Unusual because of the quatrafoil braid and gold chinstrap, this Paris-made cap was worn by Col. Orlando C. Risdon of the 53rd Regt. U.S. Colored Troops. JHK (Above right) This rather low-crown cap, also decorated with braid, was made by Green and Green of Louisville, Kentucky. JCG

The jaunty, low crown "chasseur" or "McClellan" cap was a favorite among officers such as these: (Above) 2nd Lt. John M. Flanigan, Co. F., 5th N.J. Vols., (Right)1st Lt. Carl A. Rosander, Battery L, 3rd Rhode Island Heavy Artillery, (Below right) 1st Lt. James R. Campbell, Co. E, 140th N.Y. Vols. CPL

> outside and 1/2 inch inside, strongly soldered on inside of scroll; a double ring of stout brass wire, 1/2 inch diameter, passed through the outer loop, from which to hang the tassel cord.

While the manual went to great lengths to provide makers with everything they needed to know to produce the caps for enlisted men of light artillery, this was not the case for officers; a practice typical for all branches throughout the entire period. It is not surprising, then, that like other wartime headgear, the officers' versions tended to differ from those of the rank and file. For one thing, the plaits and the cords were of gold wire for officers, and the insignia gold embroidered. For the most part the type of crossed cannon devices and the *Arms of the United States* style of eagle that was used to loop up the 1858-pattern officer's hat brim were typically used for artillery officers' caps. The "tulip" likewise lacked the shell and flame. It appears that some officers did not have leather tops or reinforcing bands around the base of their caps either. Because officers obtained their uniform components from numerous sources, the quality and certain details differed from one man to the next.

As we have seen, large numbers of Union soldiers took it upon themselves to forego issue headgear in lieu of items they personally obtained or altered what they were issued to suit their tastes. This undercurrent toward change was given vent when Special Orders No. 31 from the Adjutant General's Office (February 11, 1862) called together several high ranking officers to deliberate "what changes or additions should be made to the uniform of the Army."[60] Board members included Daniel Butterfield, Winfield Scott Hancock, Irvin McDowell, Philip Kearny, George Stoneman, and George Sykes. These men made many recommendations, some inspired, of course, by what the French were doing.

Their divergent opinions echoed previous debates on the topic. As an example, Hancock opted for forage caps for general officers, evidently not finding the chapeau de bras or 1858-hat to his liking.[61] In fact the entire board was unanimous in its desire to abolish the dress hat universally, and cease issue of the forage cap to infantry, who in turn were to be given a new hat similar to the French shako. But, the consensus was that the forage cap was adequate for mounted soldiers. It was also felt the light artillery cap should be continued for this organization with the same insignia and cords as in the past but evidently of a slightly different design because the board had a sample of their version made. Discussion even included the Signal Corps, an arm that had been under consideration but not yet established, with crossed silver flags being proposed for officers of the department as their insignia for both the cap and collar. Despite the board members' intentions, their suggestions were tabled and nothing came of their deliberations, at least during the war years.

The soldiers' spirit of individuality extended to the headwear's insignia and its placement. The previously mentioned General Orders No. 6 set forth that officers would wear their respective branch-of-service badges on the front of their caps and enlisted caps were to secure a brass 1-inch company letter there. In practice, however, there was great variation in the size, type, and placement of the insignia. Officers generally

(Top and bottom, left) General George G. Meade, Army of the Potomac commander at Gettysburg, chose this chasseur cap made by Wanamaker's of his native Philadelphia and placed a wreath with the two stars of a major general on the front. The quilted silk lining is typical of that found in officers' caps. (Top and bottom, right) Lt. Col. Thomas Scott Martin of the 11th Pa. Vols. wore this rather plain chasseur cap by James Smith of New York City with an unusually elaborate maker's imprint inside. Martin was killed at Second Manassas on August 30, 1862. CWLM chose devices of gold embroidery on black velvet or dark blue wool, ranging from impressively large to understatedly miniature. Occasionally they would select metal, with a gilt finish, made to simulate embroidery. Enlisted men arranged their brass company letters and regimental numbers on their forage caps according to regimental or brigade regulations or to their individual whims; sometimes spelling out their military occupation (such as "BAND" or "COOK"), unit initials ("KB" for "Keystone Battery"), or their state affiliation ("MASS" or "MICH"). Regimental numbers and branch of service insignia, intended by regulations for the hat, were used as a matter of course on the cap. As the photographs in this chapter show, soldiers also added other customizations and, with the advent of corps badges, raised the trimming of their hats to a form of folk art. One such inspired soldier was Private Marius K. McDowell of the 100th Pennsylvania, who remembered being quartered in South Carolina with his comrades in an "elegant, well furnished home" which had two pianos. He wrote "...we took the ivory off the keys of one and cut out ivory figures of '100' to put on our caps..."[62] With such resourceful men under them, no wonder commanders constantly struggled for uniformity.[63]

Brass insignia and imaginative soldiers sometimes produced memorable results, as was the case with Sgt. Henry T. Peck of Co. K, 118th Pa. Vols. Captured at Shepardstown, W. Va., in September, 1862, prisoner Peck had some time on his hands as he awaited parole. He obtained a cap from the 118th that had been found on the battlefield, removed one of the brass "1" numerals from its crown and carefully placed it opposite his own cap insignia, marking him as a member of the 1,118th Pa.

The stylish chasseur cap was not limited to officers. Period images and these examples show that the rank and file of some regiments were issued them as well. (Top and bottom, left) Private Frank Lefler, Co. I, 47th Pa. Vols. wore this cap which strongly resembles the Model 1872 forage cap of the future. However, the quilted lining and pre-war riflemen's buttons (an eagle with an "R" in the shield) on the chinstrap indicate early manufacture. The cap was accompanied by a tintype of Lefler wearing this cap and a small photo album of men in his unit showing others in chasseur caps. CPL (Top right) The cap of Ammi B. Baker of the 15th Conn. Vols. has small silver regimental numerals affixed to the front. There is an indication that a similar letter for his company, B, was secured above them at one time as well. CPL (Above) The cap of Pvt. Thomas Drew, Co. C, 4th Mass. Vol. Cav., has a one inch brass regimental number and company letter sewn to the crown, while the branch insignia is affixed by pushing the loops on the back through the pasteboard backing and bending them over. DT

a

b

c

d

e

f

g

h

Also called a "McClellan Cap," the chasseur cap, like most of the headgear worn by the citizen-soldiers of the Union Army, had endless manifestations depending on maker or owner. The examples on these two pages illustrate just some of the variations. (a) The cap of Brevet Brig. Gen. Charles M. Prevost, former commander of the 118th Pa. Vols., has a dark blue velvet band around the base. It was made by Sullender and Pascal of Philadelphia. CPL (b) Col. O. S. Woodward, commanding the 83rd Pa. Vols., had a cap with two lines of braid and a large embroidered infantry horn with applied numerals on the front. The specimen bears the marking "Comstock" inside the crown, believed to be supplier Marcus L. Comstock of Buffalo, N.Y. PHMC (c) An unknown officer wore this cap with gold braiding and the insignia for staff officers and generals: a large Old English US within a wreath. DT (d) Col. John Glenn wore this subdued looking cap while serving with the 23rd Pa. Vols. ("Birneys Zouaves"). CPL (e) First Lt. Leonard Schoonmaker, Co. E, 51st N.Y. Vols. may have been wearing this cap when he was wounded at Fredericksburg, Va., on December 13, 1862. CPL (f) This cap, worn by Capt. Sellick White, Co. I, 10th Conn. Vols., was made by Leary and Co. of New York City. White was killed leading his company in an assault on Confederate rifle pits at Deep Bottom, Va., in August, 1864. CPL (g) The chasseur cap was particularly popular among officers of zouave regiments. This scarlet and gold example was worn by Capt. William Fowler, Co. C, 146th New York Vols. ("Garrard's Tigers"). DT (h) Another zouave, William H. Mallory, an Aide de Camp of the 5th N.Y. Vols. (Duryee's Zouaves) wore this cap. DT

Opposite: (a) This particularly low-crown chasseur cap was worn by 1st Lt. Peter Palen, Co. K, 143rd N.Y. Vols. Note that it bears the regimental numbers embroidered onto a small rectangular patch on the front. CPL (b) Another officer of that regiment., Capt. Jirah I. Young of Company G, owned this cap made by Baker and McKenny of New York City. Young affixed a First Division, XX Corps badge to the crown and, like Palen, has the unusual addition of the regimental number embroidered on a patch in the front. JHK (c) The color of this cap worn by this unknown officer of the 2nd Pa. Vol. Heavy Artillery is black. CPL (d) The front of the cap of Lt. Edward L. Gaul, 159th N.Y. Vols., is dominated by a large embroidered infantry horn. DT (e) The cap of 2nd Lt. William L.Howe of Co. H, 36th Mass. Vols., has no braiding and just a small, simple infantry horn and small metal numbers. It is by Williams and Lockwood of Cincinnati, Ohio. Howe probably purchased the cap in March, 1863, on his way to the siege of Vicksburg where he died of disease four months later. CPL (f) Like Howe, Capt. William H. Cunningham, Co. D, 3rd Mass. Vol. Cav., chose a plain cap and affixed his branch insignia and metal regimental number to the front. CPL (g) An unknown Rhode Island officer wore this fine cap with an embroidered Old English "RI" and wreath on the front and sidebuttons that bear the state's coat of arms. JCG (h) Although his cap was more simple, Colonel William Baker Curtis of the 12th West Virginia Vols. was also proud of his state, with "VA" inside the wreath. JCF

a

b

c

d

e

f

g

h

Pvt. Thomas Barry, Battery M, 1st Mass. Heavy Artillery holds his chasseur cap to the camera. CPL

Capt. Albert G. Cummings, Co. A, 5th N.H. Vols. wore this variation of the chasseur cap, with a long bill, a narrow cord in place of a chinstrap and diminutive infantry insignia. The cap, made by M. H. Stevens and Co. of Washington, D.C., appears as dashing as its owner, who was wounded in action at Fair Oaks, Fredericksburg, and Chancellorsville. CPL

Youthful veteran Sgt. Cornelius V. Moore, Co. B, 100th N.Y. Vols. (top left) poses with friends in an 1865 winter encampment wearing a chasseur cap. At least two of his young comrades have selected slouch hats for themselves. In a letter home he identified them only as (l-r) "a Sgt. in the 39th Ill. Regt.," a corporal "in the 106th N.Y." Vols. and "a Private in the 11th Vermont." JHK

Officers of zouave regiments favored the jaunty chasseur cap, as can be seen by the scarlet and gold cap worn here by Capt. Charles Childs, Co. G, 9th N.Y. Vols. (Hawkins Zouaves). Childs was wounded in action at Antietam in September, 1862. CPL

"These extravagant figures soon attracted attention. A Confederate officer, startled at their high proportions, inquired earnestly from what state the wearer of the cap hailed. 'Pennsylvania,' was the prompt reply. 'Great heavens!' he exclaimed; 'is Pennsylvania running into the thousands? With that state alone with 1,118 regiments in the field how can the poor Confederacy ever expect to succeed!' And he strolled on, apparently, for the moment at least, yielding to the deception."[64]

There were those who had no specific information to go by early in the war with regard to their garb. This was the case for chaplains, whose uniform finally was prescribed for the first time late in 1861.[65] Early chaplains were to have a rather nondescript outfit that included a hat or a forage cap, presumably of plain black, although a chapeau could be obtained for dress wear. Three years later the War Department's General Orders No. 247 (August 25, 1864) allowed chaplain's headgear to bear the staff officer insignia of the Old English "U.S." in a gold wreath applied to a black velvet background. Again the chapeau could be substituted "on occasions of ceremony."

Medical staff, such as ambulance drivers, likewise received some attention in terms of their headgear. For example, in August 1862, privates and non-commissioned officers serving with the corps in the Army of the Potomac were authorized: "a green band, one and one quarter inches broad, around the cap...."[66] By January, 1864, the Army of the Cumberland issued General Orders No. 2 that adopted the scheme established for the Army of the Potomac's ambulance train. The ambulance train for the XVIII Army Corps in the Department of North Carolina took a slightly less elaborate approach, simply calling for a broad red band, knotted on the right side, to be applied to the hat.[67] By the time Congress created an Ambulance Corps for the Union army in 1864, the secretary of war was given the latitude of providing a suitable uniform design for the officers and men, although no such action seems to have been taken.[68]

Another new organization, the Invalid Corps, was launched on October 10, 1863, "recruited in the main from partially disabled soldiers in general hospitals and convalescent camps in various states" where these men provided guards and staffs for Union medical facilities. Later, in March 1864, the name changed to the Veteran Reserve Corps, in part because the old designation was abbreviated "IC," shorthand for "in-

The Union cavalry officers in this carte d'visite camp scene reveal the variety of head gear available to them. The officer on the left wears his 1858 Dress Hat, complete with ostrich plumes, while the pipe smoker next to him protects his cap with a rain cover. Their friends wear chasseur caps, McDowell Caps, and slouch hats. CPL

This panel from an E. and H. T. Anthony stereo view entitled "Warrior's Rest" indicates how varied headwear choices among the volunteers could be, at least when lounging around in camp. The corporal washing his tinware wears a chasseur cap. Two of his friends have obtained broad brimmed slouch hats, and the serious looking soldier on the right sports a fez or "smoking cap." The remainder wear the ubiquitous government issue forage cap. CPL

spected and condemned," a term that had been used by the military for discarded surplus. The other motive for the renaming was expansion of eligibility to veterans who although able bodied did not wish to reenlist for combat duty at the expiration of their first term of service. Under the new title, their mission expanded to guarding bridges, prisoners of war, railways, and government property, among other assignments.[69]

Early on, a uniform was prescribed for enlisted personnel of the Invalid Corps, including the standard forage cap.[70] Some bandsmen in these units, however, evidently adopted colorful non-regulation uniforms and images from the period, as previously mentioned, show the men wearing adaptations of the 1860 French leather shako imported early in the war from Paris.[71] Moreover, the chasseur style forage cap was favored by some of the veteran volunteer men and officers alike, according to extant specimens and period photographs.

The birth of the Signal Service did not result in any new item of headgear, but did give rise to new cap insignia.[72] On August 22, 1864, General Order No. 36, Headquarters of the Signal Corps, called for a badge to set off commissioned officers. This was to be an embroidered wreath of gold on a black velvet background encircling crossed signal flags, one red with white center and one white with red center 3/4-inch square with a lighted torch of gold embroidery and with 1 1/16th-inch gold embroidered staffs for the flags.

Another Civil War insignia initiative arose from a desire for identification beyond company and regimental level organizations. The mag-

This view of veteran campaigners of the 110th Pa. Vols. was taken by the army's only "official" photographer, Capt. A. J. Russell, at Falmouth, Va., in the early spring of 1863. Corps badges have begun to appear and many of the men turn out in wide brimmed hats. JHK

Inserts were among the devices created by inventive Yankee minds to keep the soldier cool under their notoriously hot headgear. The insert on the left was patented in 1860 by James S. Smith and Sons, a New York City military goods manufacturer and importer, and was found inside the McDowell Cap shown on page 94 (bottom). DT In 1862, W. H. Richards patented an "Improvement in Head Cushions to Prevent Sunstroke." The cloth covered insert, shown at right, has a cork layer to help repel heat and a "sponge or other equivalent liquid absorbent" layer to hold moisture. The covering of the cork side was flannel, and the other side linen. This example, which found its way into a Confederate soldier's cap, is now on display at the Gettysburg National Military Park visitors center. It is marked: "Richards/Anti-Sun Stroke/Cushion/Patented June 11, 1862/Bent & Bush/sole manufacturers/Boston, Mass./Directions/Wet the cushion with water./During the day wear the linen/side next to the head./At sun set/reverse it." Its effectiveness is unknown. GNMB

nitude of the war had resulted in the establishment of divisions, corps, and armies. Badges to identify corps eventually were adopted to produce unit identity, build cohesiveness, and instill esprit. Perhaps a somewhat more tangible reason was to prevent "injustice by reports of straggling and misconduct through mistake as to the organizations" that such individuals belonged to, or so one corps commander reasoned.[73]

At first this practice began informally with Major General Philip Kearny's Third Division, III Corps. The general, according to one account, dressed down an officer he presumed to be under his command, only to learn that the man was from another unit. Supposedly Kearny wished to avoid a recurrence of this awkward episode. On June 28, 1862, he ordered a red flannel, 2-inch square swatch sewn to the caps of officers serving in his corps.[74] Just days after Kearny was killed in action at the Battle of Chantilly in September, 1862, his replacement, Gen. David B. Birney, directed that the practice would continue in honor of the fallen general. Eventually many enlisted men in the III Corps elected to follow suit, even though no orders existed authorizing this action. Thus the so-called "Kearny Patch" was born.[75]

By February 10, 1863, the First Division of III Corps likewise opted for a square or diamond patch to set off their personnel. The use of corps badges began to spread as the Army of the Potomac reorganized under its new commander, Gen. Joseph Hooker, in early 1863. Hooker's chief of staff, Gen. Daniel Butterfield, took note of how distinctive the III Corps looked with their "patches" and convinced Hooker that the practice should be spread throughout his command. In an order dated March 21, 1863, Hooker directed the adoption of distinctive cloth badges "to be worn on top of the cap" for his entire command; the I, II, III, V, VI, XI, and XII Army Corps. The badges of the First Division would be red, white for Second Division, blue for Third, green for Fourth and orange for Fifth. From then on, corps after corps gradually inaugurated its own version of the badge. Cloth for making the badges was shipped to the Army of the Potomac's Quartermaster from the Army Clothing and Equipage Office in Philadelphia on March 30, followed later by metal dies "with mallets and plates" so they could be cut quickly and consistently for all the troops. These devices included circles, crescents, shields, crosses, stars, and other signs that in past times had mystical

A creative but now unknown Northerner devised a brass "ventilator" to encourage air to flow under the soldier's hot cap. It was installed by cutting a hole in the pasteboard crown, inserting the device and crimping two rings of tabs around each side to hold it in place. An outer disk could then be rotated to either open or close the holes. A number of these are known in private collections, seen in period photographs, and excavated by relic hunters, testifying to their popularity. The example shown on this commercial forage cap was worn by young Capt. Lindley Coleman, Co. B, 19th Maine Vols. It still retains traces of a thin gilt finish, most likely due to the fact that Coleman died of disease in camp on October 18, 1862, just seven weeks after enlisting. (see also pages 106, 132) CPL

This volunteer is ready to battle the Southern sunshine with his brass ventilator firmly in place. CPL

symbolism, perhaps unconsciously suggesting the corps badge was a lucky charm! Eventually there was a great variety of designs, materials used in construction, methods of wearing the badges, and levels of artistry (or lack thereof) making the corps badge a topic worthy of its own book. They began to be seen in quantity by the Battle of Chancellorsville in May, 1863, and by the last years of the war they appeared in proliferation on both caps and hats. By the conclusion of the fighting all but two corps had some form of badge available as a morale booster and identifier.[76]

As with other parts of the uniform, the ingenuity of the citizen-soldier interacted with corps badges as well. Captured at Cold Harbor in 1864, Pvt. William Henning of the 118th Pa. Vols. found his captors were confiscating the greenbacks of their prisoners before their departure for Andersonville. Many of his comrades were unable to find places to conceal their money that the Confederates could not find and Henning had $7 which he did not want to lose. "After considerable cogitation on my part I ripped the corps mark which I wore on the side of my cap, half off, then cut the cloth and put the notes between the cloth and the lining. Both being old notes they could not be detected in the cap by feeling. I then sewed the corps mark on again over the cut in the cloth." Henning was later thoroughly searched, but kept his money, thanks in part to his V Corps badge.[77]

When the war halted in 1865, forage caps and slouch hats, most with corps badges affixed, could be seen on just about all of the rank and file, worn proudly as battered symbols of the fight to preserve the Union. Some, bearing the marks of minie balls or shell fragments, were carefully stowed away in knapsacks or sent safely home as souvenirs of a great adventure.

Looking Westward

As the guns fell silent, the United States government found itself with warehouses filled with all types of uniforms and equipment. For economic reasons, this large quantity of unissued headgear would continue to be distributed to regular army troops until the supplies were exhausted.[78] Only when sizeable numbers had been expended could something new be considered, although even then Quartermaster General Montgomery Meigs doubted that a majority really desired to "throw aside the uniform in which officers & men so well and gloriously served and saved their country...," motives that Meigs thought outweighed "changing tastes." He reinforced this belief suggesting that the old uniform "was good enough to make campaigns in, and it ought to be good enough for the more inactive duties of the present military state of the country."[79]

Despite Meigs' conservative stand on the matter, many others opposed continuation of old patterns, and often expressed their dissatisfaction in the pages of the *Army and Navy Journal*, the semi-official voice for mid-nineteenth-century American military men.[80] Several letters to the editor appeared in the publication venting dissatisfaction with U.S. Army attire and denunciation of the regulation garb which remained on hand from the Civil War was widespread (and not too different than the wartime complaints of the Union Army's volunteers). One critic expressed his abhorrence to troops being permitted "to wear every imaginable style and color of hat or cap that he may be possessed of."[81] Other officers much preferred the traditional staff officer's chapeau as a replacement for dress wear.[82]

Another advocate waxed eloquent over the merits of the metal helmets worn by Cromwell's roundhead cavalry in England during the seventeenth century, reflecting the fine "effect of a regiment of cavalry equipped like the Ironsides, with the addition of an eagle, in dark metal, surmounting a steel cap.[83] He went on to lavish praise on the helmet of the Czar's army that he thought "exceedingly beautiful and serviceable" as was that of the Austrian dragoons which supposedly was "well ventilated, sword-proof, and graceful, and not expensive," in contrast to the "ugly and heavy" model won by the Kaiser's forces.[84] Two more letters to the editor called for Russian-style helmets for cavalry and pasteboard-stiffened caps with pompons.[85]

Expanding on this "Euro-centric" viewpoint, and taking a more scientific and medical focus on the subject of clothing as well, a report issued by the U.S. Army's surgeon general offered new perspectives and directions that previously had received little consideration in the

Corporal James P. Tilton, Co. K, 128th Pa. Vols. had this lightweight canvas cap cover to help keep him comfortable during his nine-month enlistment. It was probably a gift from someone at home. CPL

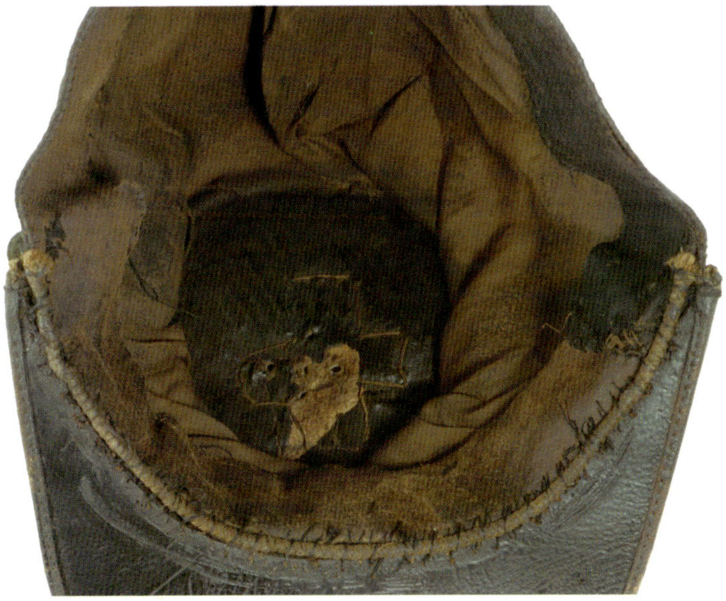

Soldiers dealt with the problem of circulating air in their own way. Many simply cut holes in their headgear as seen in these examples. (Top left, right) During the Gettysburg campaign, Pvt. Robert Elliot, Co. C, 23rd Pa. Vols., removed the First Division, VI Corps badge from the crown of his privately purchased cap and punched five small holes in the center, later adding the small, stippled brass figures and letters. CPL (Center left) Pvt. Frank Elliot of Pennsylvania's "Keystone Battery" punched eight holes around the insignia on the crown of his government issue forage cap. CPL (Center right) Lt. Matthias Johnson, Co. B, 165th N. Y. Vols. (2nd Duryee Zouaves) carefully cut diamond-shaped vents in and around the gold braiding on the top of his scarlet chasseur cap. CPL (Bottom left, right) Pvt. John McLain, Co. M, 6th Ohio Vol. Cav., made adjustments to his Army Hat to include several ventilation holes. JCF

United States. Based on the opinions and observations of 168 officers this document bespoke of a general complaint about the quality of the uniform.[86]

Eventually, the persistent call for change resulted in some modifications to the Civil War issue. As an example, some companies and individuals ceased wearing the 1858-pattern hat albeit without approval from on high.[87] Like his Civil War counterparts who found nothing to commend those tall *pilgrim hats*, one fellow dubbed it an "unsightly abortion" that would be propelled "spinning across the parade to the intense disgust of the wearer" by even a slight gust of wind. He went on to call it a "sombrero feo" (ugly hat).[88] Another writer thought the hat was "unwieldy, ill-shaped, and a perpetual nuisance to the wearer, because it is either knocked off, blown off, or out of gear in some way." Further, he condemned it as "bereft of beauty." Another avowed it was "the most ugly, uncomfortable, and unsoldierly covering that a malignant spirit could have devised for the heads of suffering humanity."[89] A third commentator indicated that in his cavalry regiment it "was tabooed even for full dress."[90]

Yet it seems other units continued to wear it, as indicated by an 1872 request to have the brim looped up on the right side for both mounted and dismounted troops alike rather than on opposite sides depending on whether the wearer was a cavalryman or a foot soldier, as had been the previous requirement. The change was approved because of the "carry arms" and "right shoulder" arms movements for infantrymen tended to displace the hat when the musket moved passed it for these evolutions.[91]

Such a slight alteration in regulations may have been ample for some commanders, but not others. In the case of Brigadier General C.C. Augur, men serving under him in the Department of the Platte in 1869 were allowed to dispense with the hat all together, even for dress occasions. Instead they would wear the forage cap.[92]

Still others, however, would have disliked Augur's solution. The tall crowned enlisted forage cap was not a thing of beauty in the eyes of many men as reflected in an 1872 ditty that might have been sung to the tune of *The Star Spangled Banner* (not at the time the national anthem). Some of the verses ran:

> O, say have you seen the unique forage cap
> that good Uncle Sam on his Army doth clap?
> Some turn up its visor, and some turn it down,
> still it gives each poor wearer the air of a clown.
> It looks like a scarecrow—good reason why

Nathanial Prentiss Banks left his position as Governor of Massachusetts in January, 1861, when President Lincoln named him a major general of volunteers. Like the volunteers he commanded, Banks felt free to make whatever adjustments to his headwear he felt necessary, despite what army regulations dictated. An existing image of Banks shows he first wore this officers quality Army Hat with only the gold hat cords of a general officer and the left simply turned up by means of a small hook on the brim which attached to a loop of thread on the side. Apparently the heat compelled him to make some alterations when he took command of Union forces around Port Hudson, Louisiana, in 1863. First, it appears Banks simply cut "flaps" in the sides and back to encourage the flow of air. Later he sewed them up and inserted round, 5/8 inch, brass "vents" at those points. He also punched eight holes in the crown for additional ventilation. JHK

the enemy saw it, took fright and did fly.
But the flag of our Union in triumph shall wave,
when each cap and contractor shall lie in one grave.[93]

The dissatisfaction with the forage cap's floppy design prompted some officers and enlisted men to again procure the chasseur pattern with its lower crown.[94] Other deviations from regulations related to the forage cap had to do with insignia. As during the late war, officers were to wear their branch or corps device with the regimental numeral, all in embroidery or simulated embroidery, while enlisted men were to display only the brass company letter.[95] In certain instances soldiers added their branch device from the 1858-pattern hat, and in at least one situation troops at a post in Wyoming Territory were told to place their regimental numeral on the crown of their cap and the company letter below. The hunting horns of infantrymen that evidently had been used by many, if not all of the men previously, were to be removed.[96]

Another reference to cap insignia came from San Francisco, where the adjutant of the Second Artillery asked for lyre and harp devices for the regimental band, a request that was denied by the Quartermaster Department as being outside the authorized items of issue.[97] Such a divergence might have been commonplace among the Civil War's volunteer regiments, but this, now, was the *regular* army. Another query to have twenty-four light artillery caps sent to the Fourth Artillery band at Fort McHenry likewise was turned down, this time because regulations allowed this type of headgear for mounted artillerymen only.[98] When other non-artillery units made similar requisitions for light artillery caps, they also were refused.[99] While these applications for the artillery cap for bandsmen were denied, an exception for a similar type of headgear was allowed for the musicians at the U.S. Military Academy.[100] This atypical allowance for the Academy's band was granted because that organization was the only one officially recognized by statute, all other bands of the era existing on a sort of ad hoc status.[101]

Not only bandsmen were regularly outfitted with non-government funds. Winter clothing, at least for extreme cold, was not available through the quartermaster, with the exception for a brief period when woolen mittens were distributed until stocks obtained during the Civil War ran out.[102]

In a report prepared for the surgeon general's office by military doctor Alfred Woodhull, the need for "those posts where the cold is represented by twenty-five degrees below zero, and lower, in the winter" to be supplied with garments such as buffalo robes that would entirely "envelop the wearer" was called for.[103] Dr. Woodhull maintained

The government supplied cap covers of glazed silk for its soldiers to use in foul weather, as seen on this infantryman (left) and a first sergeant of the 5th N.Y. Veteran Vols. (right). CPL Many soldiers also wore them around camp or on the march to keep their caps clean.

Some militia units entered service with their own rain gear. The entire body of this tall chasseur cap is made of glazed silk and was purchased by the "State Fencibles" of Philadelphia to outfit their unit in 1855. CPL

this type of cold weather gear should be issued by the government, rather than purchased from the meager pay of the soldier. Another 1868 advocate of special gear among other things suggested fur caps. He also felt that the army should make these items available to the troops much as certain European powers did for the health and comfort of the men.[104]

Field duty was not the only time such requirements came about, as indicated by one garrison where the men resorted to a sort of pseudo havelock to cut the chilling winds that buffeted the head and face. This was a piece of cloth with three button holes to attach it to the rear of the forage cap, and a drawstring at the front bottom to close the appendage as protection for the ears and part of the face, not unlike the flap that had been affixed to some of the 1839-pattern forage caps years earlier.[105] A surgeon at one post discovered another means to provide what Uncle Sam did not. He recalled: "My cap was made from beaver's skin and is the respectable feature of my outlandish outfit."[106]

If dealing with the bone chilling Northern Plains were not enough to tax the quartermaster, the opposite extremes of heat presented another puzzlement. The surgeon general noted that the 1858-pattern hat and the forage cap were found objectionable by many officers, "a light straw hat, during the warm weather, a period that varies with locality," being deemed optimum as a "defense against the direct rays of the sun."

(Left) Corp. Henry S. Perham, Co. H, 6th Mass. Vols. owned this glazed cloth cap cover to keep him dry. Like those called for back in 1851 (see page 49) it closed in the front by ties. CPL (Center) Corp. Charles Little, Co. B, 48th Mass, used this more substantial rubberized cloth havelock with a small hook and eye in the front to close it just below the chin. DT (Right) Perhaps it was raining outside when this unidentified Massachusetts officer posed for the photographer. CPL

The army-issue headgear also offered little protection from the cold. These two officers have obtained fur hats to help them endure winter in the field: 2nd Lt. James L. Mast of Durell's Battery, Pa. Lt. Art. (left) and Capt. Edward Wertheimer, Co. E, 54th N.Y. Vol. Inf. CPL

Such a hat had been granted to the Fort Monroe garrison prior to the Civil War (and as described earlier, was presented to an entire regiment of New Yorkers during the war by their major). Thereafter use of straw hats continued informally out "of necessity of substituting *something* for the uniform [hat or cap], its accessibility, and its low cost."[107]

Another answer to this problem, according to the surgeon general's office, was: "either a kepi or casque or light brimmed hat, essentially the style of a Malay hat. To be made of some stiff, light material with pearl-colored cover and an air-space of half an inch between the ring and the head."[108] Such a headpiece was not adopted officially, however, for more than a decade.

The same statement was true of yet a second recommendation found in Woodhull's 1868 report. This was "A light-colored, brimmed felt hat," a piece of headgear generally recommended by those who responded to the survey. It could be either as a simple felt slouch hat, "or looped up on the side for dress." The pattern proposed was the Andrews hat made in the Mexican War and issued for a short period in the early 1850s to the Second Dragoons. Thus, "a gray, light felt hat," in the estimation of the report, was "without a doubt, the most serviceable" solution to the problem of dealing with heat as far as the head was concerned.[109]

Even before the surgeon general's report was certain, influential officers who convened in response to Special Orders No. 523, GO, December 18, 1867 to consider a revision of all U.S. Army regulations, gave consideration to improving the uniform, including headgear.[110] The trio of men assigned this daunting duty were Brigadier General Christopher C. Augur, Lieutenant General Philip H. Sheridan, and General William T. Sherman, all noted Civil War generals who after the war were among the most senior men in the army. Sherman presided, at least until his departure for the field after January 1868.[111] Before doing so, he submitted a draft of the board's findings up to that point to the adjutant general.[112] After that, Augur and Sheridan continued for several more days. Despite the immense task at hand, and the relatively conservative nature of the three, they still reviewed prototype uniform articles during their sessions. These included a fully trimmed cadet officer's cap; new hat and various types of trim for it, that included two thistle pompons (green and red). A hair plume for cavalry, plus two cords and tassels (green and red), evidently were reviewed as well.[113]

Despite their reflections on the matter, the 1868 board disbanded, as had their 1862 counterparts, without taking any real action relative to the uniform. There was some confusion over the board afterwards, however, with certain military suppliers particularly believing that it actually had issued new directives for replacements of the previous pattern, or portions of the uniform.[114] The contractor who furnished a sample of the "Andrews" hat based upon the favorable notice for this design in the surgeon general's report, wanted to know about future directions of the uniform, and even offered to produce another sample or samples of the hat "that would combine all the requirements of *comfort* and *utility* desired, in a better quality than the previous submission that was made "only to give an idea of *shape* and *appearance*.[115]

While the rumors of a new uniform were unfounded, continued calls for change still were in the air. As one example, in 1871, Brevet Major General James A. Hardie, a West Pointer who had taught at the academy and had served in the Mexican War, Indian campaigns, and the Civil War, made a suggestion for a new cap to the adjutant general, declaring: "I dislike our present one, and equally so the French `kepi' which officers generally wear." What Hardie proposed was "a plain military fashion" that would "attract no condemnation for want of utility or of taste...."[116]

The army's commanding general also felt the time was approaching for a new cap. While William T. Sherman did not "expect soon to see a hat that will be fixed and appropriate for the Army" he did admit, "Fashions change and we must do the same." His preference was for "The old leather gig top" (evidently meaning the 1833-pattern leather forage cap).[117] However, he acknowledged this style "now would be grotesque." What seemed most practical to Sherman was a "round felt hat with a brim—for common wear—with some pompoms to be worn for *dress* parade."[118]

There were a few individuals at least who took a different approach to what constituted the ideal headgear. For instance, some light artillery officers reveled in the glory of their scarlet horsetail bedecked caps, and were the envy of others. Furnishing these coveted caps proved difficult, however, because soon after the Civil War, stocks dwindled, going from 2,886 on June 30, 1866 to none by early 1868.[119] Indeed, when the Third Artillery required 400 of the caps in San Francisco, there were not enough on hand to fill the order.[120] Permission was granted to buy the hats and attaching rings for cords, and Horstmann of Philadelphia received a contract to make sample caps.[121]

Other artillery units around the country required the caps as well. In Louisiana 200 caps had been sent to the light battery at New Orleans, leaving only 145 on hand. More were needed, as was authorization to have them produced.[122] A similar situation could be found in Richmond, necessitating an order to make more for the mounted gunners there.[123] This last communique became garbled, which caused the commanding colonel of the Fifth Artillery to think a new uniform was being produced, rather than just orders for replacement caps.[124] Part of this confusion stemmed from the correspondence to both Richmond and Fort Leavenworth stating the depleted stock of caps meant that when caps were required they were to be ordered in small quantities in that the design might be changed soon "and for that reason also it is not desirable to accumulate any more of the present style."[125] Another letter to

Two officers strike formal poses with their 1858 Dress Hats: (Left) Col. William Henry Noble, 17th Conn. Vols. and (Right) Capt. Judson Alexander, Co. B, 9th N.H. Vols. A close up look at Pitcher's cap clearly shows the yellow worsted binding found on most of the government produced products. CPL

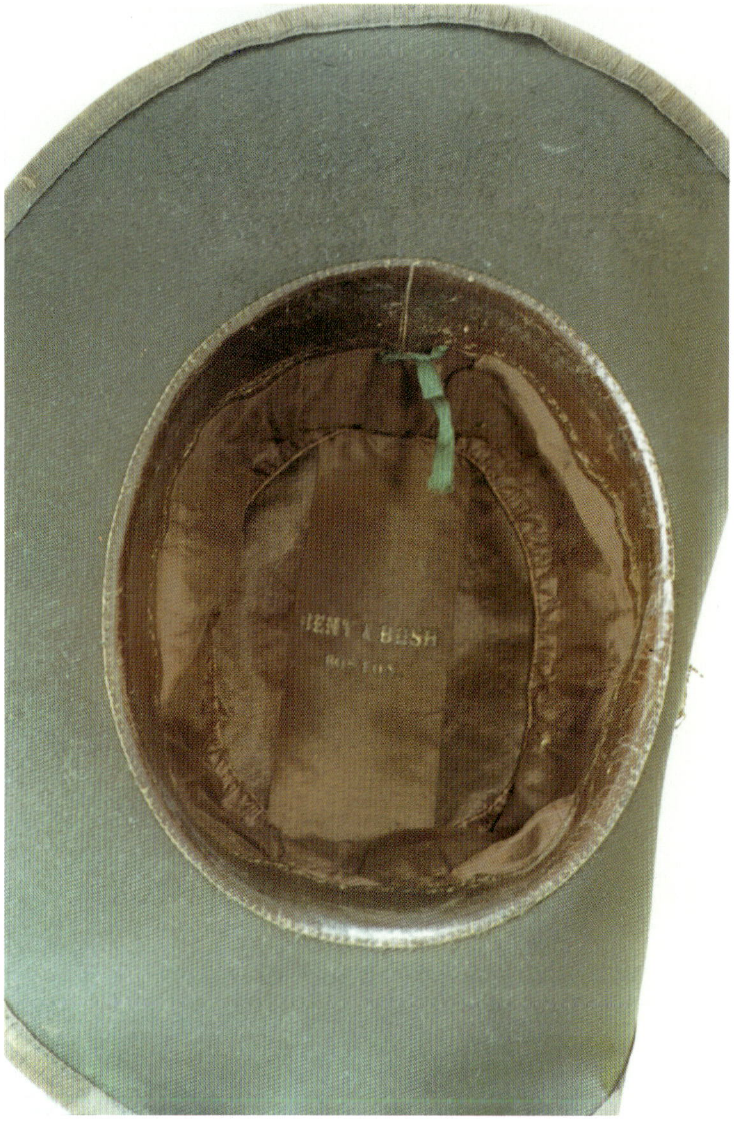

(Top left, right) Two views of the 1858 Dress Hat worn by an unknown 22nd regiment of infantry officer, as sold by Bent and Bush of Boston, Mass. DT (Bottom left) The dress hat of William Baker Curtis, 12th West Va. Vols., substitutes the state designation in place of the branch of service insignia on the front. JCF

For officers, the "Burnside Pattern Felt Hat" combined the trappings of the army hat with a more comfortable slouch hat. It enjoyed a great deal of popularity and was available from many of the military suppliers (see page 119). (Left) This example, for an infantry officer, was made by Horstmann of Philadelphia. (Right) General John Henry Hobart Ward, former commander of the 38th N. Y. Vols., owned this fine example. JCG

Here are four examples of the black felt slouch hat as obtained by officers. (Top left) This plain version, ornamented only with the gold hat cords of a general officer, was worn by Gen. Thomas Greely Stevenson. He was killed by a Confederate sharpshooter at the head of his division of the IX Corps on May 10, 1864. The purple silk lining inside is embossed in gold with "U.S. Army" over an eagle. CPL (Top right) Gen. Amiel Weeks Whipple wore a similar hat, but with the addition of a III Corps badge on the side. He, too, was killed by a Confederate sharpshooter, just six days before Stevenson at the battle of Chancellorsville. DT (Opposite left) Battered by hard use in the field, the slouch hat of Capt. Edward L. Stratton, Co. F, 12th N.J. Vols., has a II Corps badge on the side and the gold and black hat cords of an officer. RM (Opposite right) Lt. Col. Edward Cabot of the 44th Mass. Vols. also had his XVIII corps badge affixed to the side as well as the embroidered branch of service insignia at the front. RR

Like the men they commanded, officers came to prefer a soft felt hat with a wide brim for protection from the elements. Such is the case with (Left) Asst. Surgeon Thomas Cushing, 28th N.Y. Vols. and (Right) Lt. Charles A Stevens, Co. G, 1st U.S. Sharp Shooters. Note both men have only their gold and black hat cords as ornamentation. CPL

Hatter William F. Warburton of Philadelphia patented several "Army Hats" in 1862, like this one worn by Capt. Elias Hamilton of Co. E, 15th N.J. Vols. He has fastened his hat cords so that the ends stay on one side of the hat and further personalized it with a VI Corps badge on the opposite side in which he affixed his regimental number. AL

A variation on the slouch hat was the so-called "plug hat," which was essentially a wide brimmed hat with a crown that was low and rounded, rather than high and pointed. Asst. Surgeon Heinrich W. Reissberger of the 68th N.Y. Vols. is seen with one in this carte d'visite. CPL

the Third Independent Battery of Ohio Volunteer Militia was even more telling as to why some officers and contractors presumed there was a uniform change in the offing. This letter stated: "no changes have yet been made for the United States Army uniforms, though it is contemplated making some after the present stock is exhausted."[126]

Because so few light artillery caps were to be had in 1870, Sherman recommended that the 1858-pattern hat be retained.[127] In like manner the Second Artillery was informed that the cap could not be issued to any but mounted batteries.[128]

Although some of the light artillerymen may have delighted in their fashionable headgear, the time approached when replacements for this and all other forms of headdress issued to the army were being seriously contemplated. Perhaps this was one reason why a document providing descriptions of each article of clothing and equipment had been requested for use by the quartermaster general's office on the eve of yet another board being called together.[129] Special Orders No. 260, Headquarters of the Army, July 3, 1871 established another group of officers to again review army regulations, the 1868 effort having never gone forward. This body was made up of Andrew J. Alexander, Eighth Cavalry; Richard I. Dodge, Third Infantry; Henry J. Hunt, Fifth Artillery; John H. King, Ninth Infantry; and Inspector General of the Army Randolph B. Marcy, the senior member and president of the board.[130]

While deliberating on other, issues Marcy and the board asked whether they should extend its sitting to make recommendations about any changes in the uniform. To the latter inquiry Marcy asked: "Do you wish that we should bring into [the] new regulations any changes in uniform?" He went on to assert, "We think it can be improved upon and made better for service. At present so much clothing of the old pattern has been sold to citizens that they are found wearing it everywhere. If material changes were made this would not be the case...."[131] Although Marcy appears not to have received a reply to this issue, he forged ahead and requested a copy of the 1862 board's actions regarding the same subject.[132] Perhaps had Sherman not been abroad in Europe at the time this request might have been denied, he being conservative when it came to the uniform. This was not to be the case, however.

Indeed, sweeping changes in the uniform, including headdress were about to be made. In 1872, Marcy and his fellow board members would do away with the floppy bummer's cap and tall black hat with ostrich feathers for new headgear. While these replacements were not issued immediately, the patterns of the Civil War were destined to disappear before long, thereby passing into history with the soldiers who once wore them.[133]

This classic example of a "plug hat," worn by Capt. Henry M. Brewster, Co. C, 57th N.Y. Vols., bears a hand cut II Corps badge on the front with stippled metal numbers of the regiment inserted in the middle. The officer's hat cords are the "twisted" variety as shown in the Schuyler, Hartley and Graham catalogue of 1864 (see page 57). The gold embossed maker's mark inside says only "Mode de Paris." CPL

Sgt. George Lemmon, Co. D, 30th Pa. Vols. (1st Reserves) has decorated his "plug hat" with officer's hat cords, a V Corps badge on front, and an array of brass letters on the crown which proudly proclaim his unit affiliation: "1/REG/D/PRVVC" (Pa. Reserve Veteran Volunteer Corps). RP

For slouch hats and forage caps, officers could obtain their branch insignia embroidered on cloth or velvet without the tin backing, as this example worn by Lt. George W. Taylor of the 4th Battery, Mass. Light Artillery. CPL

Regulations called for the Army Hat's "ornament in front" for officers to be the insignia of the branch of service embroidered in gold on a "black velvet ground." As with the headgear, these devices varied widely in style and quality depending on the manufacturer and the taste of the owner. Those designed for the army hat were usually over a tin backing with metal loops for fastening. These three examples of infantry insignia, a bugle with the "number of the regiment in silver within the bend," follow the regulations but, as you can see, differ. (Top) The regimental number for Capt. Levi E. Kent, Co. F, 4th R.I. Vols. is embroidered. (Center) 1st Lt. Charles Luther, Co. E, 76th Ohio Vols., had metal regimental numbers. (Bottom) The bugle worn by Capt. Richard H. Lee, Co. I, 6th N.J. Vols. is of mixed silver and gold metallic thread. CPL

The eagle that looped up the side of the Army Hat was also embroidered on a black velvet oval over a metal backing (left). Photographs indicate that a variant style, embroidered on a shield, existed just before the Civil War (right). CPL

Left: This well-armed teamster has embellished his forage cap with a set of officers' hat cords. CPL

Opposite: A page from the 1864 Schuyler, Hartley and Graham catalogue shows some of the variety of headgear available to the soldiers including the old "Regulation Chapeau," an item of head dress seldom seen during the war. Note that this important military supply firm, founded in 1854, offered items as small as the "scroll pattern" brass company letters and numbers along with silver "plated metal figures for officers' caps."

Chapeaux, Hats, and Caps.

No. 56.

U. S. A. Regulation Chapeau.

No. 57.

U. S. Felt Hat.

No. 58.

Fatigue Cap, with Oiled Silk Cover.

No. 59.

Fatigue Cap, with Gold, or Silk Braid.

No. 60.

Burnside Pattern Felt Hat.

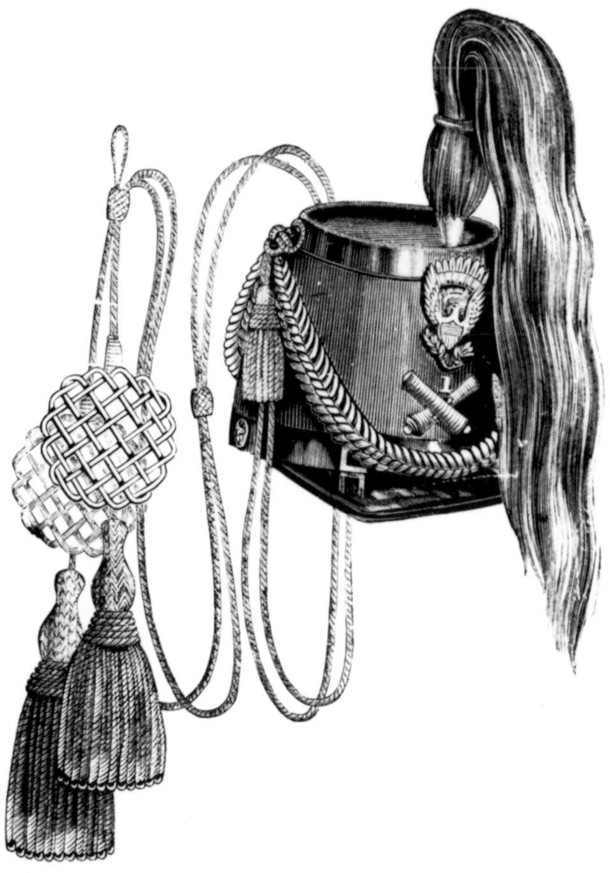

No. 60½.

Artillery Cap.

1 2 3 4 5 6 7 8 9 0

No. 61.

Plated Metal Figures, for Officers' Caps.

A B C D E

F G H I K

No. 62.

Company Letters, Brass or Plated.

Company Figures, do. do.

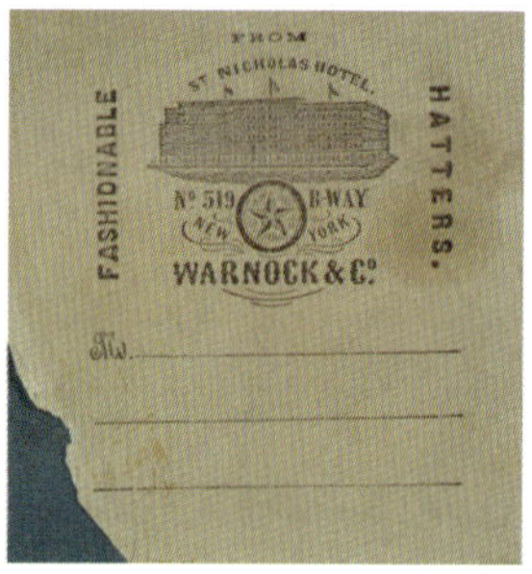

The 1861 Army Regulations allowed "officers of the General Staff and Staff Corps" the option of wearing "a light French chapeau," but few did. (Top row) This one was worn by Maj. Gen. Amos B. Eaton, who was named commissary general of the U. S. Army in June, 1864. As the label on its pasteboard box shows, it was made by Warnock and Company. DT (Bottom left, right) New York militia general John N. Knapp would become Governor of his state after the war. He wore this chapeau when serving on the staff of Gen. John Dix in 1863. Note that in place of the U. S. eagle and shield insignia, it bears the New York coat of arms. CPL

The men of Co. G, 114th Pa. Vols. donned their full zouave uniforms, complete with turbans, in this portrait taken at Petersburg in August, 1864. NA

The turban was perhaps the most unfamiliar part of the zouave uniform encountered by the American volunteer. (Above left) Drum Major John H. Naylor of the 5th N.Y. Veteran Vol. Inf. seems to be at home beneath his turban in this image taken in 1864-65. CPL (Right) Pvt. Charles Lyons of Co. I, 114th Pa. Vols. (Collis Zouaves) looks somewhat overwhelmed by his. RP

With its colorful woolen tassel, the stiff felt fez was a distinctive piece of headwear that was provided after the war got underway to a number of regiments by the U.S. Government as part of their classic zouave uniform. These four specimens were worn by (Above left) the 62nd N.Y. Vols. (Anderson Zouaves), DT (Above right) the 114th Pa. Vols. (Collis Zouaves), CPL, (Below left) Pvt. Julius D. Pitcher, Co D, 146th N.Y. Vols. (Garrard's Tigers), DT and (Below right) Pvt. David P. Davis, Co. F, 5th N. Y. Vols. (Duryee's Zouaves). CPL. Both Pitcher and Davis altered the look of their fezes by wearing them with the sides turned up, either for better fit or greater fashion. The close up of Pitcher's cap shows the yellow worsted binding found on most of the government produced products.

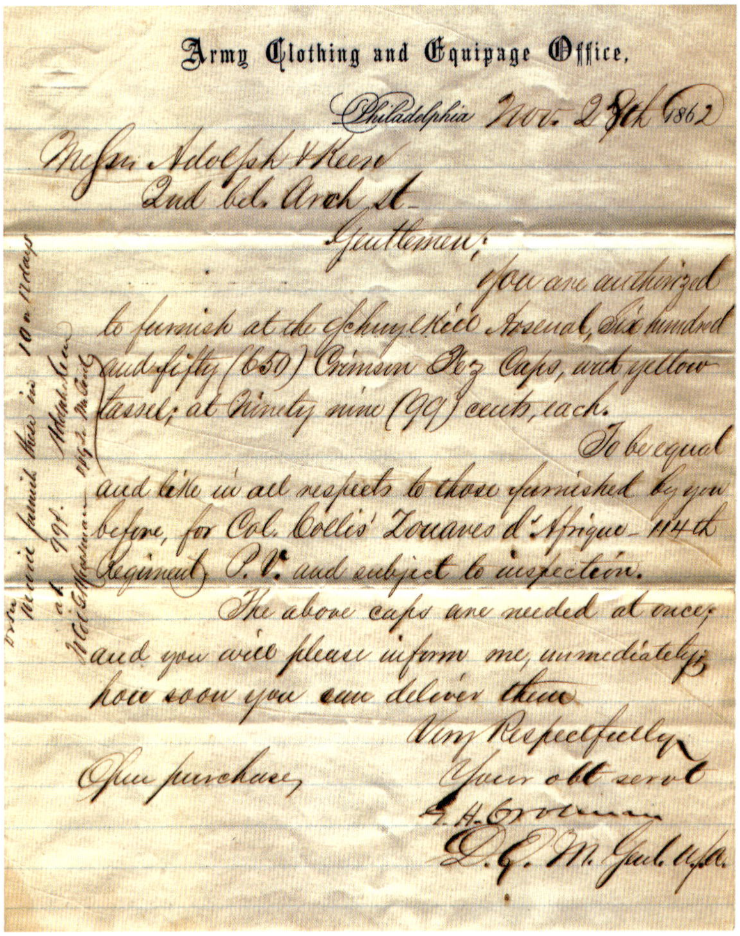

Army Clothing and Equipage Office,

Philadelphia Nov. 28th 1862

Messrs. Adolph & Keen
2nd bel. Arch st.

Gentlemen;

You are authorized to furnish at the Schuylkill Arsenal, Six hundred and fifty (650) Crimson Fez Caps, with yellow tassel; at Ninety nine (99) cents each.

To be equal and like in all respects to those furnished by you before, for Col. Collis' Zouaves d'Afrique – 114th Regiment P.V. and subject to inspection.

The above caps are needed at once, and you will please inform me, immediately how soon you can deliver them.

Very Respectfully
Your obt servt

Open purchase,

G. H. Crosman
D.Q.M. Genl. USA

Above: The Army Clothing and Equipage Office at Philadelphia's Schuylkill Arsenal issued this order to hatters Adolph and Keen for 650 "red fez caps, with yellow tassel, at ninety nine (99) cents each" for the 114th Pa. Vols. (Collis' Zouaves) in November, 1862. The company received a number of contracts for "fez caps" during the war, and most likely provided much of those issued by the Federal government. JHK

Right: First Sgt. Cyrus Butler relaxes at his unit's campsite wearing a fashionable "camp cap." Butler was a member of Co. K, 40th Pa. Vols. (11th Reserves), not a zouave. RP

Camp caps or smoking caps were fashionable among the soldiery just as they were among men in civilian life. (Top) The infantry insignia on the front flap gives this fur-trimmed folding cap a definite military look. It was worn by Col. William B. Hatch, commander of the 4th N.J. Vols. Considered "a born soldier" by his contemporaries, Hatch once held a Captain's commission in the Russian cavalry. He was mortally wounded at Fredericksburg on December 13, 1862. CPL (Center) The note that accompanies this ornate smoking cap shows it was "presented to Col. G. Sniper by Capt. A. H. Spore, 185th Regt., December 25, 1864." Gustavus Sniper and Abram Spore were both with the 185th N.Y. Vols. Around the button holding the tassel on top is a Maltese cross denoting the unit's association with the V Corps. DT (Bottom) Andrew Ryder, a 1st Class Petty Officer in the U.S. Navy, was on one of several boats used to transport the 9th N.Y. Vols. (Hawkins Zouaves) to the assault on Roanoke Island in February, 1862 . Ryder was apparently able to obtain a fez from one of the zouaves, which (sans tassel) he used when off duty. CPL

The Model 1860 French infantry shako was part of the 10,000 sets of uniforms purchased from the Godillot firm in Paris. The sturdy black leather cap was intended for dress occasions and included a round green pompon, black rooster feather plume and gilt front plate designed for the U.S. market. Like the American shakos of the 1850s, it was heavy and hot, despite having vents in the side. The 62nd and 83rd Pa. Vols. and 18th Mass. Vols. are known to have received them without the brass plates, and units in New York's Excelsior Brigade with the plates. Many of the French uniforms were too small to fit the more robust American soldier and subsequently more than 6,000 of the shakos were set aside to be sold at auction. Some found their way to various army bands, like those in the Veteran Reserve Corps. Others went elsewhere. Judging by the more colorful plume and markings inside, this specimen probably served a military band from some New England unit. CPL

(Above left) A member of one of the first three units to obtain the French uniform wears his shako without the front plate, although plainly visible is the brass reinforcement around the hole through which it was secured by a nut. Above it, a portion of the red/white/ blue metal rosette, affixed by wires, can be seen partially hidden by the feather plume. JHK (Left) Pvt. Samuel Kyle Isett, Co. F, 83rd Pa. Vols. stands tall in his complete French uniform. RP (Right) Pvt. Henry D. Campbell, Co. B, 84th Pa. Vols. wears a mixture of the French and U.S. issue clothing including the shako with brass front plate. Why Campbell was so outfitted is a mystery as no records seem to exist of the 84th being issued any of the French uniform. RP

Pvt. Charles M. Hugo, Co. M, 62nd Pa. Vols. wears the cloth M. 1860 fatigue cap issued with the French uniforms. CPL

Right: A well armed corporal has his on the table beside him. USAMHI, CPL, RB

A sargeant of the 2nd U.S. Light Artillery (above) and an unknown light artillery private (Opposite, Top right) wear their Light Artillery Shakos.

Pvt. George J. Killmer, Co. L, 62nd Pa. Vols. Pvt. Killmer apparently either lost or removed the tassel at the time the cap was worn. BCHS

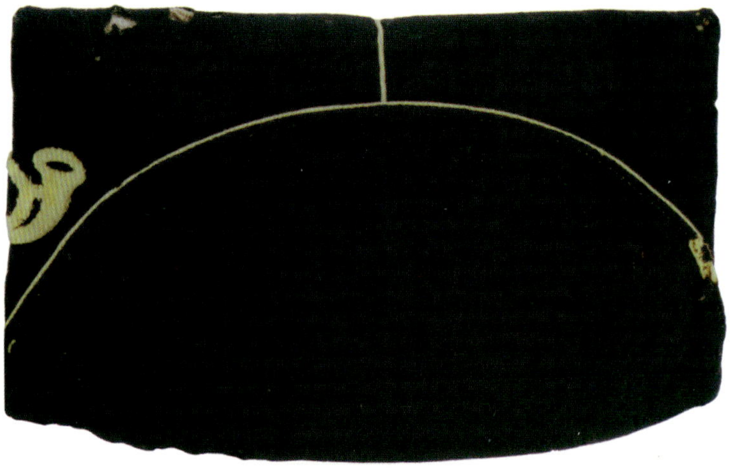

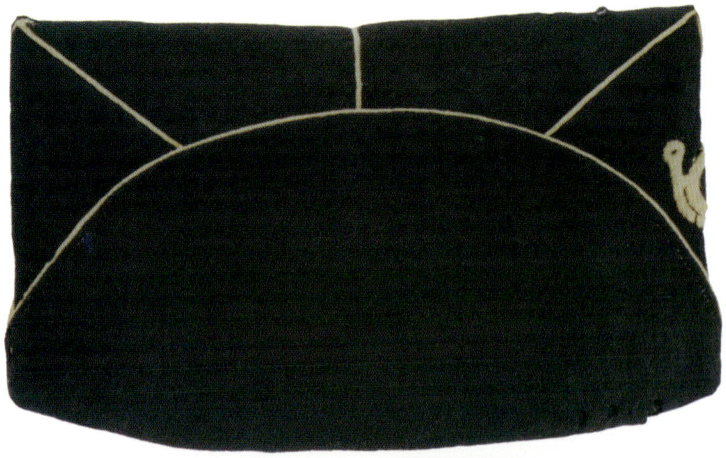

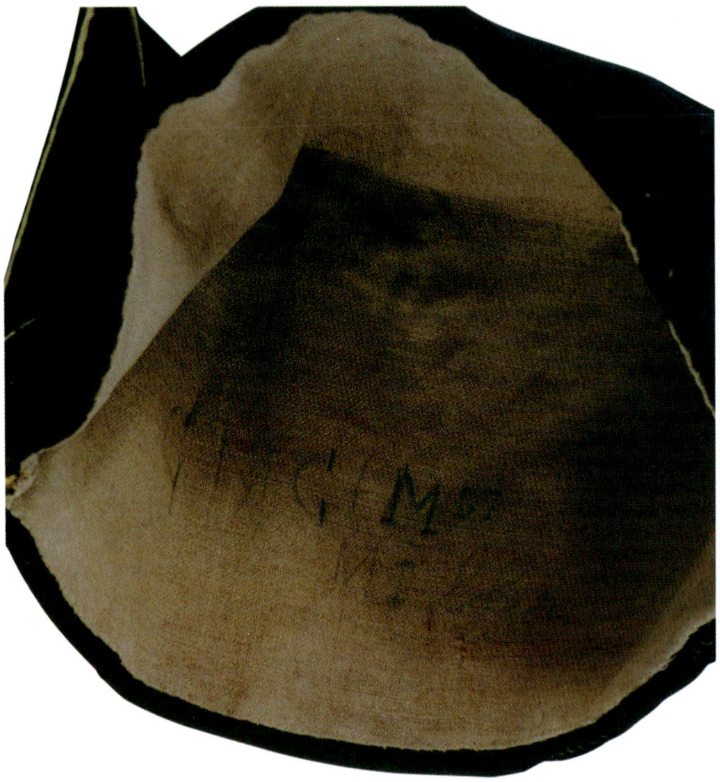

The shipment of French uniforms in 1861 included medium blue, wool fatigue caps, trimmed in light yellow piping. The front of the cap bore a yellow tassel and the same cloth bugle insignia as found on the tails of the dress coat. The caps were 5 5/8 inches tall, with the flaps rising to 4 1/2 inches, fastened to the sides by hooks and eyes. It had a simple cloth lining, without sweatband. This example was worn by Pvt. George J. Killmer (see p 127). BCHS

Bvt. Capt. Ballard Smith Humphrey of the 1st U.S. Light Artillery, posed with his Light Artillery Shako in this 1865 photograph (above). The view of an unknown officer of a 4th Light Artillery regiment (right) clearly shows the use of embroidered insignia on the cap. USAMHI, CPL

The 1864 Light Artillery Shako was an elegant piece of military headwear that recalled the army of antebellum America. It was made by Philadelphia hatter William C. Dare. An additional contract was given to Philadelphia's Horstmann Brothers in 1867. RB, CPL

The most striking ornament on the Light Artillery Shako was the 15-inch-long scarlet horse hair plume. It was secured to an eight-inch-long whalebone shaft that passed through the top of cap. CPL

One of the more famous embellishments worn on a soldier's cap was a deer's tail. First adopted by the 42nd Pa. Vols. as a sign of their marksmanship, the "bucktail" gave the unit its nickname and was later worn by two additional regiments from the Keystone State, the 149th and 150th. On the left Sgt. John Steele, Co. A, 42nd Pa. Vols. proudly wears his bucktail in what appears to be a chasseur cap. CPL The inscription on the reverse of the bucktail on the right indicates it was "Captured from the Penn. Bucktails by Stonewall Jackson's men 1863" and was found with the effects of Capt. Francis Key Shaaf of the 15th Alabama Vols., CSA. PHMC

The bucktail adorning the cap of this soldier of the 149th Pa. Vols. is remarkable for its size. RP

C
63

63

128

F
15

William. H. Hosford.
Co F. 15 N.Y. Cavalry

5
K
129

5
K

Opposite: Soldiers customized and personalized their headgear in endless ways, as these forage caps illustrate. (Top left, right) A now unknown member of the 63rd Pa. Vols. gave this cap worn at the battle of Gettysburg to a young boy there at a reunion in the early 20th Century. The crown has a brass company letter affixed over an early III Corps badge (truly a "red patch" as first ordered for that organization), along with 5/8" brass regimental numbers. He also sewed a cord of thread from the crown to the base of the cap so that the top would always sit at a "jaunty" angle and proudly display his unit identification. CPL (Second left, right) Pvt. Jacob Muschbach, Co. F, 128th Pa. Vols. added a brass ventilator to the insignia on his cap to get some relief from the heat. Underneath the sweatband he kept a needle and thread at the ready. CPL (Third left, right) Pvt. William H. Hosford, Co. F, 15th N.Y. Cav. carved his name and unit deeply into the underside of the visor. DT (Bottom left, right) An unknown member of Co. K, 129th Pa. Vols. carefully carved the "eagle" portion out of a pewter button from one of the uniforms the North purchased from France, and placed it in the center of his V Corps badge, along with a small stippled brass "5" for good measure. JF

Above: The State of New Hampshire issued its rank and file a commercial grade forage cap of moderate height, ornamented with a specially produced set of distinctive silver insignia that included "N.H.V." in 5/8" letters for "New Hampshire Volunteers." (Top left, right) The cap of Corp. John C. Blake, Co. A, 15th N.H. Vols. has the full array of state insignia including a "simulated embroidery" infantry horn with silver finish. They are secured to the crown by brass wires bent over the quilted lining inside. CPL (Bottom left) This 14th N.H. Vols. cap has utilized the standard brass infantry bugle. DT (Bottom right) This cap of the 9th N.H. Vols. has only the letters of silver. The bugle and regimental number are of the common brass variety. JCG.

In varying arrangements, the insignia on their caps proclaim that these are men from New Hampshire. (Above left) This private from the 13th N.H. Vols. has his forage cap fully trimmed. (Above right) Pvt. George Drew, Co. A, 1st N.H. Vol. Heavy Artillery uses letters and numbers of varied sizes on his cap. (Left) Battle-ready Corp. William A. Rand, Co. K, 16th N.H. Vols. has only the state's silver letters on his cap. CPL

Two men from New York, an officer of the 137th and a private of the 146th, have each used a wreath around their regimental numbers.

The insignia on the cap of Colonel Robert Nugent, commander of the famed Irish 69th N.Y. Vols., was the regimental number within a wreath of shamrocks. CPL

Special insignia for a new branch of service, the Signal Corps, was first called for in August, 1864. As seen on this rather low crown commercial forage cap (left), it was a pair of crossed signal flags with an arc of 13 stars above and "U.S." in Old English letters below. PR The officer's cap patch shown at right follows the style of the period, with the emblem embroidered on black velvet. CPL

In August, 1862, privates and non commissioned officers serving with the ambulance corps in the Army of the Potomac were authorized to wear a cap with a broad green band around the cap. Such a band has been added to this forage cap by Murphy and Griswold of New York City. DT

This attractive chasseur cap with State of New York side buttons bears the insignia mandated for officers of the Corps of Engineers, "a gold embroidered wreath of laurel and palm, encircling a silver turreted castle." GL

This volunteer has the enlisted version of the Corps of Engineers insignia, a castle of stamped brass, on his hat. CPL

A Sargeant of the Ordnance Department stands beside his cap which is ornamented by the regulation "shell and flame" in brass, for enlisted men. CPL

This V Corps badge was worn on the cap of young drummer George D. Massey, Co. K, 31st Pa. Vols. It is handmade of blue wool over a thin pasteboard backing with a spun wire border and has a 5/8" brass scroll style "K" affixed to the center. CPL

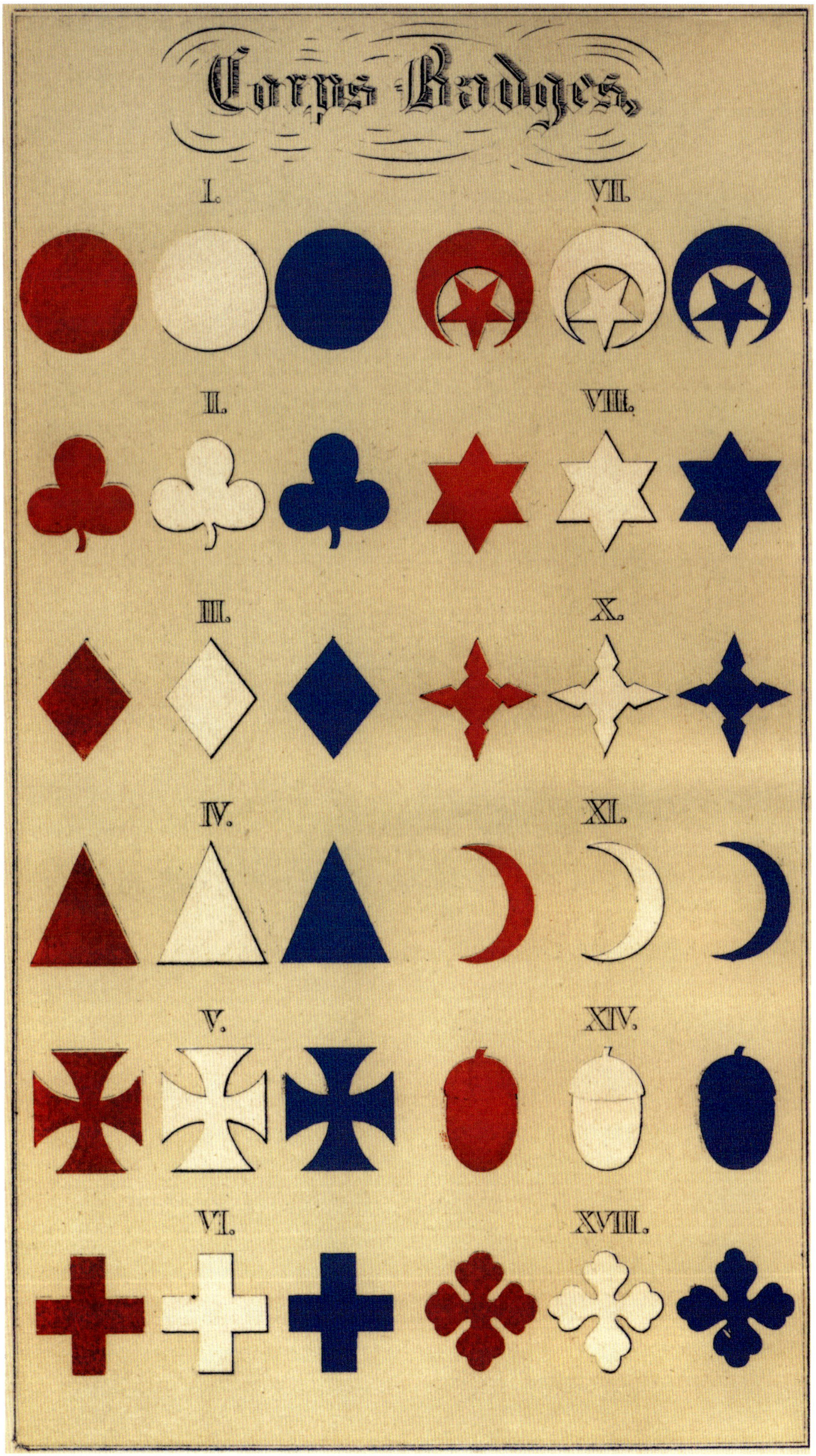

When first introduced in early 1863, corps badges were intended to be worn on the caps and hats of the troops of the Army of the Potomac. The practice soon spread to almost every Union Army corps by the end of the war.

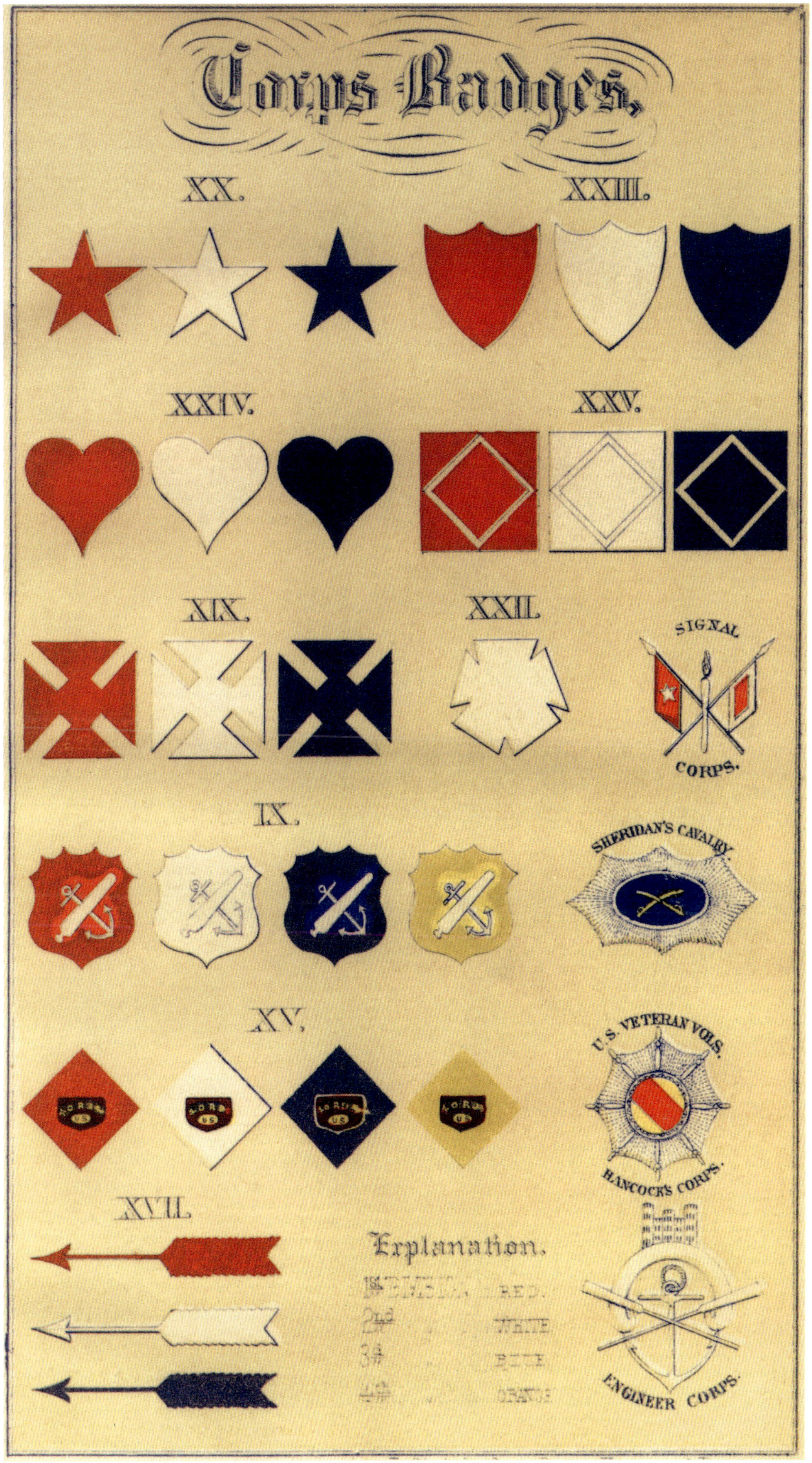

These pages, from Samuel Bates' *History of Pennsylvania Volunteers*, show the great variety of designs adopted by 1865. Red marked the first division of a corps, white the second, blue the third, and green the fourth.

A soldier of the 56th Pa. Vols. wears his I Corps badge on the crown of his commercially made forage cap, with the number of the regiment in the center (left). Young Pvt. Albert F. Brock of the 11th Mass. Battery proudly displays his cap to the camera with a IX Corps badge beneath his brass insignia (right). Pvt. John Clancy, Co. C., 29th Pa. Vols. (below) has placed his XX Corps badge on the side of his cap and pinned a silver version to his vest as well. Note, also, the small letters and figures of stippled brass on the crown of the cap, typical of many Pennsylvania troops in the latter years of the war. CPL

Stamped brass, painted corps badges with ribbing to approximate embroidery were quite popular. These comercially produced examples are for: Head-quarters, II Corps; Third Division, XIX Corps; and First Division, VI Corps. It is believed they were made by the Philadelphia firm of H. G. Clagston. Examples for the I, III, V, and XII Corps are also known. CPL

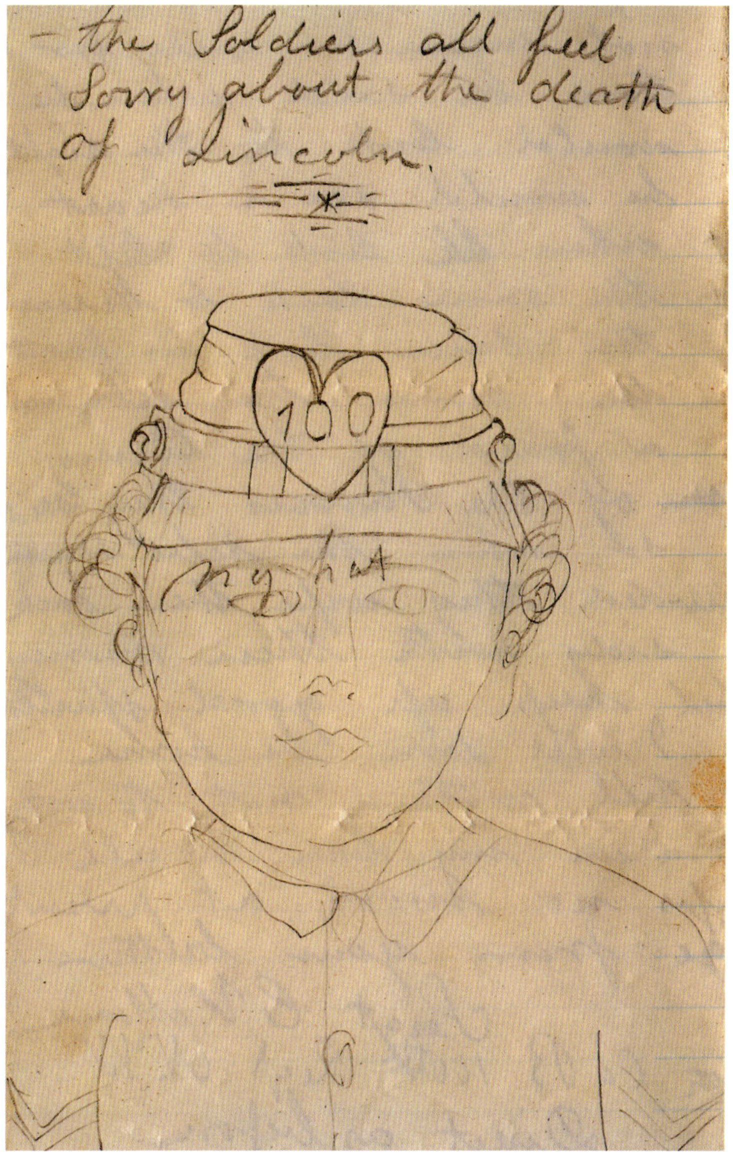

(Above) A sketch in a late April, 1865, letter from Sgt. Cornelius V. Moore, Co. B, 100th N.Y. Vols. suggests he wore his heart-shaped XXIV Corps badge on the front of his chasseur cap on which was affixed his regimental number. With the war essentially over, Moore proudly wrote his brother from outside Petersburg, Va., that "there was a rebel ask me what corp I belong to and I told him the 24th and he said hearts was trumps…" JHK

Pvt. James Malone, Co. C, 95th Pa. Vols. poses in the uniform of Gosline's Zouaves with a VI Corps badge placed above other insignia on his cap (Above left). A God-fearing 1st Lt. Matthias Lambson, Co. E, 3rd N.J. Vols. (left) has chosen to use a Christian cross on his slouch hat to represent the same corps. He also inserted a "6" in the center of the cross probably to underline its dual meaning. Similar devices were sometimes used by chaplains and, well after the war, by certain fraternal organizations. CPL

Pvt. George W. Parker, Co. F, 57th Pa. Vols. obtained a high quality black felt hat, complete with officer's hat cords, on which he has placed a large III Corps badge that appears to have a metal frame. Parker was wounded in action at Gettysburg on July 2, 1863. CPL

Right column: The chasseur cap of Col. George C. Burling, 6th N.J. Vols., bears a III Corps badge with a testimonial to his unit's old division commander, Gen. Joseph Hooker, embroidered in the center. The unit was a proud member of Hooker's division from October, 1861, to March, 1862, and then part of the III Corps until March, 1864. The cap was made by Charles Oakford and Son, Philadelphia. GNMB

(Top left, right) Major Elliot C. Pierce of the 13th Mass. Vols. served at his corps' headquarters and pinned a red/white/blue silk and gold embroidery I Corps Headquarters badge to his chasseur cap. The cap was made by Shute and Son, Boston. DT (Center left) Second Lt. James P. Newkirk, Co. C, 10th N.J. Vols wore a cap bearing a VI Corps badge. Inside the cap is the maker's marking "J.W. Currier/Dealer in Officer's/Clothing and Equipments/City Point Va." SCHS (Center right) This dashing forage cap was made by McCormick and Brothers of Baltimore. It was worn by Maj. Samuel S. Linton of the 39th Ill. Vols. who affixed a hand-cut X Corps badge to the crown. CPL (Bottom left) Capt. James A. Cook, Quartermaster of the 2nd N.H. Vols., wore this cap by Warnock and Co. with a III Corps badge pined to the crown. JHK (Bottom right) A well made, embroidered IX Corps badge is on the top of this staff officer's cap, its black decorative trimming faded to brown. DT

Broadcloth for making corps badges was forwarded to army quartermasters along with mallets and metal dies for stamping them out. This forage cap worn by a soldier from the 188th Pa. Vols. has two examples of these thin, die-cut emblems affixed to the top: a blue heart for the Third Division, XXIV Corps, and a red cross for the XVIII Corps. The regiment, formed from the 3rd Pa. Heavy Artillery in April, 1864, served in both corps and the original owner probably wanted to keep both badges as testimony to his service. The brass "3" was inserted in the XXIV Corps badge to further denote the division. CPL

Here are a two examples of the diverse use of corps emblems on forage caps. (Left) Pvt. Daniel P. Doyle of the 9th Battery, Mass. Light Artillery, had his V Corps Artillery Brigade badge painted above his brass insignia. DT (Right) This cap of Co. 1, 40th Mass. Vols. has a Third Division, XXIV Corps badge on top with a brass "Y" added to further indicate the division. DT **Opposite:** Additional examples of the corps badge (Top, left) Sgt. John C. Dittler, Co. K, 51st Pa. Vols., had a simple, thick felt IX Corps badge on his cap. CPL (Top, right) Likewise, Gettysburg native Corp. Joseph H. Baker, Co. K, 30th Pa. Vols., used a blue wool, handmade V Corps badge, cut perhaps from a piece of trowser material. CPL (Center, left) Pvt. John A. Wiedersheim, Co. F, 119th Pa. Vols. applied a cloth VI Corps badge with gold tape edging. DT (Center, right). A large, hand cut VI Corps badge was sewn to the cap of Pvt. Levi Hines, Co. G, 10th Vt. Vols. DT (Bottom, left). Pvt. William Button, Co. K, 5th N.J. Vols. was mortally wounded in action at Gettysburg. His cap had a III Corps device and company letter in the center. WM (Bottom, Right) has an XI Corps badge is sewn to the side of this forage cap. JO

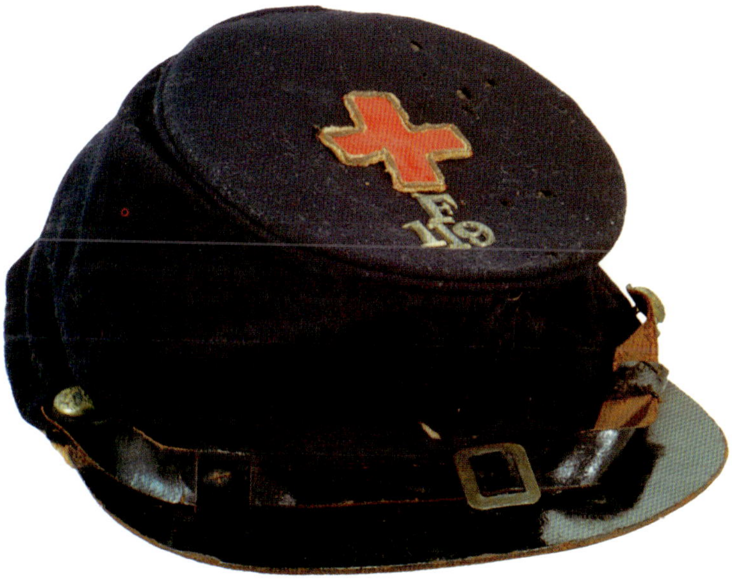

The faded chasseur cap of Pvt. George Wilde Linn, Co B, 107th Pa. Vols., shows the effect of a minie ball which passed through it at Petersburg, Va., in 1865. Linn kept the cap as a souvenir of a close call and wore it with pride a short time later when the Army of Northern Virginia surrendered at Appomattox Court House. PHMC

Light artillery units retained the ungainly cap with horsehair plume and scarlet cords after the Civil War, as seen in this parade ground view of members of the Third U. S. Artillery at the Presidio of San Francisco, around 1866. GGNRA

Officers in the immediate post Civil War era, such as this group at Ft. Bridger, Wyoming Territory, during the winter of 1866-67, continued to procure a variety of caps and insignia. In this case one wears a commercial forage cap and the other three chasseur caps. Note the diminutive infantry device on the officer seated at the center of the group. GS

Fig. 5. The cloth detached from the cap, showing its attachment by button holes and tapes.

The report on the "uniform and clothing" of the U.S. Army submitted in January, 1868, by Asst. Surgeon Alfred A. Woodhull, suggested the adoption of a removable neck piece "of wadded cloth" for warmth, an expedient being used in cold weather by some U.S. troops on the plains and much like the neck flap that had formed part of the 1839-pattern enlisted cap. NA

According to the 1868 Woodhull Report, some types of foreign headgear seemed desirable for adoption by the U.S. Army, such as a "Stiff Dress Hat," after the French and English shakos (Above left), a "Cloth Fatigue Cap" (Above right), and a "Scotch Cap with Visor" (right). NA

"Ventilated or Eastern Hats" such as those adopted by the British in India "after the style of the Malay hat," were possibilities discussed in the Woodhull Report. NA

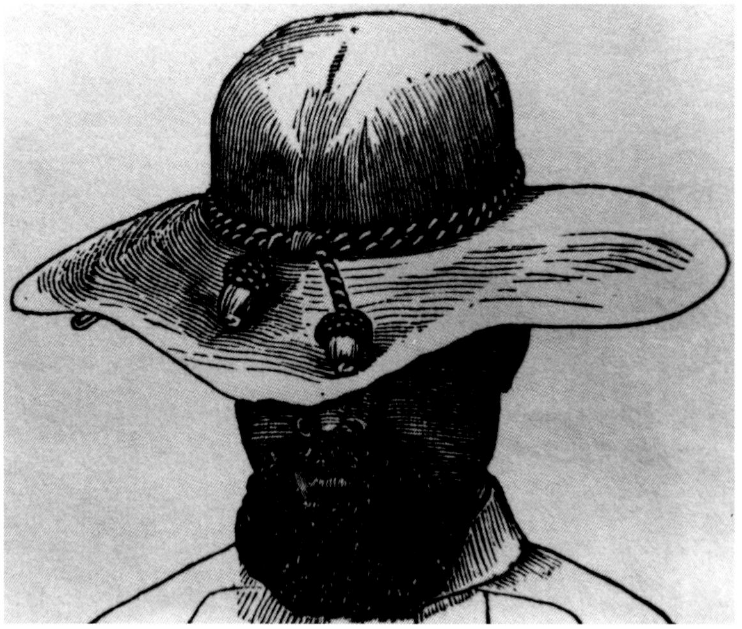

Another item reviewed in the 1868 Surgeon General's study was a broad brimmed folding hat based on the short-lived version designed by Col. T. P. Andrews and used in Texas in 1853. The report deemed it "probably the most serviceable hat ever used by the United States Army..." NA

Opposite: Pillbox caps, similar to those first seen in the British and Canadian armies in the 1850s, began to appear on the heads of some Union officers in the last days of the conflict. They were privately purchased and, although they continued to be seen sporadically in the decades after the war, were never called for in regulations. This one is worn by 1st Lt. William E. Gibson, Co. B, 4th U.S. Colored Troops. Gibson became a 1st Lt. in this unit on March 29, 1865, and was mustered out on May 4, 1866. USAMHI

Notes:

1 The *zouave* style that had been so popular on the eve of the war was one such holdover from the days of antebellum pomp. In the 1830s, North African-based troops were first drawn from Berber warriors known as *Zouava*. They donned the distinctive *Tirailleurs Algerian* (Turcos) garb associated with the region where they served. Soon, "the French Zouave regiments captured the romantic fancy of the world much as the Foreign Legion of today...." Michael J. McAfee, "What Is A Zouave," I *Military Images* No. 2 (September-October 1979): 14.

2 Just to offer a few examples of this early-war diversity: The First Minnesota marched off in shirts "of the kind then affected by steamboat men" and frontiersmen "very fancifully ornamented with crescents, stars, trefoils, etc." A wealthy German-born patron of the 41st New York saw to it that the entire regiment was supplied with green and gray uniforms, trimmed in red, modeled after the Prussian Army. The Colonel of the Second Massachusetts had a hard time convincing others that the unit's uniform should be blue, not gray. He was finally successful. Almost every company of the Sixth Massachusetts wore a different uniform as the unit was an amalgamation of independent militia companies. At the insistence of Gen. Benjamin Butler, Massachusetts Governor Andrew finally provided the entire unit with gray overcoats to give it some semblance of uniformity.

3 James Swales, 10th Illinois Vol. Inf., to David Swales, August 29, 1861, James M. Swales Papers, Illinois State Historical Library. The authors are greatly indebted to Brian White of Cincinnati, Ohio, and Greg Schuler of Peoria, Ill., for bringing the Loomis connection and related documents to their attention.

4 Carrington, George D., Company B, 11th Illinois Infantry, manuscript diary, 21-22, Chicago Historical Society,

5 The Whipple model omitted the buttons on the crown for looping up the brim.

6 In fact, no definitive earlier work exists covering Union headgear, but a number of sources are available which provide ample indication of the numerous styles employed. In addition to titles cited elsewhere in this study readers should find the following works of interest: John Elting, ed., *Military Uniforms in America, Volume III Long Endure: The Civil War Period 1852-1867* (Navato, CA: Presidio Press, 1982); Frederick P. Todd, *American Military Equipage, 1851-1872 Volume II State Forces* (New York: Chatham Square Press, 1983); Robin Smith, *Brassey's History of Uniforms American Civil War Union Army* (London: Brassey's Ltd., 1996); and Henry Woodhead, ed., *Echoes of Glory: Arms and Equipment of the Union* (Alexandria, VA: Time-Life Books, 1991).

7 For a brief overview of the havelock read, Don Dillion, "The Havelock," III *Military Images* No. 4 (January-February 1984): 14-15.

8 Ibid.

9, 10 Livermore, Mary, *My Story of the War* (Hartford, CT.: A. D. Worthington & Co., 1888), 112-3.

11 Collis, Septima M., *A Woman's War Record*, 1861-1865 (New York and London: G. P. Putnam's Sons, 1889), 13.

12 Boston Post, July 24, 1861, 2

13. U.S. Sanitary Commission, *Report of a portion of the Volunteer Forces near Washington, No 17, July 9, 1861* (Washington, DC: U.S Sanitary Commission, 1861), 3.

14 Livermore, *My Story, 112-3.*

15 General Orders Circular No. 4 (War Department, Richmond, January 24, 1862).

16 Smith, John Day, *The History of the Nineteenth Regiment of Maine Volunteer Infantry* (Minneapolis, MN: Great Western Printing Co., 1909), 3.

17 *Report on a portion of the Volunteer Forces Near Washington*, 7.

18 Wiley, Bell Irvin, *The Life of Billy Yank* (Baton Rouge: Louisiana State University Press, 1952), 59.

19 Mann, Albert, *History of the Forty-Fifth Regiment Massachusetts Volunteers* (Jamaica Plains, Mass.: Brookside Press, 1908), 366.

20 Davis, Charles, *Three Years in the Army. The Story of the Thirteenth Massachusetts Volunteers* (Boston: Estes and Lauriat, 1894), 9.

21 Hays, Gilbert Adams, *Under the Red Patch. The Story of the Sixty Third Regiment Pennsylvania Volunteers 1861-1864* (Pittsburg: Sixty-third Pennsylvania Volunteers Regimental Association, 1908), 30.

22 Sneden, Robert Knox, *Eye of the Storm* (New York: The Free Press, 2000), 7 (Charles F Bryan Jr and Nelson D Lankford ed)

23 Davis, *Three Years*, 14.

24 Boyle, John Richards, *Soldiers True. The Story of the One Hundred and Eleventh Pennsylvania Veteran Volunteers, and of Its Campaigns in the War for the Union* (New York: Eaton and Mains, 1903), 25.

25 Wert, Jeffrey D, *A Brotherhood of Valor* (New York: Simon and Schuster, 1999), 101.

26 Stevens, Charles A, *Berdan's United States Sharpshooters in the Army of the Potomac 1861-1865* (Dayton, Ohio: Morningside Bookshop, 1984), 277-278.

27 Archambault, Alan H., "The First Regiment Rhode Island Detached Militia," LIII *Military Collector and Historian*, No. 3 (Fall 2001), 104.

28 *United States Army and Navy Journal*, November 14, 1863, 180. Hereafter referred to as *A&NJ*, date, and page.

29 Ibid., September 12, 1863, 26.

30 Billings, John D., *Hard Tack and Coffee* (Williamstown, Mass.: Corner House Publishers, 1984), 277.

31 Goss, Warren Lee, "Going to the Front," *The Century War Book* (New York: Arno Press, 1978), 20. Goss served in the 2nd Mass. Heavy Artillery.

32 Boston Evening Journal, September 14, 1861, 4

33 *Report of a Portion of the Volunteer Forces near Washington*, 6-7.

34 Howell, Edgar M., *United States Army Headgear 1855-1902* (Washington D.C.: The Smithsonian Institution, 1975) 15.

35 Frederick C. Gaede, "A Model of 1858 Federal Forage Cap," LI *Military Collector and Historian* No. 2 (Summer, 1999), 66-67.

36 Coates, Earl J. and James L. Kochan, *Don Troiani's Soldiers in America*, (Mechanicsburg, Pa.: Stackpole, 1998), 136.

37 The National Tribune, Nov. 12, 1891.

38 Braun, Robert, "Evidence of McDowell-pattern Forage Caps in the Western Army, 1863," *The Watchdog* (Winter, 2000): 12. The Mitchell letters are in the collection of Jan Mitchell, Northfield, Minn. Copies are in the Milwaukee County Historical Society.

39 Smith, J.L., *History of the 118th Pennsylvania Volunteers* (Philadelphia: J. L. Smith, 1905), 11.

40 Donald, David Herbert, ed., *Gone for a Soldier. The Civil War Memoirs of Private Alfred Bellard* (Boston: Little, Brown and Company, 1975), 262. Bellard began his army career in the Fifth New Jersey Volunteers, was wounded in the leg at Chancellorsville, and transferred into the Veteran Reserve Corps afterward.

41 The Chicago Tribune, May 1, 1861, 4.

42 Howell, Edgar, *Headgear 1855-1902*, 20.

43 More information on this regiment of Ohio cavalry can be found in Don Troiani's *Regiments and Uniforms of the Civil War* (Mechanicsburg, Pa.: Stackpole Books, 2002).

44 Rogers, Larry and Keith Rogers, *Their Horses Climbed Trees* (Atglen, Pa.: Schiffer, 2000), 171. This was one of the companies of the "California Battalion" of volunteers that served with the 2nd. Mass. Vol. Cav. The men brought with them a sizeable company fund which also enabled them to procure boots, overalls and was "used in every way for the men's comfort."

45 Romano, Victor, *Long Marches, Short Rations, the Letters of Pvt. Samuel Tomlinson*. Forthcoming.

46 Campbell, Eric, ed., *A Grand and Terrible Drama, From Gettysburg to Petersburg: The Civil War Letters of Charles Wellington Reed* (New York: Fordham University Press, 2000), 178-179.

47 Boston Evening Journal, September 14, 1861, 4.

48 Moore, Jonathan, Special Orders No. 58, December 15, 1863. Colonel Moore's Special Order was found in an online article "Hats OFF! To the Thirty-third!" By Robert A. Braun, an especially interesting study of the headgear worn by that unit.

49 Curtis, Newton Martin, *From Bull Run to Chancellorsville: The Story of the 16th New York Infantry* (New York: G. P. Putnam and Sons, 1906), 114-115.

50 The regulations also stated that officers "of the General Staff and Staff Corps" had the option to wear a "light French chapeau" like the fore-and-aft hats of previous decades. Few ever seem to have done so and, then, probably only for dress occasions.

51 There were a number of *exceptions* made to the uniforming of Federal troops, which probably drove the Deputy Quarter Master General at the Philadelphia Clothing Depot, Lt. Col. George Crosman, crazy. The influential DeWitt Clinton Baxter got the government to take over the clothing of his unit (the 72nd Pennsylvania) with their zouave uniforms when they began to wear out. Another respected Philadelphian, Peter Lyle, convinced the government to supply his regiment (90th Pennsylvania) with its own distinctive button.

52 Bazelon, Bruce and William F. McGuinn, *A Directory of Military Goods Dealers and makers 1785-1915* (Manassas: Bazelon and McGuinn, 1990), 1. Alfred W. Adolph and Eli Keen in Philadelphia had numerous contracts for hats and caps, including 2,500 "fez hats" in August and October, 1863. Jonathan F. Whipple of New York City had contracts for 3,500 that same year.

53 Porter, John T., et. al. *Under the Maltese Cross* (Pittsburg: The 155th Regimental Association, 1910), 224-226.

54 Russell, William Howard, *My Diary North and South* (Boston: T.O.H.P. Burnham, 1863), 416.

55 Billings, *Hard Tack and Coffee*,277.

56 Troiani, Don, "French Uniforms, Cloth and Equippage in the Union Army" XXVI *North-South Trader's Civil War* No.2 (1999), 38-50.

57 A photograph of the 10th Veteran Reserve Corps Band, taken in April, 1865, appears on page 87 of *A Pictorial History of Civil War Musical Instruments and Military Bands* by Robert Garafalo and Mark Elrod (Charleston: Pictorial Histories Publishing Co., 1985). The bandsmen wear the shako with a pompon and the red/white/blue rosette, but without any brass frontplate. They also wear alterations of the coat issued with the French uniform. In author Loane's collection is a shako with rosette, plate, and falling white and blue feather plume believed to have been worn by a musician in the 3rd Maine Vols.

58 Todd, *American Military Equipage*, II, 377.

59 Howell, *Headgear 1855-1902*, 23 and 25.

60 Ibid., 24-5.

61 Other boards of the period assembled from time to time to investigate such things as "the merits of certain military hats," as was called for by Special Orders (SO) No. 308, AGO, November 18, 1862; SO No. 31, AGO, February 11, 1862, for the purpose of reviewing Lieutenant Colonel W. King's "Cavalry Raiding Equipment;" SO No. 22, AGO, January 22, 1865, to study Woods' infantry equipment; and SO No. 62, AGO, February 8, 1865, regarding the matter of Weston's shoulder brace equipment. The fact that these bodies periodically were summoned bespoke of a willingness to look to new solutions for uniforms and equipment.

62 M.C. Meigs to E.M. Stanton, January 22, 1862, Consolidated Correspondence Files, Box 1170, Office of the Quartermaster General, Record Group 92, NA, hereinafter referred to as CCF, OQMG, RG92, NA.

63 Gavin, William Gilfillan, *Campaigning with the Roundheads*, (Dayton: Morningside Bookshop, 1989), 71.

64 A nice example of an attempt to regulate the placement of cap insignia on a brigade level can be found on page 37 of Stanley S. Phillips 1982 publication *Civil War Corps Badges and Other Related Awards, Badges, Medals of the Period, Including A Section on Post Civil War and Spanish American War Corps Badges.*

65 Smith, J.L., *History of the 118th Pennsylvania Volunteers*, 90-91.

66 GO No. 102, WD, November 25, 1861. For examples of several variation of uniforms worn by Union chaplains see, Michael J. Winey, "Clergy in Uniform," IV *Military Images* No. 6 (May-June 1983): 8-12.

67 GO No. 147, Head-quarters, Army of the Potomac, August 2, 1862, Camp Near Harrison's Landing.

68 GO 85, XVIII Army Corps, December 30, 1862.

69 Todd, *American Military Equipage*, 398.

70 Ibid., 411. Also see, Philip Katcher, "'They were well thought of...' The Veteran Reserve Corps, 1863-1866," VI *Military Images* No. 1 (July-August 1984): 20-4.

71 GO No. 124, WD, May 15, 1863.

72 Todd, *American Military Equipage*, 412.

73 It is interesting to note that the one exception to the Signal Corps' preeminence in communications was the telegraph, a separate Military Telegraph Service being established in November 1861 to operate this means of transmitting information. Because the service was "in the main civilian" no uniform was prescribed, although GO No. 14, Army of the Tennessee, July 5, 1864, allowed an undress uniform for operators in the Department of Tennessee. Todd, *American Military Equipage*, 402.

74 Circular, Army of the Potomac, March 21, 1863. This document directed that a crescent would represent the XI Corps, with the first division having red, the second division white, and the third division blue versions, according to a plan that paralleled other corps. The XI Corps' badge was to be affixed to the top of the forage cap, and inspectors were to ensure that the devices were "worn as directed." Moreover, when the "badges were lost or torn off" they were to be replaced immediately. Additionally, provost-marshalls were to "arrest as stragglers all other troops found without badges, and return them to their commands under guard." This same approach was taken by the Department of the Cumberland, GO No. 62, April 26, 1864.

75 D. Townsend, *Anecdotes of the Civil War in the United States* (New York: D. Appleton and Company, 1884), 168-9, and John D. Billings, *Hardtack and Coffee* (Boston: George M. Smith Co., 1888), 256.

76 Todd, *American Military Equipage*, 93-4. For additional information on corps badges consult, Wendell W. Lang, Jr., "Corps Badges of the Civil War," Pt. 1, VI *Military Images* No. 6 (May-June 1986): 16-25; Pt. 2, VIII ibid. No. 1 (July-August 1986): 8-15; Pt. 3, VIII ibid. No. 3 (November-December 1986): 16-26; Pt. 4, IX ibid. No. 3 (November-December 1987): 6-15; Marius B. Peladeau and Roger S. Cohen, Jr., "Corps Badges of the Civil War," XXIII *Military Collector and Historian* No. 4 (Winter 1971): 103-12; John M. Wike, "The Wearing of Corps and Division Insignia of the Union Army, 1861-1865," IV *Military Collector and Historian* No. 2 (June 1952): 35-8; and Stanley S. Phillips, *Civil War Corps Badges and Other Related Awards, Badges, Medals of the Period: Including A Section on Post Civil War and Spanish American War Corps Badges* (Lanham, MD: S.S. Phillips, 1982).

77 Phillips, Stanley S, *Civil War Corps Badges and Other Related Awards, Badges, Medals of the Period, Including A Section on Post Civil War and Spanish American War Corps Badges* (Lanham, Md: S.S. Phillips, 1982), 2-4.

78 Smith, J.L., *History of the 118th Pennsylvania Volunteers*, 663.

79 Todd, *American Military Equippage*.

80 M.C. Meigs to General of the Army, June 9, 1869, LS, C&E Br., Vol. 31, OQMG, RG92, NA.

81 For a treatment of this important publication and its extraordinary founding editor see, David Nevis Biegloe, *William Conant Church and the Army Navy Journal* (New York: Columbia University Press, 1952). Gordon Chappell, *Search For The Well-Dressed Soldier 1865-1890* (Tucson: Arizona Historical Society, 1972), 1-25, should be read for additional insight into the continued debate about uniforms and equipment in the immediate post Civil War era. Likewise see, Douglas McChristian, *The U.S. Army in the West, 1870-1880: Uniforms, Weapons, and Equipment* (Norman: University of Oklahoma Press, 1995), 9-77. Also of importance is Donald E. Kloster, "Uniforms of the Army Prior and Subsequent to 1872, Part 1," XIV *Military Collector and Historian* No. 4 (Winter 1962): 103-12; and "Uniforms of the Army Prior and Subsequent to 1872, Part 2" XV *Military Collector and Historian* No. 1 (Spring 1963): 6-14.

82 Ibid., January 19, 1867, 345.

83 Ibid., September 9, 1865, 39; February 1, 1868, 377; January 9, 1869, 326; and T.H Neill to E.D. Townsend, July 27, 1868, LR, A723, Box 1279, File 9, AGO, RG94, NA, who also advocated a change in regulations that would allow all "General Officers whether by Brevet or otherwise," as well as Officers of the General Staff and Staff Corps" to wear a light French chapeau.

84 *A&NJ*, September 23, 1865, 71.

85 Ibid.

86 Ibid., December 23, 1865, 282; and March 28, 1868, 506, respectively.

87 Ibid., 25.

88 *A&NJ*, September 28, 1867, 90; March 7, 1868, 458; and March 28, 1868, 506.

89 Ibid., February 1, 1867, 377.

90 Ibid., August 31, 1872, 42.

91 Ibid., September 7, 1872, 55.

92 J. Schindel to Adjutant General, March 7, 1872, LR, AGO, RG94, NA.

93 Circular No. 2, Department of the Platte, December 20, 1869, Circulars and Orders, Fort Fetterman, Wyoming Territory Records, Microfilm Copy, Wyoming State Museum, Cheyenne.

94 *A&NJ*, March 2, 1872, 54.

95 Chappell, *Search For the Well Dressed Soldier*, n51, 45.

96 *Revised Regulations* 1863, paragraph 1521, set forth this requirement as pointed out in A.J. Perry to G.V. Henry, December 31, 1867, Vol. 30, LS, C&E Br., OQMG, RG92, NA.

97 GO No. 35, August 1, 1870, Headquarters Fort Fred Steele, W.T., General Orders, 1870, Fort Fred Steele, Records of U.S. Army Commands, RG393, NA.

98 A.J. Perry to J.F. Calef, Vol. 30, LS, C&E Br., OQMG, RG92, NA.

99 J.C. McPherson to E.A. Bancroft, October 15, 1867, ibid; and A.J. Perry to H. Brooks, October 29, 1867, ibid.

100 A.J. Perry to R.S Stranger, November 10, 1868, Vol. 31, ibid; J.J. Dana to A.R. Eddy, June 22, 1869, ibid; and M.C. Meigs to G. Sykes, August 5, 1870, Vol. 32, ibid. The last letter noted approximately 500 light artillery caps remained in stock, and these had to be kept for the mounted batteries. This careful attention to restricting the artillery cap also can be seen in a request for sizes of the men in Battery I, First Artillery and Battery F, Fifth Artillery stationed at Fort Riley, Kansas and Washington, DC respectively, to provide a list of sizes for the gunners in case new ones had to be made. A.J. Perry to S. Van Vliet, January 5, 1870, ibid.

101 A.J. Perry to G.H. Crosman, April 12, 1867, Vol. 29; A.J. Perry to E. Schriver, February 9, 1869, Vol, 31: J.D. Bingham to T. McCrea, May 19, 1870, Vol. 32; and J.D. Bingham to E. Schriver, May 26, 1870, Vol. 31, ibid. The uniform adopted consisted of a white coatee with collar, cuffs, lace on the chest, breast cords, and worsted shoulder knots, all of scarlet. Double scarlet leg stripes along with Austrian knots accented the white trousers. The drum major had a scarlet coat trimmed with white, a bearskin, a baldric, and gold epaulets. Frederick P. Todd, *Cadet Gray* (New York: Sterling Publishing Co., Inc., 1955), 32.

102 Thomas C. Railsback and John P. Langellier, *The Drums Would Roll: A Pictorial History of US Army Bands on the American Frontier 1866-1890* (London: Arms and Armour Press, 1987), 15-6.

103 A.J. Perry to B.C. Card, November 30, 1867, Vol. 31, LS, C&E Br., RG92, NA; and A.J. Perry to J.L. Donaldson, January 19, 1869, ibid. Card was serving with the quartermaster department at Fort Leavenworth, Kansas, the forward depot for supplying the remote posts on the Upper Missouri River, while Donaldson was with the St. Louis Depot which had been responsible for considerable supply in the West during the Civil War. Also see two letters from, A.J. Perry to D.H. Rucker, both dated January 7, 1870, Vol. 30, ibid., indicating no woolen mittens were in stock nor were these items of issue. However, twelve buffalo overcoats were authorized in this correspondence for Fort Snelling, not to be charged to the enlisted men, and Fort Sully was to receive 400 pairs of overshoes that were to be sold to the troops. A third letter on this date from Perry to Rucker permitted twenty buffalo coats for Fort Totten, Dakota Territory, at no charge to the men, but disallowed a request from that post for 300 pairs of buffalo mittens.

104 Alfred A. Woodhull, *A Medical Report upon the Uniform and Clothing of the Soldiers of the U.S. Army* (Washington, DC: Surgeon General's Office, 1868), 23, hereinafter referenced as the "Woodhull Report".

105 *A&NJ*, March 7, 1868, 485.

106 "Woodhull Report," 6-7. Ibid. 5-6, also noted the Scottish Glengarry cap as a good option for winter by being "pulled down over the ears and back of the neck...." Likewise, a bag cap (the precursor to the overseas or service cap) used by French and Austrian troops had "side flaps" that could be turned down against the cold, but unfortunately was "not suited for exposure to sun in hot climates." This drawback pointed out the difficulty of furnishing clothing that would meet the diverse needs of the American soldier.

107 Maria Brace Kimball, *A Soldier-Doctor of Our Army James P. Kimball* (New York: Houghton Mifflin Company, 1917), 46. Similarly Second Cavalry officers Edward Spaulding and Henry Noyes were described as being encased "in fur from head to foot," when stationed at Fort Reno, Dakota Territory in 1867. "Reminiscences of Elizabeth Burt," (Typescript, Fort Laramie National Historic Site, c. 1912).

108 "Woodhull Report," 5.

109 Ibid., 7.

110 Ibid., 7-9.

111 SO No. 523, HQ of the Army, December 18, 1867.

112 W.T. Sherman to Adjutant General, January 28, 1868, LR, AGO, RG94, NA; and U.S. Grant to Secretary of War, January 29, 1868, LS, HQ of the Army, RG108, NA.

113 W.T. Sherman, P.H. Sheridan, and C.C. Augur to E.D. Townsend, February 3, 1868, LR, A723, 1866, Box 1279, Pt. 8, AGO, RG94, NA.

114 A.J. Perry to P.H. Sheridan, February 10, 1868, Vol. 30; A.J. Perry to E.D. Townsend, January 18, 1868; and A.J. Perry to D.G. Thomas, February 5, 1868. LS, C&E Br., OQMG, RG92, NA.

115 Examples include, A.J. Perry to Stiehl and McBride, September 2, 1868, LS, C&E Br., Vol. 30, OQMG, RG92, NA; Perry to Shannon, Miller, and Crane, September 3, 1868, ibid.; and Perry to Horstmann, November 11, 1868, Vol. 31, ibid.

116 W.R. Cole to L. Thomas, June 6, 1868, LR, A 723, 1866, Box 1279, File 8, AGO, RG94, NA. The writer of the letter was the proprietor of Wm. R. Cole and Co., Fur Wool and Straw Hats, No. 30 Sharp Street, Baltimore, MD.

117 J. A. Hardie to Adjutant General, March 27, 1871, LR, 1871, AG0, RG94, NA. At the time Hardie was the inspector general for the Military Division of the Missouri.

118 W.T. Sherman to Adjutant General, March 28, 1871, ibid. A sketch of a cap with a visor and round top similar to that worn by U.S. Navy officers and civilian %3ng men, as well as railroad conductors and some police forces was included in this piece, and was not unlike the cap ultimately adopted in 1895 for the army at large.

[119] Ibid.

[120] Howell, *op. cit.*, 27. As further indication of the depletion of stocks, by early 1867 the New York supplies had been reduced to only eight tulips to hold plumes, twelve plumes, and twelve pairs of rings. A.J. Perry to G.H. Crosman, November 11, 1867, Vol. 30, Letter Book, LS, C&E Br., OQMG, RG92, NA.

[121] A.J. Perry to G.H. Crosman, December 11, 1867, ibid. The order also included 500 cap rings to suspend the scarlet cords from the artillery cap, 2,000 neck stocks, 2,000 ponchos, 20,000 forage caps, 500 cavalry hats cords, 5000 for artillery, 500 ordnance, and 800 for infantry, as well as 5,000 stable frocks, 50 pairs of sergeants major of cavalry chevrons, 50 pairs of regimental quartermaster chevrons, 200 first sergeants, and 50 quartermaster sergeants. Like numbers of artillery sergeants major, regimental quartermasters, and first sergeants, were called for, along with 500 pairs of chevrons for artillery sergeants and corporals each, 10,000 untrimmed 1858-pattern hats, 5,000 castles for the engineers stationed at Goat Island, 5,000 sabers for cavalry troops in the command, and 10,000 bugles for the infantry, with that many ostrich feathers, too. Finally, 50 sets of artillery bugle cords, a regimental color for artillery and two cavalry regimental standards were to be shipped from the best stock by sailing ship around Cape Horn.
Previously 25 artillery caps had been sent to Philadelphia from New York, as part of a transfer of material that also included 1,000 oilcloth forage cap covers, and 1,000 pairs of sergeants major chevrons. At the same time, New York supplied another 1,000 cap covers to Fort Monroe, Virginia. A.J. Perry to D.H. Vinton, February 26, 1867, Vol. 30, ibid.

[122] A.J. Perry to G.H. Crosman, December 16, 1868: and D.H. Rucker to A.J. Perry, December 16, 1867, ibid.

[123] A.J. Perry to R.N. Batchelder, April 3, 1868, Vol. 30, ibid.

[124] A.J. Perry to J.M. Moore, May 11, 1868, ibid.

[125] A.J. Perry to J.A. Moore, July 9, 1868, ibid.

[126] A.J. Perry to B.C. Card, May, 9, 1868, ibid. This letter further related purchases should be made "from time to time only as they are actually required for issue and not to provide a surplus of them for any of the depots."

[127] A.J. Perry to J.S. Totten, July 9, 1868, ibid.

[128] Ibid. With but 1,200 caps on hand as of January 25, 1870, this made sense. Ibid.

[129] E.D. Townsend to Commanding General Military Division of the Pacific, February 16, 1871, ibid.

[130] J.D. Bingham to S. Van Vliet, June 14, 1871, LS, C&S Br., 1871, OQMG, RG92, NA.

[131] Alexander began his career on July 26, 1861 as an officer with the mounted rifles, then moved his way steadily upward to brigadier general of volunteers. Among other appointments, he served on Major General George McClellan's staff and James Grant Wilson's Cavalry Corps. Hunt was a Mexican War veteran who had been breveted for his participation in that conflict in which he had been twice wounded. Subsequently, in 1856, he served on a board to revise light artillery tactics. Five years later, during the Civil War he saw considerable service at such places as Gettysburg, Rapidian, and Petersburg, raising to the rank of major general during the conflict. King's career started in 1837 as an infantry officer in Florida, then in the West, and through the Mexican War. He was a major when the Civil War began, and ended as a major general. Mark M. Boatner, III, *The Civil War Dictionary* (New York: David McKay, Inc., 1959), 6, 418, and 463.

[132] R.B. Marcy to Secretary of War, September 14, 1871, Office of the Secretary of War, RG 107, NA.

[133] Howell, *Headgear 1855-1902*, 33.

[134] For more on the headgear adopted in lieu of Civil War types see, John P. Langellier, *HatsOff: U.S. Army Headdress, 1872-1912 (Atglen, Pa.: Schiffer Military Books, 1999).*

Bibliography

Primary Sources

Unpublished

Record Group 92. Records of the Office of Quartermaster General. National Archives. Washington, DC.
Record Group 94. Records of the Office of the Adjutant General. National Archives. Washington, DC.
Record Group 107. Records of the Secretary of War. National Archives, Washington, DC.
Record Group 108. Records of Headquarters of the Army. National Archives. Washington, DC.
Record Group 112. Records of the Office of the Surgeon General. National Archives. Washington, DC.
Record Group 391. Records of U.S.Army Mobile Commands. National Archives. Washington, DC.
Record Group 393. Records of U.S. Army Continenal Commands. National Archives. Washington, DC.
Tomlinson, Samuel. Letters home from a soldier in the 12th New Jersey Vols., Victor Romano Collection.

Published

Alter, J. Cecil. Ed. *The Utah War Journal of Albert Tracy, 1858- 1860.* Salt Lake: Utah Historical Society, 1945.
Annual Report of the Secretary of War. Volume I. Washington, DC: U.S. Government Printing Office, 1865-1872.
Bieber, Ralph P. Ed. *Frontier Life in the Army.* Glendale, CA: Arthur H. Clark, 1932.
Billings, John D. *Hardtack and Coffee.* Boston: George M. Smith & Co., 1888.
Boston *Evening Journal*, September 14, 1861.
Boston *Post*, July 24, 1861.
Boyle, John Richards. *Soldiers True. The Story of the One Hundred and Eleventh Pennsylvania Volunteers and of Its Campaigns in the War for the Union.* New York: Eaton and Mains, 1903.
Brackett, Albert G. *History of the U.S. Cavalry.* New York: Harper & Brothers, 1865.
Callan, John F. *The Military Laws of the United States, Relating to the Army, Volunteers, Militia, and to Bounty Lands and Pensions from the Foundation of the Government to the Year 1863, To Which are Prefixed the Constitution of the United States. (With an Index Thereto,) and a Synopsis of the Military Legislation of Congress During the Revolutionary War.* Philadelphia: George W. Childs, 1863.
Collis, Septima M. *A Woman's War Record, 1861-1865.* New York and London: G.P. Putnam's Sons, 1889.
Curtis, Newton Martin. *From Bull Run to Chancellorsville: The Story of the 16th New York Infantry.* New York: G.P. Putnam and Sons, 1906.
Davis, Charles. *Three Years in the Army. The Story of the Thirteenth Massachusetts Volunteers.* Boston: Estes and lauriat, 1894.
Dubois, John Van Deusen. *Campaigns in the West, 1856-1851.* Tucson: Arizona Pioneers Historical Society, 1949.
Frazer, Robert W. Ed. *Mansfield on the Condition of Western Forts 1853-54.* Norman: University of Oklahoma Press, 1963.
_____. Ed. *New Mexico in 1850: A Military View.* Norman: University of Oklahoma Press, 1968.
Gavin, William Gilfillan. *Campaigning with the Roundheads.* Dayton: Morningside Bookshop, 1989.
Hafen, Leroy R. Ed. *The Utah Expedition 1857-1858: A Documentary Account of the United States Military Movement Under*
Hays, Gilbert Adams. *Under the Red Patch. The Story of the Sixty Third Regiment Pennsylvania Volunteers 1861-1864.* Pittsburg: Sixty Third Pennsylvania Volunteers regimental Association, 1908.

General Orders and Circulars. Adjutant Generals Department, 1846-1872.
Hafen, Leroy R., Ed. *The Utah Expedition 1857-1858: A Documentary Account of the United States Military Movement Under Colonel Albert Sidney Johnston, and The Resistance by Brigham Young and the Mormon Nauvoo Legion*. Glendale, CA: The Arthur H. Clark Company, 1982.
Hammond, Otis G. Ed. *The Utah Expedition, 1857-1858 Letters of Capt. Jesse A. Gove, 10th Inf., U.S.A., of Concord, N.H. to Mrs. Gove, and special correspondence of the New York Herald*. Concord: New Hampshire Historical Society, 1928.
Hine, Robert V. and Lottinville, Savoie. Eds. *Soldier in the West: Letters of Theodore Talbot During His Services in California, Mexico, and Oregon, 1845-53*. Norman: University of Oklahoma Press, 19.
Kimball, Maria Brace. *A Soldier-Doctor of Our Army James P. Kimball*. New York: Houghton Mifflin, 1917.
Kip, Lawrence. *Army Life on the Pacific: A Journal of the Expedition Against the North Indians...in the Summer of 1858*. New York: Redfield, 1859.
Langley, Harold. Ed *To Utah With The Dragoons*. Salt Lake: University of Utah, 1974.
Livermore, Mary. *My Story of the War*. Hartford: A.D. Worthington, 1888.
Long, Oscar F. *Changes in the Uniform of the Army 1775-1895*. Washington, DC: Army & Navy Register, 1895.
Lowe, Percival G. *Five Years A Dragoon And Other Adventures on the Great Plains*. Norman: University of Oklahoma Press, 1965.
A Medical Report upon the Uniform and Clothing of the Soldiers of the U.S. Army, 15 April 1868. Washington, DC: Surgeon General's Office, 1868.
"Movement of Troops." Sacramento *Daily Union*. May 29, 1860.
New Orleans *True Delta*. November 13, 1864.
Nelson, Henry Loomis. *The Army of the United States*. New York: B.M. Whitlock, 1890.
_____. "Army Uniforms in the United States." *Harper's Weekly*. March 1, 1890.
"New Uniform for the U.S. Army." *Gleason's Pictorial Drawing-Room Companion*. March 22, 1852.
Porter, John T. *Under the Maltese Cross*. Pittsburg: The 155th Regimental Association, 1910.
Regulations for the Army of the United States 1857. Staten Island: Manor Publishing, 1973.
Report of the Secretary of War, Communicating the Report of Captain George B. McClellan, (First Regiment United States Cavalry) One of Officers Sent to the Seat of War in Europe 1855 and 1856, Executive Document No. 1, Senate, Special Session. Washington, DC: A.O.P. Nicholson, Printer, 1857.
Russell, William Howard. *My Diary North and South*. Boston: T.O.H.P. Burnham, 1863.
Smith, John Day. *The History of the Nineteenth Regiment of Maine Volunteer Infantry*. Minneapolis: Great Western Printing Co.,1909.
Sneden, Robert Knox. *Eye of the Storm*. New York: The Free Press, 2000.
Stevens, Charles A. *Berdan's United States Sharpshooters in the Army of the Potomac 1861-1865*. Dayton: Morningside Bookshop, 1984.
Survivors Association. *History of the 118th Pennsylvania Volunteers*. Philadelphia: J.L. Smith, 1905.
Tome, Robert. "The Fortunes of War." XXIX *Harper's New Monthly Magazine*. June 1864.
Townsend, E.D. *Anecdotes of the Civil War in the United States*. New York: D. Appleton & Company, 1884.
United Service Gazette. April 13, 1850.
United States Army and Navy Journal. 1863-1872.
United Sates Sanitary Commission. *Report of a Portion of the Volunteer Forces near Washington,* No 17, July 9, 1861. Washington D.C.: U.S. Sanitary Commission, 1861.
Viele, Teresa G. *Following the Drum: A Glimpse of Frontier Life* Lincoln: University of Nebraska Press, 1984.

Secondary Sources

Books and Monographs

Brinckerhoff, Sidney B. *Military Headgear in the Southwest, 1846- 1890*. Tucson: Arizona Pioneers' Historical Society, 1963.
Campbell, J. Duncan and Howell, Edgar M. *American Military Insignia 1800-1851*. Washington, DC: Smithsonian Institution, 1963.
_____. *A Dictionary of Military Uniforms*. New York: Charles Scribner's Sons, 1977.
Chappel, Gordon. *Search For The Well-Dressed Soldier, 1865-1890*. Tucson: Arizona Historical Society, 1972.
Coates, Earl J., and Kotchian, James L. *Don Troiani's Soldiers in America, 1754-1865*. Mechanicsburg, PA: Stackpole, 1998.
Coffman, Edward M. *The Old Army: A Portrait of the American Army in Peacetime, 1784-1898*. Oxford: Oxford University Press, 1986.
Cunliffe, Marcus. *Soldiers & Civilians: The Martial Spirit in America, 1775-1865*. New York: The Free Press, 1973.
Delano, Marfé Ferguson and Mallen, Barbara C. *Echoes of Glory Arms: and Equipment of the Union*. Alexandria, VA: Time- Life Books, 1991.
Davis, William C. Ed. *The Image of War 1861-1865*. Garden City, NY: Doubleday & Company, 1981-83. 5 Volumes.
Donald, David Herbert Ed. *Gone for a Soldier. The Civil War Memoirs of Private Alfred Bellard.* Boston: Little, Brown and Company, 1975.
Elting, John R. Ed. *Military Uniforms in America The Era of the American Revolution, 1755-1795*. San Rafael, CA: Presidio Press, 1974.
_____. *Military Uniforms in America Years of Growth, 1796- 1851*. San Rafael, CA: Presidio Press, 1977.
_____. *Military Uniforms in America Long Endure: The Civil War Period, 1852-1867*. Navato, CA: Presidio Press, 1982.
Emerson, William K. *Encyclopedia of United States Army Insignia and Uniforms*. Norman: University of Oklahoma Press, 1996.
Haythornewaite, Philip J. *Uniforms of the Napoleonic Wars in Color, 1796-1814*. New York: Hippocrene Books, Inc., 1973.
_____. *Uniforms of the Retreat from Moscow, 1812*. New York: Hippocrene Books, Inc., 1976.

Bibliography

Howell, Edgar M. and Kloster, Donald E. *United States Military Headgear to 1854 Catalog of United States Army Uniforms in the Collections of the Smithsonian Institution,* Volume I. City of Washington: Smithsonian Institution Press, 1969.

Howell, Edgar M. *United States Army Headgear 1855-1902: Catalog of United States Army Uniforms in the Collections of the Smithsonian Institution.* Volume II. Washington, DC: Smithsonian Institution, 1975.

Kohn, Richard H. *Eagle and Sword: The Beginnings of the Military Establishment in America.* New York: The Free Press, 1975. Langellier, John P. *Redlegs: The U.S. Artillery from the Civil War to the Spanish-American War, 1861-1898.* London: Greenhill Books, 1998.

Lewis, Waverly P. *U.S Military Headgear 1770-1880.* Devon, CT: Printed by the Author, 1960.

Lord, Francis A. *Civil War Collector's Encyclopedia: Arms, Uniforms, and Equipment of the Union and Confederacy.* New York: Castle Books, 1965.

McChristian, Douglas C. *The U.S. Army in the West, 1870-1880: Uniforms, Weapons and Equipment.* Norman: University of Oklahoma, 1995.

Matloff, Maurice, Ed. *American Military History.* Washington, DC: Office of the Chief of Military History United States Army, 1969.

Mollo, John. *Military Fashion.* New York: G.P. Putnam's Sons, 1972.

The Oxford Universal Dictionary of Historical Principles. Oxford: The Claraden Press, 1955. 3rd Ed.

Parks, Joseph H. *General Edmund Kirby Smith.* Baton Rouge: Louisiana State University Press, 1954.

Phillips, Stanley S. *Civil War Corps Badges and Other Related Awards, Badges, Medals of the Period: Including A Section on Post Civil War and Spanish American War Corps Badges.* Lanham, MD: S.S. Phillips, 1982.

Price, George F. *Across the Continent with the Fifth Cavalry.* New York: D. Van Nostrand, Publisher, 1883.

Prucha, Francis P. Ed. *Army Life on the Western Frontier: Selections from Official Reports Made Between 1826 and 1845 by Colonel George Croghan.* Norman: University of Oklahoma Press, 1958.

Rankin, Robert H. *Military Headdress: A Pictorial History of Military Headgear from 1660 to 1914.* London: Arms and Armour, 1976.

Risch Erna. *Quartermaster Support of the Army.* Washington, DC: Office of the Quartermaster General, 1962.

Sadies, Stanley. Ed. *The New Grove's Dictionary of Opera.* Volume II. New York: Grove's Dictionary of Music Inc., 1992.

Sefton, James E. *The United States Army and Reconstruction.* Baton Rouge: Louisiana State University Press, 1967.

Todd, Frederick P. *American Military Equipage 1851-1872,* Volume I New York: Charles Scribner's Sons, 1980.

_____. *American Military Equipage, 1851-1872.* Volume II. N.P.: Chatham Square Press, 1983.

_____. *Cadet Gray.* New York: Sterling Publishing Co., Inc., 1955.

Wilkinson-Latham, R.J. *Collecting Militaria.* New York: Arco Publishing, Inc., 1976.

_____. *The Indian Mutiny.* London: Osprey Publishing, 1977.

Wiley, Bell Irvin. *The Life of Billy Yank.* Baton Rouge: Louisiana State University Press, 1981.

Periodicals

Addington, Larry H. "The U.S. Coast Artillery and the Problem of Artillery Organization, 1907-1954." *Military Affairs* LX No. 1. February 1976: 1-16

Akers, Monte. "That Crazy Cap." *Military Images* V No. 4. January- February 1984: 16-19.

Anon. "Michael Bremer's Ante-bellum Daguerreotypes." *Military Images* I No. 3. November-December 1970: 18-25.

Baird, L.C. "The Philadelphia Quartermaster Intermediate Depot." *Quartermaster Review* VI No. 6. May-June 1927, 18-19.

Ball, Leonard F. "William M. Boyce, First U.S. Infantry, 1822-1836." XXIV *Military Collector and Historian* No. 2. Summer 1972: 44-47

Bazelon, Bruse S. "The Original War of 1812 Insignia Dies from the Kirk Collection—A Plausible History." *Military Collector and Historian* XXVI No 2. Summer 1974: 81-85.

Campbell, J. Duncan. "Second Pattern Cap Plate U.S. Light Artillery, 1814." *Military Collector and Historian* XXVI No. 1. Spring 1974: 6-9.

Chappell, Gordon. "Dress Hat of the First Regiment of Mounted Rifles, 1858-1861." *Military Collector and Historian* XXII No. 2. Summer 1970: 58-59.

_____. "The 'Pillbox' Cap in the United States Army c. 1866- 1902." *Military Collector and Historian* XXXII No. 1. Spring 1980: 4-15.

Chartrand, René. "Canadian Volunteer Infantry c. 1863-1870." *Military Collector and Historian* XXXVII No. 1. Spring 1985: 25-36.

Cureton, Charles, and McMaster, Fitzhugh. "4th Cavalry Regiment, South Carolina Militia, 1841." *Military Collector and Historian* XXXII No. 3. Fall 1981: 123.

_____., and Schultz, William. "Dating The Regulars." *Military Images* XVII No. 4. January-February 1996: 8-11.

Darida, R., and Donnelly, Ralph. "United States Marine Corps Dress Cap Model of 1859." *Military Collector and Historian* XXVI No. 2. Summer 1974: 110.

Dillon, Don. "The Havelock." *Military Images* III No. 4. January- February 1982: 14-15.

Gero, Anthony. "The Elusive Pillbox Cap, 1870-1900." *Military Images* XIX No. 3. November-December 1997: 24-26.

Lang, Wendell W., Jr. "Corps Badges of the Civil War." *Military Images* VI No. 6. May-June 1986: 16-25; VIII No. 1 (July-August 1986): 8-15; VIII No. 3. November-December 1986: 16-26; IX No. 3. November-December 1987: 6-15.

McAfee, Michael J. "3rd Regiment, Massachusetts Volunteers Militia." *Military Images* XIX No. 2. September-October 1997: 35.

_____. "What is a Zouave," *Military Images* I No. 2. September-October 1979: 14

Madaus, Howard Michael. "Dating the Earliest Use of the 'Pillbox Cap' in the United States Army." *Military Collector and Historian* XXXII No. 4. Winter 1980: 177-179.

Maples, Philip G. "The Dress Regulations for the Connecticut Militia, 1812: A Background Study." *Military Collector and Historian* XXXI No. 2. Summer 1979: 74-77.

_____. "Uniform of the 5th Regiment Cavalry Connecticut Militia ca. 1835." *Military Collector and Historian* XXXIV No. 4. Winter 1982: 176-177.

_____, and Gero, Anthony. *Military Collector and Historian* XXXII No. 4. Winter 1980: 155-156.

Osman, Stephen E. "Two Regular Army Musician's Coattess of the 1821 Pattern." *Military Collector and Historian* XXXII No. 2. Summer 1980: 78-81.

Peladeau, Marius B. and Cohen, Roger S., Jr. "Corps Badges of the Civil War." *Military Collector and Historian* XXIII No. 4. Winter 1971: 103-112.

Powell, John T. "Regiment of Riflemen Cap Insignia, 1808-1812." *Military Collector and Historian* XXVII No. 4. Winter 1975: 180.

Ross, Leroy E. and Emerson, William K. "Hat Cords of the U.S. Army." *Military Collector and Historian* XXVII No. 4. Winter 1976: 148-153.

Staff and Contributors. "Heavy Headgear." *Military Images* XVII No. 6. May-June 1997: 6-18.

Stamatelos, James. Whipple's Patent Military Cap. *Military Images* V No. 6. May-June 1984: 13-15.

Thatcher, Joseph M. "U.S. Light Dragoon Belts Plates and Helmets, 1808-1812." *Military Collector and Historian* XXVII No. 1. Spring 1975: 16-19.

Todd, Frederick P. "Uniforms in Connecticut, 1784-1820." *Military Collector and Historian* XXV No. 3. Fall 1973: 126- 139.

Townsend, F.C. and Todd, Frederick P. "Branch Insignia of the Regular Cavalry, 1833-1872." *Military Collector and Historian* VIII No. 1. Spring 1956: 1-5.

Wike, John M. "The Wearing of Corps and Division Insignia of the Union Army, 1861-1865." *Military Collector and Historian* IV No. 2. June 1952: 35-38.

Index

NB Number followed by "n" and numeral indicates page number and corresponding endnote number